PENG

Here'

'Artful, entertaining and often enlightening – one of the few memoirs by a senior Irish office-holder that's actually worth reading' *Sunday Times*

'Riveting . . . A fiercely urgent reminder to the world – and the Government – that peace must never be sacrificed for politics'
*Daily Telegraph*

'What an incredible life lived by an outstanding role model. I ate this book up' Sinéad Moriarty

'A fascinating story and well worth the read . . . Details much about her extraordinary career with her customary mixture of frankness and folksiness' Diarmaid Ferriter, *Irish Times*

'Engaging' *Irish Independent*

'[A] chatty, provocative and embraceable biography . . . Warm, witty, wise and often very, very funny' *RTÉ Guide*

'A meticulously researched and recorded history of the past half-century in Ireland and the story of a life passionately committed to working for peace' *TLS*

'Full of conviction and isn't afraid of plain speaking . . . Priests, popes, paramilitaries and Ian Paisley are all held to account' *Herald Scotland*

'Excellent' Matt Cooper, *Irish Daily Mail*

'So authentic, so believable . . . I was enthralled and absorbed by this memoir' Mary O'Rourke, *Sunday Independent*

'McAleese is clearly a class act. *Here's the Story* displays many of the qualities that made her such a popular president: energy, empathy and total professionalism' *Business Post*

'An immensely readable effort from that rarest of figures – a politician you actually like and admire' *Hot Press*

## ABOUT THE AUTHOR

Mary McAleese was born in Belfast in 1951. In 1975 she was appointed Reid Professor of Law at Trinity College Dublin, and in 1987 she became Director of the Institute of Professional Legal Studies at Queen's University Belfast. She was elected President of Ireland in 1997, and re-elected unopposed in 2004. Since stepping down as President in 2011, she has earned a PhD in canon law while remaining an influential advocate for peace and equality.

# Here's the Story

*A Memoir*

MARY McALEESE

PENGUIN BOOKS

PENGUIN BOOKS

UK | USA | Canada | Ireland | Australia
India | New Zealand | South Africa

Penguin Books is part of the Penguin Random House group of companies
whose addresses can be found at global.penguinrandomhouse.com.

First published by Sandycove 2020
Published in Penguin Books 2021
001

Typeset in 11.7/13.8 pt Garamond MT Std
Typeset by Jouve (UK), Milton Keynes
Printed and bound in Great Britain by Clays Ltd, Elcograf S.p.A.

The authorized representative in the EEA is Penguin Random House Ireland,
Morrison Chambers, 32 Nassau Street, Dublin D02 YH68

A CIP catalogue record for this book is available from the British Library

ISBN: 978-0-241-98620-2

www.greenpenguin.co.uk

MIX
Paper from
responsible sources
FSC® C018179
www.fsc.org

Penguin Random House is committed to a
sustainable future for our business, our readers
and our planet. This book is made from Forest
Stewardship Council® certified paper.

This book is dedicated to the memory of the late
Father Alec Reid CSsR, priest and peacemaker

People have notions about the place where I was born and raised: Ardoyne, north Belfast. During the Troubles, Ardoyne was rebranded in the mass media as 'The Ardoyne'. It became the area with the highest per capita incidence of sectarian murders and gained a reputation as a place apart.

Ardoyne was not a place apart. It was – and still is – the canary in the mine. Looking back, I can see it for what it was: a dangerously overlooked corner of the United Kingdom where the lives of many decent people of all persuasions fell or were shoved into the crevices of a turbulent history they did not create. Ardoyne is sometimes characterised as a Catholic ghetto, but that is to mistake part of it for all of it. My family was Catholic, but for as long as we lived in Ardoyne we lived among predominantly Protestant neighbours who belonged to a kaleidoscope of different churches and gospel halls. Growing up there in the 1950s and 60s, I learned from first principles that by failing to build bridges to our estranged neighbours, we lived with a dangerously (and deliberately) restricted view of life. In a divided society, the contest for hearts and minds begins with the recruitment of its children to intolerance of others.

I was raised as a Catholic whose identity was Irish, not British. I grew up among Protestant neighbours whose identity was mostly British, not Irish. I hoped the island of Ireland would one day be reunited. My neighbours could not imagine anything worse. They were loyal to the Crown and the United

Kingdom. So there were those who were loyal and those who were disloyal, those who could be trusted and those who could not. Little or nothing matched between us, or so it seemed. If we managed to live and work together, it was often because we obeyed the mantra captured by Seamus Heaney: 'Whatever you say, say nothing.' We dug our respective trenches deeper and deeper, handing on to the next generation batons of fear, contempt, hatred, self-righteousness and entitlement with which to beat to death any hope of a peaceful and egalitarian future.

And yet, for many years of my childhood it was not uncommon for most of us to find ways of navigating the problems presented by our differences of religion and politics so that we became good neighbours and lifelong friends. My closest early childhood friends were all Protestant. The family we shared a rented holiday home with year after year was Protestant, our next-door neighbours in fact. There was no unease in our relationships, no nervousness around our differences.

My parents were not Belfast natives. My mother's roots were in rural County Down and my father's in County Roscommon: not just different counties but different jurisdictions. My father had to secure a work permit to migrate north, and for many years he needed a pass for his car, known as a 'triptych', when he crossed the border to visit his parents. My parents' relative unfamiliarity with urban Belfast was probably an important factor in our good relations with our Protestant neighbours, for the cultural and experiential wells we drew from as children were a bit wider and deeper than Northern Ireland's standard sectarian bunkers. The principles of tolerance inculcated by our parents seemed to provide an effective resistance to the tendency to see things exclusively from one perspective.

None of us – I was the eldest of nine siblings – ever embraced or even countenanced paramilitarism, though we suffered its consequences. We all became convinced pacifists, and we all maintained strong cross-community friendships from childhood through to adulthood, even in circumstances where those friendships invited danger.

Patrick Joseph (Paddy) Leneghan, my father, was the eldest of five children. His parents, Frank Leneghan and Brigid McDrury, grew up as neighbours in a remote wooded clachan (cluster of cottages) called Ardglass, near Croghan in rural north Roscommon. The Leneghan clan could trace its roots in that area back at least a millennium thanks to the *Annals of Lough Key*, which told of Maelciarain O'Lenachain, a chief priest of Tuaim-mná (now Tumna), who ran a house of hospitality for 'ecclesiastics and strangers'. He died en route to nearby Ard-Carna in 1249 and was buried on Trinity Island in Lough Key, a rare honour.

Frank's father, Patrick, was born in Ardglass in 1847, into a family that would shortly be devastated by the Great Famine. Records at the Strokestown Park Famine Museum show that Patrick's widowed mother begged for food from the Pakenham-Mahons at Strokestown House. Having presented references from local worthies, she was given a bag of Indian corn. It was indigestible, as it turned out, and was the likely cause of death of Patrick's sisters.

Frank's mother, Annie Flanagan, was from a neighbouring large family in Duneoin, Ballinameen. She was a midwife, and judging by the number of people I've met in adulthood who tell me she was present at the birth of someone belonging to them, she delivered legions of children around Ballinameen, Rinn, Kilmore, Ardcarne, Ardglass and Dooneen. But the only thing I ever knew about my great-grandmother when I was growing up was that she could keep a secret.

When my father was thirteen, he took his father's new pony and turf cart for a spin without permission. Annie went with him, which says something about her daredevil nature – or perhaps her death wish. She sat dressed in her widow's weeds on a bench in the back of the cart, likely praying. Having carefully navigated the winding one-donkey track, my father finally reached the equally winding but somewhat wider metalled road that led eventually to the local metropolis of Boyle. There he succumbed to the temptation to go full throttle.

As the pony broke into a gallop, Annie was catapulted out of the trap at the first pothole and onto the side of the road. My father always maintained that that was the occasion of his first heart attack. He was sure she was dead, but in fact she survived without much damage, and on returning home re-assured my petrified father that the matter would not be reported to his parents. Nor was it, probably because she was a willing accomplice, an accessory before the fact and therefore as culpable as he was. I wish I could say that sobering experience made my father sympathetic to the youthful follies of his own children, but in fact if any of us had had the temerity to take his car without permission (which we did not), we knew that a volcanic eruption visible from Vesuvius would result. My father inherited his own father's quick, scorching temper, but thankfully also his somewhat redeeming sense of humour.

Frank's three sisters emigrated to the United States, following in the footsteps of their maternal and paternal aunts and uncles. A generation later, the memory of all of them had faded into oblivion. We heard almost nothing about them or from them.

Access to the clachan at Ardglass was by a rough track. A few years later, the family moved a couple of fields away, to a newly built council cottage on a proper, albeit very minor, road built along a high ridge that looked down over the sweep of the plains of Boyle and the River Shannon and ran all the way down to Ardcarne church on the main road to Sligo. My father remembered carrying, in a tin can, the still burning cinders from the last fire in the old house to light the first fire in the new, following an old tradition. The role fell to him as the eldest child, but the thought of arriving at the new home with only dead ashes scared the daylights out of him. It worked out, though, and that open fire, with its deep ash pit, French flue, narrow shelves on either side, and crane on which hung blackened pots and kettles, came to be the hub of family life for four successive generations. My grandparents were bare subsistence farmers with a donkey and cart for transport; their children were all early school-leavers and emigrants who returned to help with the hay- and turf-cutting in the summer; their grandchildren and great-grandchildren were well-educated car-driving occasional visitors.

My father's father was fond of saying that he had 'enough land for two cattle and enough water for two hundred' – the latter a reference to the persistent rain and boggy ground on their meagre subsistence farm. The cottage was adjacent to the Kirkwood family's Woodbrook estate, the decline of which was skilfully described by David Thompson in his book *Woodbrook*. My great-grandfather worked there some-times as an ostler. Granda Frank himself sometimes worked at a local lime kiln or on local relief work projects, building the miles of dry-stone walls in the area. There was a lot about his personality that was dry and stony.

My grandmother Brigid's mother was a McGreevy – a descendant of the Mac Riabhaigh clan, who were once chieftains and probably lords of Moylurg, a north Roscommon kingdom of which they were dispossessed in the thirteenth century when, according to the genealogist Edward MacLysaght, they were 'subdued' by the neighbouring MacDermots – or robbed, according to my father's cousin Brother Bede McGreevy, who often held forth on the subject. The injustice was legendary, at least in our house. When I brought my father a book on the MacDermots of Moylurg, he pretended to dismiss it unopened, saying he preferred fact to fiction. But he devoured its every word and took issue with more than a few of them. Brother Bede, the least vain or narcissistic of men, took mischievous delight in having the words 'Lords of Moylurg' engraved on the large Celtic cross headstone that marks the McGreevy family plot at Ardcarne graveyard. The price for doing so was having to endure a lot of mockery and teasing, not least from my father, who thereafter greeted him as 'your lordship'.

My father was baptised in Ardcarne parish, at the Roman Catholic St Michael's Church in the village of Cootehall, where I now live; but the Ardcarne graveyard of his forebears sits on the main road to Sligo and surrounds the quaint little Church of Ireland church of St Beo-Aedh. The graveyard hosts, in the everlasting silence of the dead, Catholic and Protestant, Planter and Gael, Leneghans, McGreevys and MacDermots alike. It also hosts the plot my husband Martin and I have pre-emptively chosen as our final resting place, despite accusations of mawkish morbidity from our children. God knows where that crowd would land us if left to their own devices. I had thought my father would want to be buried there, given that for all of our lives he was adamant there was no place on God's earth like Roscommon, and no visit there was complete without tours of the old Ardcarne graveyard and of the new graveyard a few miles away at Drumlion, where his parents are buried. But when push came to shove and death was stalking him, and I organised a choice of Roscommon graves, he did the thing designed to maximise internal family mischief by choosing to be buried in Rostrevor in County Down, where he had lived since the early 1970s.

Each of my father's siblings, and most of his childhood friends and relations, emigrated: to England, America, Australia and New Zealand. He himself left home at fourteen to follow his mother's three sisters to Belfast and to begin work as an apprentice barman. Those three aunts – Mary, Nora and Sarah Jane – had gone to Belfast one after the other. They lived on Kinnaird Terrace, just off the Antrim Road not far from Ardoyne. Among their neighbours and good friends was the prosperous McMahon family. Owen McMahon had a pub in the city centre, the Capstan Bar – pub ownership (thanks to mythical Protestant abstemiousness) being more open to Catholics than most other businesses. Owen and his wife Eliza had six sons and a daughter. They lived through cruel times, and like their close friend Joe Devlin, the nationalist MP, they abhorred the feverish sectarianism and violence that pervaded the Belfast of their day.

On the evening of 24 March 1922, Belfast was a nervous city. The night before, the IRA had murdered two police officers. In the petty scheme of things, that action meant there would be a reprisal against Catholics. This time it was visited upon the innocent McMahon family. Uniformed police officers broke into their home in the early hours of the morning. They murdered Owen, four of his sons, and a young Donegal barman who was staying with them. Two sons survived, one badly wounded, as did Owen's wife and daughter.

The McDrury girls, recently arrived from a thatched cottage in a field in the middle of a wood in the middle of nowhere in north Roscommon, were a long time recovering from that night. In its aftermath they rapidly bailed out of Kinnaird Terrace and moved to Ardoyne – which, as it turned out, was not the best move they could have made. That repugnant event may partly explain why my grandmother Brigid remained in Roscommon, the last of a once large McDrury clan to do so. She eschewed joining her sisters in Belfast or her dozens of cousins recently emigrated to New Zealand, instead living with her McGreevy cousins in their thatched cottage at Boher. Those who stayed in Ireland and those who emigrated endured great loneliness, some of it apparent in the melancholy that seemed to inhabit their homes in varying degrees of intensity.

Once settled in Ardoyne, the McDrury sisters revealed an entrepreneurial streak in the family: Mary (known to us as Mrs Cassidy) ran a grocery store, Sarah Jane (aka Doll) had an off-licence, and Nora (Sis) – with whom my father moved in when he arrived in Belfast – a hairdressing salon. The three sisters' businesses were all within a few yards of one another for a number of years, until some time later Mary moved to the Falls Road and the bustling boarding house where I as a child encountered many a pharmacy student 'up from the country' and an elderly celebrity neighbour, Cathal O'Byrne, who often rambled in and sang or recited passages from his then famous book, *As I Roved Out*.

My mother, Claire McManus, the middle child of eleven, was born in Maghera, County Derry. Her father, John McManus, and mother, Cassie Rogan, had grown up far from Derry, in small families on adjacent sheep farms in the Dromara Hills of County Down. Attacks on Catholics were a recurring hazard there, and mixed-marriage families were a particular target. My maternal great-great-grandparents had such a marriage, and of their huge family my great-grandmother, Cassie McCullough Rogan, was the only one who never took the boat to North America. One bonus of this diaspora is the ridiculous number of relatives I have in Boston and in Halifax, Nova Scotia, two places where I always feel at home.

My grandfather's membership of the IRA and active service during the War of Independence made long-term residence among their clans in the Dromara Hills hazardous for his young wife and family. He shuttled between County Down and Scotland, where he got labouring work, until the offer of a job with Bernard Hughes's bakery brought him to Maghera in 1927 with their first two children, Arthur and Cassie. Seven more children were born in Maghera, including my mother and a little sister, Bernadette, who died in infancy. Ten years later the bakery transferred my grandfather to Belfast, where attacks on Catholics had forced many from their homes and into the shelter of overcrowded ghettos such as the Falls Road area and the older part of Ardoyne.

The newly built Glenard estate, which extended Ardoyne on its northern flank, was occupied mainly by Protestants, though many houses were still in the course of being built when a large group of displaced Catholics moved in as squatters. The Protestant residents resisted, and for some time afterwards the area was synonymous with civil strife, so much so that when things settled down all the street names were changed to erase the notorious Glenard label (though we never referred to it as anything else). My grandparents' street, previously Glenard Drive, became Dunedin Park. A particularly nasty rent strike in 1937 had made the area the least desirable address in Belfast. When my grandparents came from Maghera it was the only place available, and so with deep misgivings they took up residence in one of the terraced houses in the estate.

With eight children already, and the arrival of two more in a two-bedroomed house with a kitchen the size of a wheelie bin, space was limited. During the Second World War, my mother, aged eight, and her sister Cassie, aged fifteen, were dispatched to live with their maternal grandparents the Rogans in Dromara, on a hard-working sheep farm on the tranquil slopes of Slieve Croob.

Like my father's birthplace in north Roscommon, Slieve Croob holds seams of age-old stories, and carries today the faint trace of ancient lives and customs in the large cairn at its summit and the traditional gatherings there at Lughnasa. Neither Ardcarne nor Slieve Croob allows dwellers or visitors to easily forget their weightlessness on this earth, or the brevity of the span from first breath to last that returns us to the soil as a mere sprinkling of dust. Both places silently pose vast questions about existence, final destiny, beauty, God and our stewardship of nature. But what God opened up for perpetual wonderment, others closed down for irredentist politics. In schools, homes, communities and churches, carefully bundled formulae saw to it that no one, not even the best of neighbours, could easily detach from the adversarial bunkers birth had allocated each of them to. Neither the outstanding natural beauty of those places nor the uncomplicated story of peace on earth and goodwill to all men could suppress the sectarian politics of attachment. The Dromara Hills were full of such politics.

My mother's older sister Cassie stayed in Granny Rogan's house, where the Lagan river rises right at the front door, beside a clump of hazel bushes, with no hint of its ultimate destiny as one of Ireland's major waterways. My mother moved to the farm next door, presided over by my grandmother's only sister, Mary Agnes, who was married to a local man, James McKinney. Theirs was a busy, prosperous farm, and Aunt Mary Agnes, while very likeable, always struck me as being slightly grandiose. Nowadays she would be described as 'high-maintenance'. She was a dab hand at delegating hard work and had a weakness for fashion. Cartloads of clothes would arrive on approval from F&F Wadsworth's drapery in Newcastle, especially in advance of a wedding or dinner dance. On the morning of one family wedding, my Aunt Una enquired of her droll husband Sammy Coulter as to what the weather was like. He opened the curtain and replied: 'It's the kind of day your Aunt Mary Agnes wouldn't know what to put on her.'

The McKinneys already had one housemaid, but my mother became an unpaid second, and without the protection of her older sister she sometimes had to run the gauntlet of unwelcome advances from one or two of the seasonal farm labourers. She attended the small country school at Munina-bane beside her paternal grandparents' home. She was fond of her gracious Uncle James, his well-dressed wife and their four children; but large and comfortable as their home was, she sorely missed the company of her own mother, father and siblings, whose visits in those carless, petrol-rationing days were rare.

At the end of the war in 1945, aged fourteen, she begged to return to Belfast, a city she barely knew, and found herself squeezed into the tiny house in Ardoyne with eight siblings and more yet to come. School was Holy Cross Girls' School near Ardoyne chapel, five minutes away at a busy urban intersection that could not have been more different from Muninabane. She left school at fifteen and became apprenticed as a hairdresser to my father's Aunt Sis. But part of her heart remained in the Dromara Hills, and during my childhood we paid dutiful visits to Aunt Mary Agnes, sometimes spending holidays with her.

Mary Agnes's younger son Peter later became head gardener at Hillsborough Castle, the home of Governors General and Secretaries of State. He was particularly friendly with Secretary of State Sir Patrick Mayhew and his wife Lady Jane, who, typical of their affability, arrived unannounced to Aunt Mary Agnes's house to wish her a happy ninetieth birthday in 1997. She was thoroughly delighted, but nervously hoped that the Mayhews, Tory grandees that they were, would not notice the ornamental harp on her mantelpiece, made for another of her birthdays by a grand-nephew when he was a republican internee in Long Kesh prison. Its inscription, '*Tiochfaidh ar lá*' (a well-known republican mantra meaning 'Our day will come'), was not exactly intended to encourage afternoon tea with British secretaries of state; but thankfully by then we were moving towards peace, helped by people like the Mayhews and McKinneys who saw the good in people before they noticed the politics. My mother's middle-of-the road political views probably owe something to Slieve Croob. The harder edge of Ardoyne and the sectarian hatred she encountered there never provoked a scintilla of resentment, just bewilderment at the stupidity and inhumanity of it all among so-called Christians.

My father had left Belfast for Dublin during the war years, moving in with the family of Frank McKenna, a Tyrone man to whom he had been apprenticed in Ardoyne. Frank bought a pub in Milltown in south Dublin, and my father got digs there, joining the local church confraternity and making many friends. When I gave a talk in the same church sixty years later, I was surprised at the number of men and women who came up to me and told me they had been friends of my father's when he lived there. When the McKennas bought a pub in Dun Laoghaire, my father moved with them; it would become our favourite family bolthole during the Troubles. My father's brother Dan joined him in Dun Laoghaire before heading off on the immigrant trail to America along with the older McKenna boys. My father was tempted to go with them, but the offer of a job as a bar manager in Belfast brought him back to Ardoyne.

The pub, called the Alderman, was situated on the Crumlin Road, a few blocks downhill from his aunts' homes and businesses. The aunts all had full houses and no room for a new lodger (Aunt Sis's lodger was a pharmacy assistant called Mick Donaghy – an avid amateur photographer who in later years would entertain us children with his fascinating slide shows), so my father took lodgings round the corner in Butler Street with a Mrs Hughes, whose daughter-in-law, Christina, the mother of eight children and a volunteer engaged in cross-community reconciliation, would be murdered in 1975 by loyalists looking for easy Catholic targets.

Seán Mac Diarmada, a Leitrim man, had once lived in Butler Street while working as a bus conductor at the local depot, five minutes' walk away. It was in Belfast in 1905 that Mac Diarmada was sworn into membership of the Irish Republican Brotherhood, and while the effects of polio kept him from significant military action, he was one of the seven signatories of the 1916 Proclamation and one of the sixteen leaders of the Easter Rising who were summarily executed by the British, actions that precipitated the War of Independence and the extrication of twenty-six of Ireland's thirty-two counties from British rule. These days, Martin and I regularly walk past the memorial to Mac Diarmada on Carrick-on-Shannon's Main Street as we go about our shopping. The people of Carrick-on-Shannon today are as unaware of his Ardoyne connection as the people of Ardoyne are!

Visiting his Aunt Sis's house as he often did, my father eventually ran across her apprentice, Claire McManus, and that was that for the next sixty years – or, as he used to put it, the equivalent of three life sentences for murder. On 5 June 1950 they were married in Holy Cross Church, directly across the road from the salon. She was nineteen and he was twenty-five. Their two-year courtship had consisted in the main of attending novenas in Clonard Monastery off the Falls Road, a twenty-minute walk away, on a Thursday night, and the local Holy Cross Monastery in Ardoyne on a Tuesday night, when he could make it on his evenings off. He was in the Catholic Men's Confraternity, which met one night a week to say prayers. She was in the Ladies' Sodality, which met on another night, also to say prayers; and with his long bar hours she seems to have spent a lot of her free time knitting.

They had so little money that my father had to get an advance on his weekly wages of £11 on return from their honeymoon in the Isle of Man. But in short order they went from living in the single rented room that was my initial home to owning the first of the five Ardoyne houses I was raised in. To gather up the deposit, my mother cleaned the new houses being built further up the Ardoyne Road, at half a crown a time. Ardoyne was losing its glens and fields with the onrush of suburbanisation. As the builders finished each house, leaving rubble and dust behind them, my mother moved in to make them habitable for their new occupants. To help pay the mortgage, we took in lodgers, among them a student of pharmacy, Tom Connolly, who went on to become the treasurer of the SDLP. My parents were young, hard-working, energetic, hope-filled, and anxious for a better life. For a while, that seemed to be enough to maintain a steady upward trajectory towards the unexceptional, unpretentious life they wanted for themselves and their children.

On Sundays they went to Mass in the Holy Cross chapel and then rambled up the open fields that would soon be full of rows of those new houses that were rapidly changing the contours of Ardoyne.

## 2

Between 1951 and 1969, my mother had eleven pregnancies, from which came nine live children: five boys and four girls. I was the eldest. Then came Nora, John, Damien, Catherine, Patrick, Claire, Phelim and Clement.

I was born in the Royal Maternity Hospital on the Falls Road on 27 June 1951. It was the Feast of the Mother of Perpetual Succour, and since my parents' social life revolved around the weekly Clonard Monastery novena to the said Mother, they named me Mary in honour of her and of my father's only sister, his maternal and paternal aunts and his great-aunt, all Marys. My second name, Patricia, was after my father, Patrick, and his grandfather.

In those days Christian names were chosen from a slim volume. When I started primary school there were nine Marys in my class. The Patricia add-on was useful from time to time to make it clear who the teacher was yelling at, and so I was occasionally called Mary P. or Mary Pat, but at home and everywhere else I was – and still am – Mary. A famous Northern Ireland golfer at the time was Fred Daly, first Irish winner of the Irish Open. His wife gave birth to their son in the same hospital that week, and according to my mother, he and I both cried so loudly and incessantly that we were placed together in the maternity unit bathroom overnight to let the other better-mannered babies get their beauty sleep. I at least had the excuse that I was being brought home to Ardoyne, which, given what lay ahead, would have made anyone cry.

If I could have thrown a rattle from my hospital cot, it would have landed close to the second-level convent school I would later attend, the hospital trust's boardroom where I would much later serve as a director, my father's pub where I also served, and the parish church of my father's Protestant minister friend, the Reverend Canon Jimmy Arbuthnot. In later years, less innocent things would be thrown at the church and my father would spend many an hour helping Jimmy scrub paint off his walls.

Ardoyne then still had the characteristics of a village, though two busy major urban arteries ran right through it, connecting the city centre and the airport. The two arterial roads, the Crumlin Road and the Shankill/Woodvale Road, both of which we lived on at various times, merged into the Crumlin Road at the apex of a triangle of high land on which sat the Catholic Holy Cross Church and Passionist Monastery. On its relatively short journey from the direction of the city centre to Ardoyne, the Crumlin Road passed the very substantial edifices of Her Majesty's main prison in Northern Ireland, the city coroner's office, and Antrim County Courthouse. It was, in other words, no suburban backwater. The entrance to the Crumlin Road at Carlisle Circus in my day hosted the statue of Roaring Hanna, a nineteenth-century evangelical Presbyterian given to stirring up riots with his anti-Catholic rhetoric. Though I passed the familiar black marble figure every day for years, I knew nothing about him until he fell victim to an IRA bomb in 1970; but by then his twentieth-century doppelgänger Dr Ian Paisley had brought Roaring Hanna back to life. After its ascent past the grim linen mills and Holy Cross Monastery, the road continued on countrywards past a row of small shops on the right, behind which was the warren of tiny terraced houses and back lanes of Glenard housing estate where I started life.

The political dynamics that shaped our lives in Ardoyne started long before I was born, and at some distance from Ardoyne. Edward B. Fiske, trying in 1971 to explain the then two-year-old Northern Irish 'Troubles' to readers of the *New York Times*, started his account in the sixteenth century (four centuries late by some reckonings!): 'Relations between the two branches of Christianity in Ireland inevitably bear the scars of troubles that began shortly after the English Reformation in the 16th century when English settlers imported Anglicanism and Scottish settlers Calvinism into a land that had been staunchly loyal to Rome since the days of St Patrick in the fifth century.' That large-scale importation of English and Scottish settlers is better known as the Plantation, and the settlers themselves as Planters. The Plantation was essentially a reward system for mercenaries: for their service to the English Crown, the migrants to Ireland were awarded lands taken from the native Irish. That history contributed instead to a siege-and-defence mentality on the Planter side and to a victim-and-vengeance mentality on the native side. Both perspectives have shown themselves to have exceptionally long shelf-lives.

A war of attrition between Planter and Gael prevailed for generations, with the former, though a minority, garnering and holding most of the political power. However, it was the eruption of Anglo-European politics on Irish soil in the form of the Williamite war at the end of the seventeenth century that left the deepest sectarian legacy, one that still haunts to this day. The war had a number of battlefields, but it was the Battle of the Boyne, which took place in 1690, that was decisive. It should have been long forgotten by the time I was born 261 years later; in fact, it was still being fought. A fierce and bloody skirmish between William III, the Dutch Protestant King of England and Scotland, and his Catholic father-in-law James II, the recently deposed monarch, was in the main a battle about things European, not Irish. But this final defeat of James II – and by extension of the Catholic claim to the throne – created the foundation for legal discrimination against Irish Catholics, and for the concept of 'Protestant ascendancy'.

No sooner had I taken my first breath than, as a result of tradition, circumstance of birth and parentage, I was assigned to one side of the Boyne battlefield: the Catholic Jacobite side. Not that any of us were familiar with the fields around the Boyne where the battle had raged. Today the site is an important heritage attraction, but that is a very recent phenomenon and symbolic of times changing for the better. For most of my life, the descendants of the losers did not visit the Boyne battle site, for reasons to do with having lost and not wanting to remember. The descendants of the Protestant Williamite winners, among whom I lived, never visited it either, for although they assiduously remembered the event, the battle site's location, near the town of Drogheda, was south of the border.

The biggest public holiday in the South was St Patrick's Day, and the parade along Dublin's main thoroughfare, O'Connell Street, was a vast national spectacle, featuring bands from all over Ireland and from America. Most years we travelled to Dublin to watch the colourful parades of marching bands, Irish dancers and community floats, and to hear songs sung that harboured hopes for a reunited Ireland and lamented the centuries of baleful British imperial rule. North of the border, meanwhile, St Patrick's Day was routinely ignored. The big public holiday event there occurred on the Twelfth of July, when the Orange Order celebrated William's victory at the Boyne with militaristic parades featuring columns of bowler-hatted and orange-sashed men marching to the throbbing massive Lambeg drums with their ferocious rat-a-tat-tat. They were accompanied by sashaying tartaned flute bands and, usually, a rabble wont to sing blood-curdling folk songs. It was not a Catholic-friendly event, but as a youngster I accompanied those of my Protestant friends whose parents allowed them to watch the parades. I learned early that not all our Protestant neighbours were enamoured of Orangeism. Some openly despised it, others quietly ignored it, but gradually I grew in awareness that we Northern Catholics and Protestants were two separated tribes and I belonged to the one that history and sectarian politics had consigned to second-class status.

Before the bubbling lava of sectarianism revealed its full volcanic fury, there were happy times in Ardoyne. Ours was what is known as a *céilí*-ing or rambling house, which is to say it was like Victoria station at rush hour most of the time, with kids and visitors coming and going. Friends popped in unannounced, the kettle was always on, a topical discussion was easily started and less easily ended, stories were told and retold and then told again, and all the while the knitting needles were clacking or the sewing machine was whirring. My mother's parents and nine siblings were never more than five minutes away on foot no matter where we lived in Ardoyne, and were rarely away for more than five minutes. People connected with one another randomly and spontaneously, visiting without advance notice and talking face to face. I know – ridiculous, isn't it? Our house was fair game to aunts, uncles, cousins, friends, friends of cousins, anyone from Roscommon, anyone from Connacht, anyone from Dromara, Christian Brothers, priests, ministers, Plymouth Brethren, Methodists, Presbyterians, Anglicans, socialist atheists, everybody else's children and stray dogs.

My mother was a whizz at baking, and the only bought treats were a weekly packet of Marie biscuits, which had the flavour and consistency of cardboard unless dunked in sweet tea – in which case they had the flavour and consistency of wet cardboard but were just about edible. These were usually swooped upon by an army of student nurses from the nearby Mater Hospital, who came attached to our nursing cousin Bridget McManus from Dundalk. Bridget was extravagantly beautiful, and we were enthralled by the glamour of these young professional women who swanned elegantly (or so it seemed to me) from their nurses' quarters past my school each day to the hospital next door, wearing starched white caps over perfectly coiffed hair and blue woollen capes over pristine white uniforms. A day I have never forgotten was when they took me, on my own, aged about eight, on the bus into town. We had lunch in a restaurant and then we went to Woolworths, that emporium of childhood delights, where they bought me a paper parasol with exotic Chinese patterns, the uselessness of which in Irish weather was entirely irrelevant. The pure bliss of being a spoilt only child for that too-brief day, with a retinue of doting quasi-aunts, has never left me.

While the kettle whistled non-stop and my mother churned out apple tarts and Victoria sponges, the spring-sponginess of which was critiqued ad nauseam by the baker herself, it was a rare thing for my mother's people and my father's people to be in our house at the same time. Since everybody arrived uninvited in those days, there had to be some kind of automated signalling system that ensured there were no clashes. We kids learned early on that the two families were separate spheres and they had to be policed diplomatically. My mother's family always seemed to have a member patrolling the roads when I was out and about. Their intelligence system would leave the Special Branch and Mossad gasping in awe.

A discernible frostiness developed between the two sides after my mother's sister Una, another of the many hairdressers in our family, opened a salon a few metres from Sis McDrury's salon. It was hardly a rival enterprise, for Una's clientele were a generation and more younger than Sis's, but such facts were not allowed to interfere with a collective outbreak of indignation. I learned the arts of diplomacy and politics early. The men in our family had it easier, for mercifully we were only related to one barber – Frank McAreavey, whose wife was Nora Cassidy, my father's cousin. But pity the late Paddy Cassidy (another cousin) who had the sweet shop next door to the barber's: we had him tormented. The other thing the males in our family were exempted from was knitting. I doubt if any of them ever darkened Lena Magennis's shop door, but I trailed in and out of it every week buying wool for yet another matinee coat. I could knit them in my sleep, and often did while dozing late into the evening.

We children shuttled gullibly between the two sets of relatives, the unwitting carriers of gossip prised out of us by expert interrogation teams. Informing had its rewards, for we never left a relative's house or business without a coin or two jangling in our pockets. That was another thing we learned: how to maximise our limited earning capacity by exploiting the divided loyalties.

One thing the two sides had in common was a strong

allegiance to a football team that was not Antrim. On our mother's side of the family we were Down supporters to the marrow. In 1960, that team of titans brought the Sam Maguire Cup across the border for the first time, releasing into the body politic a delirium of pride that is still circulating in the stratosphere over the Mournes and wherever two or more Down supporters are gathered. We could rattle off the names of every member of the team, and over and over again the stories were told of how they snatched victory from Kerry in the closing seconds of the final with a free taken by my own particular hero, Paddy Doherty. As Paddy walked back into position after blasting the ball over the bar and putting Down a point in front, rumour had it that Kerry's Mick O'Connell asked him how much time was left. Paddy was reputed to have said, 'Three hundred and sixty-five days, Micko.' Some thought the story apocryphal. But some forty years later, when my daughter Emma introduced us to her future father-in-law, it was the first question I put to Mick – and he confirmed that it was true. It fully vindicated my unwavering half-century of devotion to Paddy Doherty, footballing virtuoso, incisive wit and Down man.

My father was not given to ruminating about what his or our life might have been if he had stayed in Roscommon, but occasionally – as when a Belfast friend bought a pub in Carrick-on-Shannon – I could see him become wistful. He and my mother were country people, and we inhabited the Mournes and north County Roscommon in our heads. We were complete in those places in a way we never were in Belfast, and we visited them often.

The half-door in Roscommon was the portal to a physically small but metaphysically enormous world where the kettle never cooled and conversation rattled on incessantly. I have a mental archive of memories stashed away, distilled from childhood visits.

It is literally cock-crow. The early-morning light is spare and gloomy through the plain net curtains that alone dress the windows recessed deeply in the thick walls of my grandparents' tiny cottage. After the tedious five-hour drive from Belfast with my father and younger sister Nora, I have slept fitfully on the lumpy settle bed that takes up most of the room.

This nine-foot-by-nine-foot space is both kitchen and living room. Granny is shuffling quietly around, hoping to waken us softly so that the bed can be packed away and transformed into an equally uncomfortable wooden bench (which she calls a 'form') and the day's work can start. Well water in the creamery can by the door is conveyed via tin can to the chipped porcelain basin on the floor, ready for us to wash. There is no bathroom, inside or out, no running water, no electricity. There are three small rooms and a storeroom. A bedroom off the living room is occupied by my father. Slightly larger is the room used by my grandparents. They share it with a china cabinet, a fold-down dining table, shelves where linens are stored and a pervasive smell of mothballs.

Over the fire in the 'main' room there is a fine clock brought back from New York before the start of the twentieth century. It is the only adornment, apart from a picture of the Sacred Heart of Jesus below, a red oil lamp perpetually lit thanks to seeds that my grandmother harvests from flowers in the front garden and grinds to oil by hand.

Now she is in my line of sight, bending over the turf fire, bringing its night embers back to life. I am startled to see her waist-length grey hair unwound, unplaited, shawled around her leaning shoulders. She looks girlish from the back as she hefts the iron kettle onto the cradle hook over the fire with its French flue. This is where she cooks hens, cocks, potatoes, boxty and soda bread, and fries bacon and sausages in inches of lard on black-crusted pots and pans. But there will be nothing to eat or drink until we have walked to Drumlion chapel for first Mass at seven o'clock. A six-mile round trip, every day, no matter what the weather.

Our mother has equipped us for a spell in rural Ireland with cardigans she has knitted, skirts her mother has sewn, and white Sunday sandals that were never designed for country life. Ruining the good shoes is not an option in those frugal times, so by day three we will have reverted to my father's barefoot childhood ways. He loved to tell the story of how he got his first pair of shoes at age fourteen, having just left school and heading for the train in Carrick-on-Shannon to take up an apprenticeship in Belfast. His father bought the shoes for him in his absence, bringing them back from town wrapped up in brown paper tied with string. In the giddy excitement my father failed to notice they were a match in neither size nor colour. He always claimed it was five years before the left fitted him and six before the right did so.

Granny adds a dollop of tepid kettle water to the washbasin: our incentive to get washed before it chills. Barefoot on the rough concrete floor, we begin the day with a mix of dread and delight – dread because of the miserable trek to Mass, delight because sometimes Granny has things to buy in Deignan's shop opposite the chapel, and therein lurks the outside chance of a shared bar of Cadbury's milk chocolate. Of course it cannot be eaten on the way home but must sit in our pockets until a clear hour has passed after taking Holy Communion.

When we get back to the cottage, around nine, Granny sets about making breakfast. Yesterday's leftover potatoes are mashed and mixed with handfuls of flour to make boxty. We hit the henhouse in search of eggs. The fields beyond the henhouse, dotted with haystacks and hungry cattle, slope down to the railway tracks and flatten into the River Shannon's Lough Eidin. We stand and look, taking a deep breath of fresh, fresh air before entering the fusty coop.

The narrow deal table pushed up against the bedroom wall serves as chopping board and dining table. There will be lard-fried eggs, fried bread, fried bacon, fried sausages, fried black pudding, fried boxty. We can almost hear our arteries clanging shut. To the left of the table is Granda's rocking chair, the cathedral from which he exercises dominion over the open fire with a long tongs. He selects the embers that will be placed and replaced on the hard shoulders on either side of the firepit, where teapots are set to brew or cooked soups and stews to simmer. He is a daunting old grump, and piously righteous. His prayer book and rosary beads are prominently displayed on the table. During the Great Famine, he tells us, the ditch in front of the house was piled with dead bodies.

We become giddy as soon as we hear the approach of the Sligo train. We want to race to the stone bridge where the train disappears on one side and reappears on the other, but Granny forbids it unless an adult is with us. Dad and Granda are hand-cutting hay with scythes, and their work cannot be interrupted for anything so frivolous. We beg Granny to accompany us, but she is determined not to. We will be adults before anyone bothers to tell us that her father, a railway worker, was killed while walking on that track.

Granny sees a car, any car, and thinks: Knock Shrine. My

father will bring her and squeeze in us children and two neighbours. Holier-than-thou Granda will not go. The neighbours arrive with the rosary beads already out, and for the next hour there will be prayers until we get to Knock. When we arrive, there will be more prayers, and on the way back the praying will start again. But what makes it all worthwhile are the stalls outside the church with their holy trinkets. In advance of our holidays, relatives have given us threepences and sixpences that are burning the holes of hell in our pockets in that remote cottage miles from shops. Knock Shrine is our early and admittedly unlikely introduction to retail therapy. But first we have to manoeuvre ourselves into position behind the neighbours and Granny as they circle the outside of the church saying the rosary. The trick is to have them slightly ahead of us as the bazaar comes into view. We slow down. The adults turn the corner out of view. We sprint to the stalls and buy a Miraculous Medal sixpenny ring each. They will have turned our fingers green by the time we get home, but we are as thrilled with our purchases as if they were diamonds from Tiffany's.

The last time we came to Knock, Granny bought a small Sacred Heart picture to replace the sooted-up one in the kitchen. As she unwrapped it, Granda enquired as to what it was. The answer enraged him: what vanity to buy a picture to replace another. He grabbed the new picture, which fell, causing the glass to shatter. Granny humbly crumbled away into a corner. I harboured homicidal thoughts towards him for the following three decades, the forgiveness and sacrifice represented by the Sacred Heart notwithstanding.

Among those who rambled into our house in Ardoyne was Father Ailbe, a Roscommon man: his father was the local doctor in Castlerea. He was the out-and-out favourite priest in our house, for he had a wonderful sense of fun and a very relaxed view of the Church. He always came in through the back door, picking up the wet dishcloth from the sink as he passed by and flinging it at the first child he encountered. That started it. He created merry mayhem every time he visited. We called two goldfish after him in succession, but both died of over-feeding. Ailbe, who was himself on the corpulent side, was worried enough to stop eating my mother's apple tart for a brief period. We were surprised to learn that he had been quite an athlete in his younger days, which were not that long before he arrived in Ardoyne. Later he presided at my wedding, and he never forgot our anniversary.

Then there was the shy Father Justin Coyne, so beloved by all the children of the parish. His skills as a preacher were limited, but one on one he was amazingly affirming and encouraging of each child he encountered, whether in the chapel or on the street. There were priests in jeans and leather jackets, but Justin was not one of them. Always dressed in black suit and clerical collar when out about the parish, or in his soutane when about the monastery, he had an ascetic quality and a shyness. Some hint of pathos and humility in him drew people to love him. He was the gentlest of gentlemen, and by chance he became my friend and mentor.

He had taught in the seminary in Ardoyne before I was born and had known my mother's family. On his return there years later, after teaching elsewhere, he was standing at the back of the chapel one Saturday as I emerged from Confession. My face seemed familiar and he asked if I was one of the McManus girls – not an uncommon question, as the youngest of my mother's sisters was a mere seven years older than me and local people often remarked on my resemblance to the McManuses. I said I was not exactly a McManus girl but that I was the daughter of one of them, and brought him up to date on all seven McManus girls, which took quite a bit of time since they were almost all now married and had busloads of children. He said he would call to the house some day to say hello to my mother. From then on he arrived on our doorstep every Sunday after evening Mass, and we were drawn in to the most candid discussions about life, death, faith, heaven, hell, philosophy, politics and religion. It was grist to my mill, for I was thirteen and full of political and religious angst. The Second Vatican Council was in full swing, and the stresses and strains that had provoked Pope John XXIII to call it were already in the ether even in Belfast, or maybe especially in Belfast.

Pat McAlister, who worked in my father's bar, was another mentor, and something of a foil to Father Justin. Pat was then in his mid fifties and unmarried. Since he lived alone and was a family friend as well as an employee, he often took his meals with us, including on Christmas Day. Pat was one of the cleverest and most interesting men I ever encountered, and though modest by nature he told fascinating stories about his days serving with the International Brigade in Spain. He was full of opinions about socialism, which he strongly espoused, and clericalism, which he despised. He had joined the Brigade in Canada and fought against Franco with like-minded Protestant socialists from Belfast. The Church's support for Franco incensed him, and when he was invalided back to Ireland in 1938 at the age of thirty, he found many doors closed to him because of his politics. A little over twenty years later, he and my father ran across each other, and he got a job as a barman and general factotum in my father's pub, the Long Bar on the Lower Falls Road. I spent each lunch hour from school as his audience of one.

It was from him that I first heard the name of the poet Federico García Lorca, as Pat recited his poetry from memory in the worst Spanish in the history of Spanish-speaking.

My mother loved Pat, but when his political instruction of her firstborn led me to embrace atheism and apply to join the Communist Party of Great Britain and Ireland, she had the head-staggers. The sorry tale was told to my then headmistress Mother Helena, who solved the problem by taking me for a personal religion class each morning. She was not in the least unkind or hectoring, just very persistent. 'God is in the inkwell! God is in the table!' After a week of it I was prepared to concede that God was in the inkwell and the table. Helena was triumphant, and my mother was mollified. Pat McAlister countered by giving me a copy of the English lyrics of 'The Internationale', the tune of which he tried to teach me; but since he was not blessed with a lyrical voice or anything approximating to it, I never did pick up the melody.

Meanwhile Father Justin was also apprised of the dire possibility of my apostasy. I told him about the inkwell and the table. He thought it unlikely that God was there, but diplomatically suggested we give Mother Helena the benefit of the doubt so that normality could be restored. I knew enough not to tell him about 'The Internationale', just in case my mother's anxieties were given another dose of oxygen. Over the following years, into my late teens, these two men, Pat McAlister and Father Justin, fed my mind, imagination and spirit.

Father Justin's terminal illness went unnoticed for a while by us self-absorbed children. His tall frame gradually became more and more stooped. We saw the effort it took for him to get up the hill to our house, how he sometimes stopped and held onto the railings at Everton School, but it never occurred

to us that he was dying. Had I been asked, I might have estimated his age to be well over seventy. In fact, when he died
on the night of 22 June 1969, he was still in his forties. It was
a Sunday, and when the door knocked I answered it expecting to see him. Instead it was an altar boy and friend from the
badminton club, Paddy Gormley, sent to tell us Justin had
died. I still remember the haunting spontaneous wail that
went up from the children as his coffin emerged from the
monastery. My only son is named after him, fulfilling a promise I made to myself that day. His picture sat on my desk
throughout my time as President, and is on my desk even now
as I am writing. Just as Pat McAlister taught me a healthy
scepticism and anti-sectarianism, Justin's saintly forbearance
and gentle nature helped me to understand better the skewed
dynamics of the world I lived in and to believe in the power
of God, prayer, goodness and love to change things for the
better.

Years later, I made an official visit to Kenya, which included
a visit to the grave of the Venerable Edel Quinn, who had
been a Legion of Mary envoy to east Africa. She had been
unable to become a nun because of the tuberculosis that
eventually killed her in her mid thirties, but chose instead to
become a lay missionary. Father Justin had been the organiser of the Legion of Mary in darkest Ardoyne. We did not do
anything heroic, just said prayers and undertook occasional
good works. Father Justin loved to tell the story of Edel's
heroic life and was delighted that at the sacrament of Confirmation I had taken her name. Every week at the meeting
of our Legion of Mary praesidium, we giddy teenagers sorely
tested Father Justin's bottomless patience by our constant
fidgeting through prayers and our invented sightings of mice
to cause a distraction. He was very much in my mind as I

walked up that day to Edel's grave. I passed through a group of missionary sisters, one of whom gently put her hand on my arm and whispered, 'I was also a friend of Father Justin's.' He might just as well have appeared himself.

The Holy Cross church and monastery in Ardoyne, run by the Passionists, was for many a comfort blanket in lives dimmed by poverty and lack of opportunity. It was our parish church, and virtually every form of charitable, social, sporting and spiritual endeavour was associated with it. It was the fulcrum of our lives. We were hooshed out to weekly Confession, Sunday Mass, holy days, retreats, missions, novenas, Legion of Mary, rosary crusades, confraternities and daily Mass. And our parish apprenticeship to lives of holiness was enhanced by collateral non-parish activities. We joined the Dominican-inspired White Star League, dedicated to eradicating misuse of the Lord's name and inappropriate use of swear words. We took the pledge of the Pioneer Total Abstinence Association, promising to avoid alcohol until adulthood. We said our morning and night-time prayers. During Lent we said the family rosary every evening, and each of the forty Lenten mornings began with our mother's daily exhortations to us to get out to first Mass and not disgrace ourselves in front of the Dinan family, who were a credit to the Church, the parish and the country: exactly the family of saints and scholars my mother wanted us to be.

God, how we resented those holy Dinans, who lived in front of the chapel and whom we knew well, for the younger ones of that large family overlapped with the older ones of ours and we were friends. Our mother had drummed into us that they were 'the purest of holy saints'. But a chance meeting some years ago in Brisbane with one of the older

Dinans – Muredach, then Pro Vice Chancellor of the Catholic University of Australia – revealed that his dear mother, God be good to her, had blackmailed the Dinan kids into attending daily Mass by upcasting the great Christian example of the Leneghan children, every one of whom, according to her, was miles holier than the Dinans! No wonder God sent the Passionists to Ardoyne, for the notorious Ardoyne Mothers Meeting (equivalent to the Supreme Court, only in our parish and self-appointed) would undoubtedly have made mincemeat of the Jesuits.

I often walked to and from Mass with my McManus grandparents, for, next to their home, Holy Cross Church was the centre of their lives. It was the centre of mine too, along with the Ovada badminton club, Pat Collins's ice-cream emporium, known as Castle Creameries, the Glenard and Gleneagle chip shops, and the wicked gossipy banter in Charlie Delaney's newsagency. Charlie ran the badminton club. I was a mediocre player, but the club produced some stars, and my friends Kathleen Boyle and Maureen Totten distinguished themselves also on our school team, which managed to win an inter-schools championship. There I am in the winners' picture, complete with large cup, though my contribution was to make it a slimmer victory than it might otherwise have been. I could claim in my defence the handicap of being very short-sighted, but as Kathleen and Maureen both wore glasses, that excuse is a bit lame.

The same lame excuse applies to my undistinguished career as a camogie player, both at school and in the parish, where I played for Ardoyne Kickhams (badly, with glasses) along with Kathleen and Maureen, who once again were stars also with glasses. Given that camogie is played by lambasting a ball as hard as a cricket ball with a mighty lump of a stick, provoking it to travel through the air at considerable speed, my concern to protect my one pair of National Health spectacles, which my parents could not afford to replace, seems adequate in explaining why my tackling and fielding of a dropping ball were spectacularly awful. Luckily in those days parents and siblings never thought to show up at matches, so there was no one at home to rub it in. That is until the day Ardoyne Kickhams met the Michael Dwyers club from the Lower Falls Road for a match in the Falls Park. Five minutes into the game there was a kerfuffle over custodianship of the ball involving players much more courageous than me; I was as far as it was possible to get from the scene without actually leaving the pitch. What exactly happened within the scrum is disputed, but suddenly we were being chased down the Falls Road by the opposing team. I stopped at a phone box outside the Royal Victoria Hospital, intending to call the police. The others all jumped on a passing bus, leaving me the only target of the approaching tribe of warrior Amazons. I expected to be battered to a pulp.

Every so often in life an event proves the existence of the Communion of Saints. This was one of them. Heaven had decreed that my father was in fact the owner of the Michael Dwyers club rooms, which were above his pub, the Long Bar on the Lower Falls. I worked weekends in the pub and often sold its legendary beef pies to club members en route to meetings or after matches. My mother wouldn't let us touch the pies for fear they would put us off our dinner. That was evidently a mistake. Many of the girls confronting me were monuments to the muscle-building capability of those pies. Luckily for me, I was recognised as my father's daughter. The Michael Dwyers girls backed off and I slithered home. Naturally they betook themselves to the Long Bar for hot beef pies, and did not miss the opportunity to apprise my father and his entire Saturday clientele of the day's events.

We had Catholic parish schools in Ardoyne, which, like the nearby Protestant schools, catered mainly for working-class children. My parents chose not to send us to them, mainly because there were no classes in the Irish language – a cultural lacuna my father and his cousin, Brother Bede McGreevy, in particular felt strongly about, since such schooling as they had received in Roscommon was through the medium of Irish. Instead, the boys went to the Christian Brothers, a twenty-minute bus ride away rather than a five-minute walk.

The girls went a mile away to the Convent of Mercy, which was wedged into a small site on the Crumlin Road dominated by a jail, a courthouse, a Catholic hospital, a nurses' home and a seminary. It seemed to have captured the worst aspects of each of its neighbouring institutions' strict regimes: judgemental, authoritarian, austere, harsh and narrow. Yet not all the teachers were unkind. All were women – some nuns, some unmarried laywomen, some married. Some were unfailingly pleasant despite large class sizes, but the menacing ambience was overwhelmingly dictated by the brutal headmistress and her batty deputy. By the time I left to move on to grammar school, I detested the place and the unnecessary anxiety it inflicted on children while drumming into their heads the 370 questions and answers of the Penny Catechism's rudimentary theology. Day after day in answer to the question 'Why did God make you?', we chanted in unison, 'God made me to know him, love him and serve him in this world and to be happy with him forever in the next.' Delayed gratification was definitely the order of the day, for happiness in this world was neither a priority nor an ambition in the Convent of Mercy.

I promised myself for years that if I had children I would never, ever send them to the Mercy(less) nuns. But by the time my girls were ready for school in Rostrevor, County Down, thirty years later and forty miles from Ardoyne, times had changed and our village school was run by altogether more congenial Mercy nuns, who were if anything lenient and indulgent to a fault. It was they who suffered the karma of having to put up with my younger daughter Sara, having been lulled into a false sense of security in dealing with the older, less inquisitorial Emma. 'I know God made the world, Sister Regina, but where *exactly* was he standing when he made it?' Poor Sister Regina still loved Sara to bits. The latter's excellent junior infants teacher Miss Walsh, in her first teaching post, decided at the end of that year to undertake a master's degree in educational psychology. When I asked her why, she answered simply, 'Your Sara.' I understood perfectly. In one of those quirky coincidences, Miss Walsh's father had been the best friend of my saintly mentor Father Justin.

I have said that Ardoyne was no backwater; but in those days it felt more like a village than a city suburb. The monastery, the fire station and the bus station, each with their own respective cohorts of uniformed men, lent a unique atmosphere to the place. We knew all those men by name and they knew us. I presumed that every parish in the country had dozens of priests until many years later I went to live in a rural one-priest parish and it dawned on me for the first time how ususual Ardoyne was in this respect. Father Honorius Kelly, a Dubliner, was responsible for our end of the parish. He was the uncle of Frank Kelly, who would play Father Jack in the comedy series *Father Ted*. It is fortunate that Honorius did not live long enough to see *Father Ted*, for his resemblance to Father Jack was sometimes commented upon.

I have no memory of the two Glenard homes I lived in – 60 Ladbrook Drive, which was behind my grandparents' house, and 22 Balholm Drive, at the top of their street – but there are photos of me outside the former in a fine Silver Cross pram, and there are stories of attempts by Billy Bates, the boy next door in Balholm, to teach me language more appropriate to inebriates or sailors or both. I have a vague memory of him, but our paths never crossed again after we moved a couple of minutes' walk away across the main road, behind the fire station, to Mountainview Gardens. I imagine my mother made sure of that. She recounts how, when Billy's mother asked her how to transform her sickly son into a healthy lump like me, she advised feeding him more fish. He almost choked to death a week later on fishbones. Later, when he was serving a prison sentence in Crumlin Road jail for serious paramilitary offences, fellow republican inmates fed him a drink of powdered glass – with the intention of making him terminally sickly – for fear he had turned state's evidence. Last I heard he was in witness protection in the United States. He is not to be confused with Billy 'Basher' Bates, a Protestant of the same name born close by, on the Shankill side of the Crumlin Road. Basher Bates became a loyalist paramilitary and a member of the brutal sectarian murder gang known as the Shankill Butchers. In jail he claimed to have found God, which may explain God's absence from the streets of Belfast; but on his release a disgruntled fellow loyalist, whose father he had apparently murdered, shot him dead.

On the left of the Crumlin Road (travelling countrywards), at its Ardoyne apex across from Glenard, was the fire station, a mecca for us local kids. We knew every piece of equipment and every drill; and like soldiers at reveille we lined up at the sound of the station alarm, thrilled to see those magic red engines dashing out onto the Crumlin Road. To the back of the fire station was the tidy Mountainview estate of newish small semi-detached houses with gardens front and back. Number 23 Mountainview Gardens became our third Ardoyne home when I was still a pre-schooler. We were the first Catholics to live on that street, for, thanks to a history of pogroms against Catholics, the main road tended (roughly) to be a sectarian dividing line. That home holds by far my happiest early childhood memories of Belfast. My parents were then young and full of fun and faith in the future. The family, though growing, was still small, and next door was an exactly matching family, the Watsons, with whom we instantly bonded. At the bottom of the street there were the Maxwell girls and halfway up the O'Neills and many other families who opened doors and hearts to us and we to them. There was the very occasional expression of sectarianism, but if it was offensive to us it was just as offensive to our Protestant friends. But the big attraction of that street was the huge field and glen it opened on to, with endless scope for childish adventures and its face to the sun.

Leaving Mountainview Gardens was traumatic, not least because my parents had omitted to tell me we were moving. I arrived home to find no one there, and no furniture. I ran to a friend's house, so distraught that I banged my head on her protruding bathroom windowsill, and then bled so profusely that her mother thought I was going to die at her back door. Within minutes there was a gaggle of neighbours and a fireman. He established that I was unlikely to die, wasn't concussed, but just needed to go home. The only problem was, I had no idea where home now was.

One of the neighbours had a vague idea that someone had heard it was among the two hundred houses on the Wood-vale Road; someone else thought it was on the Falls Road. The fireman, whose wife was a friend of Auntie Una, insisted that this was a job for the local bobby, who generally passed by on his bike every hour or so. Our neighbourhood police force, all one of him in those sainted days, duly arrived and pedalled off in the direction of Una's salon. On hearing the news, she raced out of the salon, leaving some woman half-way through a permanent wave treatment, and, still wearing her lemon shop coat with hairclips attached to the pockets, took me by the hand and set off to 142 Woodvale Road, a five-minute walk away, singing an old Marie Lloyd music hall song that had been revisited in a British war film that year, *Ice Cold in Alex*: 'My Old Man (Said Follow the Van)'. The song includes the words: 'I dillied and dallied, dallied and dillied, lost me way and don't know where to go . . . Oh I'm in such a mess, I don't know the new address, I don't know even know the blessed neighbourhood.'

It turned out that my mother thought my father had given me the new address, and my father thought my mother had. And both thought I had stopped off at my cousin Ann's house, as I often did on the way home. The upshot was that no one considered me missing. Fortunately, but also suspi-ciously from my point of view, my parents had managed between them to assemble all the other children, and for a long time I harboured (or claimed to harbour) the suspicion that there was a Hansel and Gretel element to my predica-ment. I milked the trauma for all it was worth. Still do.

The Woodvale Road house was a miserable old semi-d. I hated it, for it never saw the sun, had a mud patch of an excuse for a back garden, and no front garden at all. It was redeemed only by great neighbours: the Shaws, who were Plymouth Brethren, and the O'Reillys, Catholics who lived beside the Shaws, a few houses away from us. Both families were open and welcoming, and we ran in and out of their front and back doors daily. The two youngest O'Reilly boys, Tony and Myles, were the older brothers I never had. I adored them, adored all thirteen O'Reillys, for they were full of devilment.

A smattering of other Catholic families lived on the Wood-vale Road, including our cousins the O'Haras and my first primary school teacher, the kind-hearted Miss Matthews. The O'Haras lived at the northernmost end at number 190, twenty-five terraced houses away from us. At their end of the road was McConkey's, probably the most cheerless sweet shop on the planet, a place where children, even children with pennies to spend, were regarded as the pillaging enemy and treated accordingly. The tiny shop was stacked to the ceiling with sweets in large jars. A wooden ladder was needed to reach the top shelf, and for want of melodrama in our lives we always asked for sweets from the Matterhorn. The austere Miss McConkey, in her oversized brown shop-coat, would creak arthritically up the ladder with a countenance that would sour fresh milk. We loved to irritate her – but only occasionally, for Jean Spence's shop was two doors from our house, and although it was not overburdened with stock or choice, Jean herself was chirpy and we loved her company. Choosing where to spend the rare treat of sweet money gifted by a passing aunt or uncle or family friend was a serious task. The Crumlin Road intersection had a glut of sweet shops, and we had tried, tested and rated them all.

There were no matching houses on the opposite side of our section of the Woodvale Road, just the large monastic edifice and a rather grand adjacent house with manicured gardens that had been a family home to one of the Protestant mill owners before being acquired by the Catholic parish. A high granite wall ran the length of the house and the monastery grounds. My attic bedroom, shared with Nora, overlooked that elegant house and its tennis court. I have no recollection of ever seeing anyone enjoy the grounds or play tennis, but that could be because to see out the window I had to stand on a chair and not just peer out of the puny skylight but hang out of it. More than once, neighbours shopping in Spence's would roar at us to 'GET DOWN', some even going to the trouble of rapping on the front door and informing on us. Passengers on passing buses shook their fists too, but the lure of seeing the pretty herbaceous borders, the picture-perfect flower beds and lawn was too hard to resist, especially as a respite from homework. From our ground-level front door, all we could see of the idyll across the road was a high wall and a blank gate through which large cars came and went.

The Woodvale Road was a somewhat genteel continuation of the Shankill Road, and it in turn ended where it met and merged with the Crumlin Road. Both the Shankill and Crumlin Roads were also the boundaries of Protestant enclaves. Off both sides of the Shankill Road were the rough-and-ready little streets of small terraced houses with their front steps regimentally scrubbed, waxed and polished every Monday – mirror images of the neighbouring Catholic streets and houses of the Lower Falls Road. I lived for Saturdays, when my mother or grandmother and I would walk the Shankill Road, in and out of its shops, especially Loanes, the famous drapery shop, where we bought the fabrics that became, by our own handiwork, dresses, skirts, petticoats, pyjamas, trousers, over-coats and bedclothes. The fanciest shop in the most elegant mall has never managed to evoke in me the excitement and delight of Loanes, with its stout wooden counter stacked with bales of ex-army blankets just waiting to be turned into hand-some topcoats and matching hats by my needle-genius granny. Her Fair Isle sweaters, socks and even wartime gas-mask cov-ers, made from recycled wool, were legendary. My mother and her siblings were sometimes lined up at school to impress a visiting dignitary with their sartorial style.

At the bend in the road where the Shankill Road gave way to the Woodvale Road was Woodvale Park. It was a public park, but dear Lord, what a joyless place, where the swings and roundabouts were locked up on a Sunday in order to keep holy the Sabbath day. This in a place riddled with so much round-the-clock, seven-days-a-week, three-hundred-and-sixty-five-days-a-year sectarianism that we would have been hard put to find an entire minute that was not unholy. The other six days we ventured into the park alone at our peril, for there was always a shape-throwing gang of rough-tongued boys or girls ready to have a go at us, pushing, shoving, throw-ing stones or shouting 'Fenian bastards!' Apparently they could tell we were Catholics from any distance. I wrote a poem about it in my diary shortly before we moved to Ardoyne house number five. The poem was about Woodvale Park, but could just as easily apply to Ligoniel Park up the road, which was equally joyless and dangerous for Catholic children.

> Fenced in or fenced out
> Do not walk upon the grass
> Or put your head through
> Ramrod fences.

Flowers standing to attention
Sweet Williams wilt in serried files
Perfumed wallflowers on parade
Salute the prancing warden.

Do not cycle in this park
Or make a noise or dare to laugh
In case the owners notice
Your religion.

See saw marjerydaw
Rock the horse
Push the swing
Politely.

Lukewarm, leaden drinking fountain
Clammy goblets chained of course
Crater cloyed with heavy water
Magnetise a thirsty child.

Small, I stretch on top tiptoes
Dry-mouthed dip the stale stillness
Wary of my eyeless back for
I know I am being watched.

Our Protestant friend Florence Maxwell generally accompanied us to the park. We were in awe of her, and almost entirely dependent on her for our safe recreation there. She was courageous to the point of foolhardy, for many of those she stood up to had to be faced next day in her schoolyard. Years later, when she married a Scottish soldier, Stuart Taylor, in Thiepval barracks in Lisburn, we repaid her loyalty by attending the wedding, my sister Nora acting as her bridesmaid, even though such fraternising with British troops generally resulted in Catholics like us being tarred and feathered by other Catholics like us. No harm came to us from that ecumenical outing, and it made my parents' day to hear the minister, Reverend Sidney Callaghan, tell the congregation that he saw me more often in his church than most of his parishioners. That too was thanks to Florence, who returned the compliment by often accompanying Nora and me to Saturday Confession, sitting patiently dangling her legs from the back pew while we snaked up the long queue until finally we got into the confession box. She always had a thousand questions about what went on in there and kept a scorecard of the penances given by the priest. More than once she declared it unfair that last week's sins had only merited three Hail Marys against ten this week. She took to advising us on the best priest to go to, and was thoroughly charmed to discover from observation that Father Timothy dispensed Cadbury's Roses with his Hail Marys. On her advice we shifted to him. Florence was reared with us in our house, and we were reared with her and her sisters Catherine and Winnie in her house. We took our denominational differences in our stride, accepted our respective political identities with a touch so light they barely registered in our daily lives.

We were in Maxwells' when, some years later, the first bomb went off in Ardoyne. The Old Country Roses dinner service in the china cabinet shook and several Waterford crystal glasses knocked against each other. They were Mrs Maxwell's pride and joy, bought with scraped-together pennies, for theirs was a modest working-class home. We spent the afternoon wrapping each piece carefully in newspaper. They were put away 'until people got sense', as Florence's mother put it. People never did get sense while she was alive. Like so many of us, she and her family upped and left, going to live in Millisle on the Ards peninsula, where they kept a holiday caravan. Their grandchildren would never know the joyless delights of Woodvale Park.

The park was also a tempting shortcut to and from my second-level school, St Dominic's on the Falls Road. Early mornings were safe enough, but the afternoon return was not. Wearing my distinctive wine-coloured school uniform, I might as well have been wrapped in the Irish tricolour. I never came through the park on my own unless armed with the stick I used for playing camogie at school or for beating silly lads who, had they the remotest notion about Irish culture, would have known better than to mess with a hurler. Even a bad hurler can inflict substantial damage on a shin or calf or a retreating backside, especially in the absence of a referee.

A hundred yards uphill from the fire station, across the road and next door to the nominally state but actually Protestant Everton Girls School attended by Florence and not a few of those she routinely flailed on our behalf, stood our last Ardoyne home, right on the front of the Crumlin Road. It was a substantial semi-detached corner house with wonderful light and a large garden in which we had our own swing. Unlike those in Woodvale Park, it was never locked up; but because of the large queue that formed to use it, it regularly had an egg timer parked beside it. As did the sole bathroom and toilet. This was located at the top of the stairs, and was immediately preceded by two corner shelves on which sat large statues, one of St Joseph and the other of the Blessed Virgin. They in turn were preceded by framed prints of Pope John XXIII, President John F. Kennedy and the 1916 Irish Proclamation in ascending order on the wall. We had ample time to study this last, given its position and the amount of time spent waiting for the bathroom door to open.

Before we moved in to 657 Crumlin Road, my father installed the then rare phenomenon of a built-in kitchen, with an early version of the automatic washing machine. The first time it went into spin mode and rattled unmercifully against the shared wall, the two elderly ladies who lived next door became hysterical, believing, having lived through the Belfast Blitz, that war had returned and with it aerial bombardment. The noise from the seven exuberant children who had just moved in may also have added to their confusion. Yet they quickly got to know each of us by name. Damien instantly became their favourite and their runner, obligingly (for a small fee) going to the shops to collect their 'messages', which mostly consisted of bottles of gin from the off-licence once owned by our Great-Aunt Doll and Great-Uncle Willie O'Hara. It is a miracle Damien's teeth are as good as they are, given that his income was regularly lavished on sweets bought on the way home and only irregularly shared with his siblings as they lay in wait for his return. He was a ridiculously winning child, not least because a childhood tumour had inflicted lasting damage on one side of his face, requiring severe regular surgery through to his late teens, which he never ever complained about, always quietly and good-humouredly accepting his lot. We never begrudged him his secret stash of sweets.

To our elderly blue-rinse neighbours Damien was a hero, having saved them from being eaten by a cannibalistic mouse that had ventured into their kitchen. Alerted by a racket that would have bettered rampaging elephants, he grabbed his hurley and ran next door, firmly expecting to encounter thieves or murderers. Meanwhile I ran to get the police inspector who lived across the road. The two women were throwing pots, pans and saucepan lids as the mouse ran rings around them. Damien caught it on the rebound from an airborne baking tin and pucked it over the heads of the hysterical ladies with his hurl. When they came to, having collapsed with fright and general upset, they were in time to see our hero delicately, and with due respect for a worthy opponent, deposit the deceased mouse by the tail in their compost bin. He was lavished with gold and silver, and took several years to come down off his Superman plinth.

# 3

The numerous moves during my Ardoyne years, each house no more than a hundred yards from the one we had just left, were prompted by the need for more space as babies continued to arrive. The final two moves indicated not just an expanding family but a shift from the working to the vaguely middle class, as my father morphed from trade union activist and barman to publican, with the heavily mortgaged purchase in the early 1960s of the Long Bar, a working man's pub on Leeson Street, just off the Lower Falls Road.

Many of the regulars were on either unemployment or sickness benefit and my father quickly became an expert at navigating the bureaucracy surrounding the benefits system, for not all were literate or capable of coping with form-filling. They were exclusively Catholic, and in the early years there was more interest in horse racing than politics, with men lining up at the bar to watch the races on television. Their sole forms of exercise consisted of going to the bookie's next door to place their bets, and dodging the officials sent to check that those who were on sickness or disability benefit really were sick or disabled. When such an official was spotted on Leeson Street, the nearest agile person who was not on the sick sprinted to the pub to raise the alarm. The warning having been received, any at-risk customers could escape via the Cyprus Street exit and be tucked up in bed at home by the time the official had been stopped by random passers-by and asked for directions, a match, a light, a pencil, a pen, a shilling . . .

The racing was watched on television in the pub, pint in one hand, meat pie in the other. My father sold the best meat pies in the history of pub meat pies. My mother was believed to bake them each day in between raising nine children, a rumour my father likely started and was never heard to contradict when asked by customers to convey their compliments to his wife. In fact they were bought daily by the gross from an Ardoyne bakery. On one infamous occasion, a customer overstayed the warning about an imminent official visit as his horse was coming up on the outside and looked to have a good chance of winning. Meanwhile the district nurse had already rapped on his door and found him not there. She was on her way back up the street when he exited the pub and ran straight into her. He had a meat pie in one hand and a crutch in the other. Limping laboriously, he explained that Mrs Leneghan, the publican's wife and an old family friend, was so worried about his health and his failing appetite that she baked him a meat pie every day, but only God's holy will and the help of the Communion of Saints gave him the strength to collect it, for he did not like to disappoint her.

Women never entered the main bar area. There was a tiny snug or booth at the front where they were permitted, though they were a rare occurrence except for those trying to prise money out of their dads or spouses, or coming to buy the famous beef pies. I was usually the only female behind the bar, though Nora also worked there occasionally; but since my school, unlike hers, was just five minutes away, I spent a lot of lunchtimes there too.

My father ran a very tight ship. Licensing laws were strictly adhered to, and customers were vetted so that those wont to argumentation, foul language or fighting were quickly barred. My father had a reputation as a gentleman and he liked a gentlemanly pub. He did not encourage an excess of conversation between staff and customers. Any hanging about was seen as dodging the work. So we cleaned countertops, passed pleasantries, polished glasses, refilled shelves, pulled pints, mopped out the toilets, emptied the ashtrays, brushed the floors and kept moving to avoid that paternal look indicating displeasure at time-wasting. Between the customers themselves there was plenty of easy wit and banter, with my father as a bemused listener, a damp cloth in hand as he wiped spillages and kept the countertop clean. He was always on the move.

His role as landlord of the Long Bar was to cost him dearly. But back in the early 1960s, when he borrowed the money to buy the pub, he had no idea of what lay ahead. The purchase was about cementing the economic future of his family. It helped that the manager of the Belfast High Street branch of the Munster and Leinster Bank, which gave him the loan, was Tim McHale, a west of Ireland man and a friend.

For the year and a half before my sister Nora was born, I had a cot to myself, or so I was told. From then until I married at twenty-four, I shared a bed, any available bed, with one or other of my little sisters. They shifted about so often and so erratically that I was never sure on any given night where a space might open up for me. I casually mentioned this one night as I said goodnight to my parents and their regular evening caller, the Reverend Canon Jimmy Arbuthnot, a Church of Ireland minister who lived six doors up and worked in Drew Memorial Church, near my father's pub. General denominational decorum meant that Jimmy never drank in the Long Bar, but he often shared a late-night glass of whiskey and a lot of debate and laughter with my father in our house. It was the era of the Second Vatican Council, and Jimmy, an arch-ecumenist, was loving all the deliberations. He was one of four Protestant ministers who were our immediate neighbours when we lived on the Crumlin Road. His Anglican colleague, the Reverend T. W. W. Jones, was the rector of the Immanuel Church on Ardoyne Road to the back of us. The quietly gracious Reverend John Llewellyn Wynn lived right opposite us and ministered in Ballysillan Presbyterian Church a couple of hundred yards away until he moved to Dublin at the beginning of the seventies. The not-so-gracious Donald Gillies, a dour fundamentalist Presbyterian, was a few doors up on our side. We saw him more often on the television than on the road, and usually in virulently anti-ecumenical voice. Jimmy was brilliant at mimicking Gillies.

Even when Jimmy was moved to St Barnabas, a few miles away, he and my father remained great pals. Their friendship was severely tested, however, when my father supplied him with an assortment of donkeys (from where I have no idea) to be used for children's rides at a fund-raising festival in Jimmy's new parish. The animals were sequestered in Jimmy's garden overnight before the event, but broke free and scattered in as many directions as there were donkeys. The two men, with a posse of bemused Protestants and Catholics, spent the entire night chasing them up and down the Antrim Road until they were eventually rounded up. If the two did not die laughing that night it was a miracle. Jimmy was sure the donkeys were Counter-Reformationists, out to subvert the Anglican Communion. My father conceded only that they were 'bloody Bolsheviks with allegiance to neither church nor chapel'.

On the night that I indelicately mentioned in front of

Jimmy that I was off upstairs on my nightly search for a place to sleep, I knew I had caused some embarrassment to my parents, although nothing was said. I came home from university next day to find a new single bed squeezed in between the two double beds already in the girls' room. My euphoria was short-lived, for on going to bed that night I found three sleeping heads now distributed across three beds. Kate had commandeered the single bed and there was no shifting her – not that night, not any night. One of the overrated benefits of being the oldest is the acquisition of staying-up-late rights. The younger kids with earlier bedtimes had a clear fix on the law of adverse possession long before I studied property law.

A big part of our childhood consisted of my father touring the relatives on his days off, usually taking the kids with him – out of my mother's way as she coped with the latest baby and prepared for the next. They were all open-door homes where there was a more than even chance of running into visitors 'up from the country', meaning usually Roscommon, and where the mere idea that any one of us would have a footballing allegiance involving the county of Antrim – in which we all actually lived – would have produced an outbreak of uncontrollable laughter. Antrim? Don't be ridiculous! We might have been living there, but we regarded ourselves as temporarily displaced, for that part of my tribe inhabited Roscommon in its thinking. We supported the Roscommon football team, which had been one of the great teams of the 1940s. In preparation for their 1962 final against Kerry, in our home on the Woodvale Road where the Gaelic Athletic Association was an unknown planet to our neighbours, we sewed a plague of blue and yellow Roscommon flags, which went to Croke Park with the family members fortunate enough to get tickets.

It was the first ever televised All-Ireland final. Few houses had televisions then, but we did, and the house that day was rammed with Roscommon relatives and friends and some curious Protestant neighbours. The atmosphere was febrile. The picture was so bad it looked as if the match was being played in a snowstorm. Most of us were seeing (through a blizzard) the Artane Boys Band for the first time, seeing Croke Park for the first time, seeing the teams lining up for the first time. We were fit to burst when the whistle blew, the match started and silence descended. Thirty-four seconds it lasted, that silence, before Kerry's Garry McMahon fisted a ball into the net: the fastest goal scored in the history of the All-Ireland football final and the one that probably produced the greatest outpouring of profane language ever heard in our house. The White Star League lost out badly that day, and the Pioneer Total Abstinence Association too. It was clear that mugs of tea, ham sandwiches and apple tart were not going to be adequate to the task of getting us through the match. Naggins of whiskey were produced and the tea was duly fortified. It made no difference to mood or outcome. Roscommon lost by six points, which constitutes well beaten in anybody's money, and our flags were put away *sine die*.

Roscommon had more than one nemesis that day besides the great Garry Mc. The other was the celebrated Mick O'Connell. He moved like Nureyev and executed kicks with the accuracy of a heat-seeking missile. He had already captained Kerry to an All-Ireland win in 1959 (before losing the 1960 final, as I have mentioned, to Down); and fifty-four years later he would give the miniature silver Sam Maguire Cup he won that day as Kerry captain to Charles Jeremiah

O'Connell, his firstborn grandson – and mine. Charles Jeremiah (Charlie) is named after great-grandfathers on both sides, and two great-great-grandfathers – all long dead before he was born. When Mick's wife Rosaleen saw him shortly after he was born, she was heard to say: 'I declare to God, Jeremiah is back!', a reference to the child's strong resemblance to her late father-in-law Jeremiah, coxswain of the Valentia lifeboat and not exactly renowned for his sweet, indulgent and patient nature, as she had cause to know having lived with him in the early days of her marriage. As it happens, Charlie does seem to have a sweet, indulgent and patient nature, so far. On a visit to Valentia's little island museum, I walked through the door and straight into a portrait of the said Jeremiah and immediately understood Rosaleen's remark. The resemblance was astonishing.

Sadly for both Roscommon and Kerry, Charlie and his brother Mossie are both true-blue, hard-core northside Dubs – which is to say supporters of Dublin's superstar five-in-a-row Gaelic football team. Before they started school, my grandsons had been to Croke Park more times than they'd had birthdays. Never in my wildest Ardoyne dreams did I think this was how life would pan out: mother and grandmother to Dubs. Martin still tells them stories about Antrim, poor deluded man. But then dreams are the stuff of future winning teams, or so he says. One in a row is the current elusive Antrim ambition, and has been since the GAA was founded in 1884.

I would likely have remained semi-detached from Antrim's less than amazing fortunes in Gaelic games at national level but for two people who attached themselves to our clan in the sixties. One was my Uncle Declan's girlfriend, and later wife, Kathleen Beirne, who was part of a luminous camogie squad that put Antrim on the All-Ireland map. The other was Martin McAleese, who by the time of our first date in June 1969 was captain of the Antrim minor football team and reputedly the first minor footballer in GAA history to be flown home from his summer job in London – somewhat controversially – for an important match. (I mention this only because if I didn't there would be hell to pay in our house.) Much as Martin is thrilled to be related by marriage to Mick O'Connell, there arises the slight problem of an imbalance in the stories of footballing heroics with which he can impress our grandchildren while they are still impressionable and innumerate. He has no All-Ireland medals with which to mesmerise them; but luckily for him Mick, ever casual about fame and fortune, gave his away to charities over the years.

Martin was one of those splendid young footballers whose fate was to be the target of every groin-numbing kick, thump, push, shove, trip, wallop, knock or smack that could be administered by the opposition behind the referee's back. The object is to frighten the living daylights out of them, nobble their potential in perpetuity, turn them off football for life and (more immediately) provoke them to retaliate in front of the referee so that they are sent off for what looks like a wanton, malicious attack on an innocent opponent. Many a mighty minor never appeared in a senior match as a consequence. I mention this by way of background to my later short career as an Antrim minor, Rossa and Queen's team groupie with a reputation for incitement from the sidelines and offering unwelcome advice to referees – of which more later, possibly, when I have figured out what can and cannot be safely disclosed in print while my mother is still alive and before the statute of limitations kicks in.

Once I teamed up with Martin, my social life revolved around his football club, O'Donovan Rossa, based on the Falls Road. I learned to play bridge there while waiting for him to finish training sessions, returned there after weekend matches to celebrate or commiserate, sang there, danced there and became part of the thriving Rossa family. Pat McManus was the football team's manager and selector, and Martin had many a nervous day waiting to be reassured by a phone call from him that he had made the team. To this day, almost fifty years later, Martin still asks when he comes through the door: 'Did Pat McManus ring, looking for me?' Sad.

Among my parents' closest friends were my father's first cousin Nan (Cassidy) Bradley and her Tyrone-born husband, Leo. They lived a couple of doors from Sis. Nan's first child, Ann, and I were born just weeks apart, started school together and were inseparable until her family emigrated to Philadelphia when she was nine and I came to experience undiluted aching loss for the first time. Across the years and miles since the dark day they disappeared down the Crumlin Road to get the boat, our family friendship never wavered, nor did the sorrow. Ann's mother and father carried the burden of uncured emigrants' grief to their grave, for leaving Ireland was not what they had wished; but jobs for Catholics were hard to come by, while work in America was plentiful. More than that, Leo could not stand the abiding whiff of sectarianism in Belfast.

In Philadephia, their lives were far from easy. Leo, who had been a formidable athlete in younger days, suffered a serious work accident shortly after the family arrived in the US. It severely hampered his ability to work and meant that the placid, open-hearted Nan, a clever woman who worked as a tax official, became the family's financial mainstay. My parents himmed and hawed for a time about following them to the US but stayed put in the end, a new child every couple of years making the transition seem ever more difficult. During those months that drifted into years of deliberations my parents never intended me to overhear, I dreamed constantly of going to Philadelphia, so much so that when Brian Friel's play *Philadelphia, Here I Come!* was the toast of the town during the mid sixties, the mere mention of its title would reduce me to tears. Visiting Nan's American home for the first time as a university student in the summer of 1972, with the Troubles raging back in Ardoyne, it seemed clear to me that despite the hardships, they had made the right choice for their children's sake. But as the years wore on and we saw each other more often, I could discern in her face an anguish for home in Ireland that could not be quenched but had to be endured. Just as our growing family had kept us in Ireland, so hers kept her in Philadelphia.

Nan came back to Ireland on holiday from time to time, and we visited her in Philadelphia. The resolute Leo never returned to Ireland, though he kept a proud eye from a distance on the legendary horse-racing success of his nephew and grand-nephew, Ted and Ruby Walsh. But he could not bear the thought of going back, because leaving Ireland would have broken him all over again. His daughter Marion had visited once in the early 1980s, but Ann carried a lot of her father's hesitation, and it was only when she turned fifty that I was able to persuade her to return to Ireland for the first time so that we could share a birthday party.

It was a cathartic few days. Our husbands concluded that they had married emotionally conjoined twins, reunited after being separated at birth, with a capacity for non-stop talking

unmatched except by each other. Ann's Irish-American husband Frank Dillon remarked that his wife, after a fortnight
in Ireland, had about her a completeness he had never witnessed before. Seeing a modern, vibrant Dublin, visiting the
modest but comfortable homes of cousins, marvelling at the
terrific education they had all received without bankrupting
their parents, Ann asked out loud if her parents had made
the right choice after all, for in her case and that of her siblings, going to university had not been on the agenda. It was
too expensive for Nan and Leo. It would be the next generation, their grandchildren, who would go to university and
enter the professions. In a remarkable coincidence, I was
invited to speak at the graduation ceremony one year at
Villanova University, founded in the suburbs of Philadelphia
by Irish Augustinian priests, and a place where many a famous
Irish athlete had perfected their talents. The parade of grad-
uates was led onto the pitch by the most outstanding student
of the year, Ann's daughter Caitlin. There was a lot of crying
that day.

Nan had dementia by that time and was in a nursing
home. Leo, lost without her, visited daily, making himself
useful as a volunteer tending to the garden and plants. Each
day he stopped off at the local deli and ordered her favourite
baloney and pumpernickel sandwich, which she ate with
gusto. Two years into this everyday ritual, she asked Ann
one day, 'Who is that wee man who keeps bringing me the
baloney and pumpernickel sandwich?' Yet when Martin and
I visited her, she knew me immediately (though she may
have thought I was my mother) and within minutes we were
back in Ardoyne – visiting Sis, pushing prams from shop to
shop, going to the Forum picture house, discussing whose
fish and chips were the best (Freddie Fusco's, D'Agostino's

or McCann's), buying baby wool in Lena Magennis's shop – and Philadelphia had never happened. When one of her doctors wondered out loud if her dementia was not in fact a deep-seated emigrant's depression, I wished to God he had kept that to himself, for it was hard enough to bear thinking about what forced emigration had cost us all.

I was two months shy of my eighteenth birthday when my parents' ninth and final child, Clement, was born. His arrival was badly timed, just as I started A-level exams and Nora her O levels. Worse still, our mother was weak as water after the birth, haemorrhaging badly and, according to the doctor, in need of a hysterectomy to save her health if not her life. Our family doctor, James O'Rawe, was a Catholic and himself the father of eleven children. He referred my mother to a Protestant gynaecologist, and the operation was duly performed in a state hospital. Shortly afterwards, Father Honorius arrived in a bit of a fury. He had found out about the hysterectomy, possibly from the hospital's Catholic chaplain, and in front of us children he berated my parents, demanding to know why his permission had not been sought, since my mother was still of 'child-bearing age'. It was an unnerving scene, and the indignity of it bore heavily on my mother, not to mention on me.

Honorius was not to know it, but clerical control was even then on the wane. The passive, obedient, 'pay, pray and obey' laity were slowly but surely getting up off their knees and asserting their natural human rights to freedom of religion, conscience, opinion and belief. The Holy See would come to face persistent internal questions regarding its teaching on women, human sexuality, artificial contraception and abortion. It would face a tsunami of sexual and financial scandals.

The days of false deference and passive obedience were on their way out.

For my generation of Catholics in Northern Ireland, the game-changer was the introduction of free second-level education at the end of the 1940s. The excellent education we received in Catholic schools gave us the intellectual tools and self-confidence with which to challenge the vast presumptuousness and pomposity of the Protestant elite who governed Northern Ireland, and to critique Catholic clerical power and the many flawed man-made doctrines conveniently but erroneously attributed to God. We were the generation in which women would routinely develop careers and in which family size would be decided by a husband and wife, not by their parish priest. Most of the sixty children created by my mother and her siblings would go on to have small families of two or three children.

My father was a member of the Knights of Columbanus, an organisation of Catholic laymen. He was part of a local group that immediately saw the potential offered by the new education law and saw to it that (despite the usual sectarian resistance) Catholic schools scaled up in order to harness and harvest that potential. I got the chance to go to a Dominican grammar school that only a short time before had been a boarding school mainly for a well-to-do elite and a small number of scholarship children.

The new education system did not end elitism or wasted lives. There were a fixed number of free grammar-school places, and these were awarded to those who did best in a competitive exam called the 11-plus. (That there were considerably fewer places for girls than for boys was revealed only decades later, thanks to the legal acumen of the journalist and barrister Michael Keogh, a dear friend.) In all, about 25 per cent of children benefited. Virtually all the rest were consigned to free non-grammar secondary schools. They were popularly deemed (no matter how the Department of Education dressed it up) to have 'failed' the 11-plus. It was an evil system, which broke the spirit of more than a few children, but few people then realised how dramatically the outcome could skew a life. The collaboration of Catholic schools in particular with that system has always haunted me. Stirring stories abound of secondary schools that, through great leadership and fantastic teaching, managed to transcend the hex of not being grammar schools and helped students to achieve their potential; but they faced unfair odds.

One curiosity that was never explained to us was why children attending Catholic schools had to sit the 11-plus in a nominally state but actually Protestant school. We were marched up two by two to the now demolished Finiston Primary School on the Oldpark Road on the day of the dreaded exam. It was just one more source of stress at the tail end of a year of chronic trepidation, mostly induced by our headmistress, Mother Brendan, who was choleric at best and insane at worst, and her deputy, a lay teacher, the late Miss Marie Malone, who had the longest, reddest, glossiest, pointiest, scariest polished nails since Cruella de Vil. They frightened the living melt out of all of us. We were already so intimidated by her that the regularly administered whacks with a wooden ruler were completely superfluous. I never again met her after the day I left that school of wretched memories. If I had, I am not sure that civility would have come easily.

I remember with burning annoyance how she chided my fun-loving, giggling younger sister, then aged about five, telling her that I had more brains in my little finger than she had in her whole body. My little sister, God bless her innocence, had just donned her first school uniform and was still innocuously untutored in the wearying ways of adult bullies. The teacher in question appears to have lived a very long and healthy life, which is surprising given the unforgiving musings that predominate when two or more of her past pupils are gathered together. She made the lives of many children miserable, and for some it was a misery that hung over their lives long after they had left her controlling clutches. I was greatly relieved on moving to St Dominic's High School on the Falls Road to find that corporal punishment, which was such a central part of the Mercy culture of relentlessly belittling us children, was not permitted by the Dominican nuns.

On the day the letter announcing my success in the 11-plus brought a flood of happiness to our house, the opposite was happening in my future husband's home, where an altogether different letter had arrived. He had 'failed', and his parents were advised that he was so unsuited to academic study that they should withdraw him from school at the earliest opportunity and apprentice him to a 'low-grade trade'. His mild-mannered mother knew better. She brought him to the St Mary's Christian Brothers grammar school, where his older brother was already a pupil, and they agreed to try him for a year (which had to be paid for), after which he could do 'the review': effectively a second go at the 11-plus, since abolished. If he passed that, he would remain at St Mary's and not have to pay fees. If not, he would have to go to a secondary school. Martin passed the review at a trot, and went on to excel at the sciences and maths, as well as debating and sports.

My father's cousin Brother Bede McGreevy was deputy

principal at the school, and taught Martin applied maths as well as training him in hurling. The big prize in Ulster schools under-13 Gaelic football is the McGreevy Cup, created in Bede's memory, though he himself by common consent was an awkwardly constructed, flat-footed specimen and no great shakes as a sportsman, as my father often took pleasure in pointing out to him when they disagreed during an after-match analysis. Bede's invariable response to being told he had no business coaching teams when he himself couldn't kick a barn door (or snow off a rope, or a tin can down a hill) was to insist triumphantly that 'you don't have to be a greyhound to train one'.

Whatever about his sporting talent, Bede was better than WhatsApp for keeping the scattered Roscommon McGreevy/ Leneghan/McDrury clan up to date with the latest news, which was likely to concern the tragic demise of a milking cow, a poor turf-cutting season, a disastrous summer for hay-making, a birth, death or marriage, an exam success, a job or other family event in England/Australia/America/ New Zealand, or a new mathematical puzzle he wanted to torment us with. His regular arrival in our home brought a quirky mix of his accessible erudition across science, arts and music, his prognostications and lamentations on several sports as well as politics, his peals of laughter and the realisation that this humble genius wanted nothing more than for us to do well in life and be happy.

When Bede learned that the lad I was dating was his former pupil, my parents having made the usual enquiries of the usual suspects, he remarked, 'Congratulations, she has got herself an all-rounder.' He was right. As I type, Martin, legendary footballer (according to himself), debater extraordinaire (according to himself), physicist, accountant, dentist,

Senator, university chancellor, befriender of paramilitaries and amazing grandad (according to his two grandsons) is outside painting the gate. He finished the fence, two miles of it, at the weekend. And he brought me breakfast in bed early this morning to make up for missing our usual Saturday breakfast-out date in a local café, since he wanted to get stuck into the painting. Somebody was definitely praying for me the day I met him! The all-rounder thing does not cover cooking or ironing, however; nor does a degree in physics extend to understanding how to turn on the washing machine or where to find the tin-opener. Remarkably, on the weeks when I am away from home and he has to cope alone, there is always a neighbour or relative who turns up unasked to do that stuff for him.

Martin and I, by the sheer good fortune of having been born in the early 1950s, had the chance to enter university and to pursue a profession, options that lay far beyond our parents' reach because of their economic circumstances and despite their bright intellects. They lived under what Seamus Heaney called 'high, banked clouds of resignation', accepting and adapting to the limits on their lives. Martin and I, on the other hand, belonged to the cohort of 'intelligences brightened and unmannerly as crowbars' – another line from Heaney's poem 'From the Canton of Expectation', which charts the sudden change in Catholic fortunes wrought by the extension of second- and third-level education from the 1950s onwards.

Father Honorius was a drama queen, but he was no feminist, to put it mildly. In those days it was commonplace to leave school without much in the way of qualifications at fifteen, and as I approached that age he asked me about my future plans. I told him I intended to stay on at school, do my A levels, go to university, study law and become a lawyer. The plan amused him no end. He told me emphatically that it was ill-conceived, as I was female and had nobody belonging to me in the law. My mother, who ordinarily went into bell-ringing deferential mode whenever a cleric visited the house, suddenly became incensed and ordered Honorius out of the house. She then gave me the sole piece of vocational advice I ever heard from her. 'You,' she said, 'ignore the oul' eejit!' As career counselling goes, it has had a long shelf life.

To be fair to Honorius, his views were far from unique to him. When I did eventually get into Queen's University to study for an undergraduate law degree four years later, the first book on our reading list was *Learning the Law*, by the eminent jurist Glanville Williams. I still remember the nervous joy I felt when my preliminary first-year reading list arrived in the post. I jumped on the bus for town, got off at the bookstore, bought the book and had it almost entirely read on the journey home. It was admittedly a slender volume. Nonetheless, it was heart-scalding to reach the chapter entitled 'Women'. Needless to say, there was no equivalent chapter dedicated to 'Men', more is the pity.

The great Glanville Williams did not intend to be 'ungallant', as he said himself, but he took pains to point out that the entry of women into 'the law' was a waste of time given our obvious weaknesses, such as voices too light to carry in court. He never met an Ardoyne mammy, obviously. The only conceivable reason for a woman to aspire to being a law student was the opportunity it offered to meet a suitable future husband. Five years later, when myself and two other females were called to the Bar with the intent of practising at a time when there were no women in practice (though the odd one or two had previously tried and given up in frustration), the Lord Chief Justice gifted each of us a hardback copy of the eighth edition of *Learning the Law.* The updated edition no longer mentioned our marriage prospects. Possibly the marriageable men meanwhile had been unimpressed by our light voices and our temerity in undertaking four years of intensive study just to find a husband.

Honorius, whose Christian name was actually Phelim, was soon back on his pastoral visitations, which always included a glass of whiskey rather than tea. Peace was restored, and the next one of my brothers to be born was called after him – Phelim, that is, not Honorius. It may have been an act of appeasement, and if it was, it worked, for when I was admitted to the Faculty of Law at Queen's four years later, Father Honorius was so thrilled he took me out to dinner to celebrate, along with another parishioner and school friend, Eileen Gilmartin, who had also got a place at university.

The date was 14 August 1969.

# 4

Father Honorius drove us home from that dinner in the monastery car. At the top of Twaddell Avenue, almost home, we were shocked to see Eileen's father, Jack Gilmartin, and a group of other local Catholics armed only with hurley sticks on what turned out to be a hastily assembled patrol for the protection of Catholic homes and families in the parish.

There had been no word of such a thing when we left for dinner a short time earlier, though tensions were high after the Battle of the Bogside in Derry that week and the outbreak across Northern Ireland of pockets of Catholic protest at events in that city. The summer's Orange and Apprentice Boys parades in Belfast and Derry had ended with riots. In July, police had beaten to death two innocent Catholic bystanders in Derry. When I saw Jack Gilmartin out patrolling the neighbourhood with a hurley, I knew with a sickening certainty that things must have deteriorated closer to home, for a quieter, more reflective human being would have been hard to find.

While we were dining and debating, the Protestant police auxiliaries known as the B-Specials had entered the parish in uniform and, with gangs of loyalist thugs, set about systematically burning Catholic properties across the road from the monastery. It was clear there was no way Father Honorius would get his car in through the monastery's front gate, which was perilously close to the action. We got out of the car and stood for a couple of minutes looking down the Crumlin

Road. We could see and hear the chaotic scenes. Even that brief glimpse was chilling and terrifying, and destined to leave a lifelong imprint.

On the very night I'd been celebrating the chance to become a lawyer, Northern Ireland's uniformed forces of law and order joined with loyalist agitators in a display of naked sectarianism. They were bully boys, fired up with hatred and contempt for the defenceless community who that night bore the brunt of their wrath. Catholics were afraid for their homes and their lives, and sought to defend them, but they were ill-prepared. There was no organisation either lawful or unlawful to which they could look for help. The old IRA was just that, and the letters IRA quickly became the subject of sneering graffiti, denoting 'I RAN AWAY'. As the sectarian confrontations continued and a government of vacuous bigots kept digging bigger holes, nothing was more inevitable than what happened: the emergence of rudimentary organisations for the protection of the beleaguered Catholic community, which, as things deteriorated, gave way to a new wave of organised republicanism. Before long there was significant recruitment into paramilitaries on both sides. That night of 14 August the die was cast for a very unhappy future.

Jack Gilmartin had been minding his own business that night, watching television after dinner at home, like everyone else in the area, when the news of what essentially became a pogrom against Catholics started to filter through. He and his Catholic neighbours had gathered spontaneously to try to help people like us who were returning to Ardoyne in ignorance of the parlous turn of events. Honorius, Eileen and I were escorted to our homes, but there was to be no sleep that night, and not much for many nights to come. Jack took all the marbles my brothers could muster: his plan was to fire them at the chapel wall to imitate the sound of gun-fire, in the hope of keeping the marauders in the lower end of the parish.

The district nurse, Mrs McBrierty, and her daughter Annette, whose home was right in the middle of the mad zone, went out to offer help to pregnant women, families with young babies and people who were ill. They came back to find their own house destroyed. Our aunts came looking for clothes for them and other families who were left with nothing. We stripped our wardrobes and sat up through the night waiting in case the marbles didn't work and we would be next to feel the heel of the Reformation, the Plantation and the Boyne twentieth-century style. Clement was four months old, Phelim was three, Claire five, Pat six, Kate eight, Damien ten, John thirteen, Nora sixteen. I was eighteen. The future, which had begun to brighten with the firstborn getting to university, had suddenly darkened.

Next morning, Friday 15 August, I ventured out to inspect the damage and check on my relations. People on the street were in shock. Thirty houses, shops and pubs had been destroyed, and two local Catholic men murdered, Sammy McLarnon and Michael Lynch. No one seemed sure what to do or what was likely to happen next, but there was a suffo-cating fear. The acrid smell of smoke hung densely in the air. I passed the Ardoyne bus depot, where before the day was out, thirty buses would be hijacked by locals thrust into sud-den activism, in order to create safety barricades in case the B-Specials and the loyalist gangs returned.

At the Ardoyne shops, Honorius came walking towards me in his long black woollen cassock and his dramatic regu-lation black cloak; clearly visible was the large wooden emblem of the Sacred Heart emblazoned with the Cross and with the words JESU XPI PASSIO – the passion of Jesus. Ever a man for the theatrical, Honorius shouted: 'We were fiddling while Rome burnt.' It was an inexact use of the phrase, if he meant to compare us and our celebratory dinner to the Emperor Nero. But his gist was right. Northern Ireland had sleepwalked into mayhem and it was about to engulf us all. We did not detain each other long. Like his Passionist confrères, who had been out all night bringing help where they could, he had people to bury and families to comfort.

I had family to find. First, those in the most direct line of fire: Una's hairdresser's, Kathleen's dress shop, Sis's home and salon, Paddy's newsagent's, Frank and Nora's home and barber shop, the O'Haras' home and off-licence. The wreckage had stopped short of them – they had all avoided the disaster that had befallen friends and neighbours on the next block. I was mightily relieved as I ticked each one off, putting my head around the doors to make sure all were accounted for; and then my eyes fell on the McBriertys' burnt-out home.

In all of Ardoyne there was no woman more revered, more needed, more hard-working than District Nurse McBrierty. She had brought some of my siblings into the world, and the sight of her bustling into any house with her grey uniform and faithful bag brought not just a sense of professional order and reassurance but the presence of a most trusted friend. The idea that she and her family could be treated so abominably was unbearable. They were eventually rehoused a couple of miles away on the Antrim Road, in a house with a long-neglected front garden. By then the British Army had arrived into Northern Ireland to try and restore order. Having no time to sort the garden out during the day, Nurse McBrierty took a spade to it late into the night. She had barely shifted one sod when three truckloads of soldiers screeched to a halt on the pavement in front of her. They suspected she was burying weapons. She neither confirmed nor denied the allegation, but handed them the spade and went inside and got another one. They dug through the night and by morning her garden had been well turned over and was ready for planting out. She was thrilled. The army left empty-handed, apart from blisters and an insight into the limited value of acting on suspicion. The story kept us going for years. But we would have been happier if she and her family had been able to stay where they belonged. More than anything else, for me it was her trashed and burnt house that spelled the end of old Ardoyne that day and the end of peace of mind.

I cut through the back streets to my grandparents. Their street was completely barricaded at both ends, with double-decker buses perfectly parked at right angles to the rows of facing houses. How they were manoeuvred into place beats me, for they were awkward big brutes and there was no room to squeeze past. Even the entry (as we called the lane to the back yard) was impassable, with hastily erected barricades of prams and bins manned by grim-faced young men of the parish. I eventually reached my grandparents by taking their neighbours' garden walls and fences like a steeplechaser. Any illusions I had about getting them out of there and up to our house dwindled by the second. They were rightly of the view that our house was a sitting duck and they were as well off where they were now. Also I had no idea how I would get two elderly persons over the steeplechase course I had just about managed myself. The idea of official protection was, needless to say, risible.

Next stop was Hooker Street, where my best friend

Catherine Kane and her family lived. It was where the trouble of the night before had started, and I had no idea what to expect. What I saw was horrific. Burnt-out shells of houses. People gaunt with distress standing nervously in little groups sharing stories of the night before and, more ominously, groups of men young and old preparing a barricade and a stock of pathetic missiles – stones, bricks and bottles – with which to ward off a second attack. I was only thirty seconds into the street when I heard about Alice, whom I knew by sight: a young pregnant woman who had been beaten by a uniformed police officer at her own door. She had miscarried her baby during the night. (Four years later, a few streets away, her husband would be shot dead by loyalist gunmen.)

There was pure terror in the Kane house. They had not been harmed, for their house lay at the far end of the street, which had managed to survive the depredations of the previous evening thanks to the courage of the local men and women who tried to drive back the attackers. To stay in Hooker Street would have been insane, and so with heavy heart I helped as the Kanes began to pack a few clothes and toiletries. I borrowed our family car and drove as many as we could fit in over to Andersonstown, where a hastily organised caravan site was being made ready for refugees thanks to the charity Shelter. The Kanes were lucky enough to get a caravan to themselves, and I set off back to Ardoyne.

By the time I got home, my father had decided that it was not safe to stay in Belfast, never mind Ardoyne, and he gathered up as many kids as were home and put us in the car for Dublin. My sister Nora, who had her dream summer job as a stagehand at the Lyric Theatre on the other side of town, could not be contacted. My father spoke to Mary and Pearse O'Malley, who ran the Lyric, and they agreed to look after her until she could join us. My father had friends in the Knights of Columbanus in Dublin he hoped might be able to help us. Through them we were able to rent a house on the Kilmacud Road for a couple of weeks, to give us breathing space away from the violence being visited upon Ardoyne. Once we were safe, my father returned to Belfast and to the Long Bar. He stayed at his cousin's home on the Falls Road, phoning every evening to update us on the situation in Belfast.

Within a matter of hours of us heading south, the British Army was deployed throughout Northern Ireland, and in particular in the flashpoint areas like Ardoyne. We cheered in Dublin as we heard the news from RTÉ, for we believed the army would offer much-needed protection. We returned to Ardoyne and resumed our lives there in time for my siblings to go back to school and me to start university.

Soldiers on foot patrol were now part of the everyday landscape. Our home was very vulnerable to attack. Situated right on the doorstep of a loyalist heartland, it was exposed on three sides: ideal for anyone planning an attack and quick getaway. My mother sent the soldiers apple tarts and Victoria sponges. They had the desired effect for a while: their foot patrols were regularly routed past our house.

Our familiar city streets grew ever more frightening and nightmarish as the makeshift, unplanned defence of the Catholic neighbourhoods morphed into the organised paramilitarism of the reborn Irish Republican Army, which sought, improbably, to bring about a united Ireland by bombs and bullets. It took the best part of thirty years for the IRA to grasp the unlikelihood – never mind the immorality – of ending partition by violence visited mainly upon the very people who needed to be persuaded of the benefits of a united Ireland. That was the problem with paramilitarism: it did not generally attract the best brains or strategic thinkers; and, both sides having grown up with the Boyne dichotomy of winners and losers, it was a Sisyphean task to persuade them that an alternate strategy involving peaceful democratic politics was likely to be more effective. In the decades before that reality dawned, paramilitarism became bedded down in neighbouring Protestant and Catholic ghettos, daily life became a theatre of tragedy and melodrama, the interfaces between the two sets of ghettos became killing grounds and the tribes became more tribal.

Looking back, I see a link between the B-Specials' attack on Ardoyne and the rapid educational advancement of my generation of Catholics who came from working-class backgrounds, through university and into the professions thanks to the timely arrival of free second-level education. Casting an eye down those rows of little two-up-two-down terraced houses into which I was born and where my mother and her siblings lived, I can list off the doctors, lawyers, teachers, nurses, professors, accountants, journalists, civil servants, bankers and entrepreneurs who emerged almost from nowhere in those crossroads days. They came from families where parents had left school at fifteen to work wherever Catholics could get jobs. They came from families who believed passionately in the transformative value of education. Sadly, the very thing that engendered pride and hope in our families and community created fear and resentment in the hearts of many of our unionist neighbours. What a wonderful society we could have created if we had put all our talents together. Instead, the conflict provoked death, destruction, depression, dysfunction and dispersal.

*

Even as the Troubles began to escalate, I had no ambition to leave Ardoyne, never mind Belfast. It was, after all, home. But as homes go, it was becoming hopelessly dysfunctional and terrifyingly violent. Our days there were numbered, although we did not then know it.

Perhaps we should have known. Sectarian tensions had been rising steadily in the previous two years, with police and politicians adding fuel to the fire. From the mid 1960s, loyalists strongly linked with Ian Paisley had been trying to create the impression that the IRA was back in business, precisely to goad them back into business. They planted bombs that were blamed on the IRA. Civil rights marchers had been ambushed and beaten by loyalists on New Year's Day 1969. Unionist determination to resist equal rights for Catholics succeeded in driving the moderate unionist Prime Minister, Terence O'Neill, out of office in April of that year. Political control was not entirely in the hands of unionist politicians. It was also exercised by members of the Orange Order, a virulently anti-Catholic organisation that then counted almost the entire government among its members. An Orangeman who attended a Catholic funeral or wedding or service of any kind could be sure of swift expulsion. The number of prominent Orangemen who stood up to the Orange Order's sectarianism could be counted on the fingers of one hand.

I tried to describe the change in mood I began to intuit in my homeland in a poem I wrote in 1969, entitled 'Ulster'.

> Hatred's spumes, word bricks,
> Collarettes, necks reddened
> Veins blackened
> Eyes dart

Tight suits
Shine pressed
Narrowed lines, giddy walk,
God-talk, big boys,
Loud women, crushing drums,
Hips swagger
Poison speyed
Painted kerbstone
Stay out,
no go,
not yours,
ours, ours,
all ours
God says
God save.

There had always been more than a degree of strutting and coat-trailing around the Orange marches. The colossal Lambeg drums were banged a tad harder when the parades passed Catholic churches. I knew that within the Protestant community there were very mixed views on the Order. Some of our neighbours belonged to it, more did not. Some resolutely had nothing to do with it, and some who were not members nonetheless enjoyed the big day out on the Twelfth of July.

During my early teens I often pushed one child in a buggy and half a dozen others hanging out with me down the mile and a half to Carlisle Circus, the intersection of three roads, in order to get the best view of the Order's flute bands. The nakedly sectarian songs, the miles of Union Jacks, the pavements painted red, white and blue – none of these things intruded on our innocent enjoyment of the music and the colourful spectacle. Neighbours taking part in the march – dressed in sombre suits with immaculate sashes and walking ramrod-straight in serried ranks – waved to us. Protestant friends stood with us. We bought ice creams, and later meandered home, having been entertained.

These were the years when Terence O'Neill was Prime Minister. He was quite unlike his predecessor, the bigoted Lord Brookeborough, who wanted nothing to do with Catholics and even less to do with the independent Irish state south of the border. O'Neill was an Orangeman and a unionist, but he argued rightly that the country was at a crossroads and the best future lay in building good inter-community relationships, ditching sectarianism and working fluently with our neighbours in the Republic. He invited his Southern counterparts to Belfast, visited them in Dublin and tried to help set the scene for a new era. His was an unforced, genuine leadership that was unique within the unionism of his day.

But there was an about-turn at the crossroads, straight into the cul-de-sac of sectarian warfare and back to the future. Not far from where we had lived on the Woodvale Road, O'Neill was pelted with stones and flour by fellow unionists. By the spring of 1969, he had been driven out of office by Protestant resistance to conceding even modest reforms. At the time, Northern Ireland still had an archaic 'property franchise', which effectively discriminated against Catholics, and gerrymandered electoral districts had the same effect. Catholics were discriminated against in accessing housing and employment, were policed by a police force that was over 90 per cent Protestant, and were the main targets of special powers legislation that gave the unionist government wide powers to restrict civil rights, particularly of assembly. The Special Powers Act, first enacted as emergency legislation in 1922, had by then been made permanent and was widely seen by the Catholic nationalist citizenry of Northern Ireland as an instrument of oppression of their community.

Terence O'Neill could be his own worst enemy, for despite the sincerity of his desire for an end to sectarianism, he sometimes betrayed a belief in the superiority of his class and of the Anglican creed that did not always endear him to Catholics. In a famous interview in May 1969 he was quoted as saying:

> It is frightfully hard to explain to Protestants that if you give Roman Catholics a good job and a good house they will live like Protestants because they will see neighbours with cars and television sets; they will refuse to have eighteen children. But if a Roman Catholic is jobless, and lives in the most ghastly hovel, he will rear eighteen children on National Assistance. If you treat Roman Catholics with due consideration and kindness they will live like Protestants in spite of the authoritative [*sic*] nature of their Church.

So there it was, set out by the best of the unionists: the ambition of our little statelet was for everyone to coexist happily when Catholics learned to live like Protestants. It perfectly captured the fundamental flaw at the heart of all politics in Northern Ireland: the unfinished business of the Reformation and Counter-Reformation and the long, long shelf-life of the compulsive evangelisation culture that afflicted both sides.

Lack of imagination and fresh thinking by republicans also played a part. They reached for an outdated paramilitary handbook and shamefully played the sectarian zero-sum killing game. The IRA's contribution to the thirty years of the Troubles is an appalling catalogue of murder and destruction that served only to create further bitter division and post-pone the day a united Ireland could be mooted as realistic.

Throughout the sixties, I knew all the men who drank in my father's pub by name – until I didn't. Had I been asked to describe their politics, I would have simply said 'nationalist'; but a new politics was in the making, along with a new IRA. After August 1969, when the Catholic community felt itself to be under attack and with no effective means of protection, a different clientele started to appear in the Long Bar. The pub was tucked in off the Falls and Grosvenor Roads, both main thoroughfares, and it had exits into two different streets. Next door, above the pub, were the Michael Dwyers club rooms, where people could meet in privacy. These things made it attractive to people in search of information about what was going on in what were now being called 'republican circles'. Soon the word 'nationalist' came to be associated with the O'Connellite tradition of using politics to solve problems, while the word 'republican' was associated with the use of violence to achieve political ends. Nationalists and republicans had a common ambition to bring about Irish unity, but no shared sense of how to make it happen, or indeed what it might look like if and when it arrived.

My father warned his staff and regulars to trust none of the newcomers. He was nervous of where Northern Ireland was going and of what was now passing through the Long Bar. Journalists, civil rights activists, informers, government agents, agents provocateurs, academics, student leaders, old republicans, new republicans and local, national and international politicians – all male – began to gather there. The Michael Dwyers club rooms became a locus of growing Catholic mobilisation, including the transmission of Radio

Free Belfast, a mostly amateur student endeavour. My sole (and reluctant) contribution to its operation was giving my father my hairdryer, which was used on cold setting to keep the bockety transmission machinery from going on fire.

It was not inevitable that the conflict would explode as it did. It is a measure of how retrievable things still were on St Patrick's Day 1970 that the commanding officer of the Royal Scots Regiment, Lieutenant Colonel Robert Richardson, and three companions rambled into my father's pub for a drink in full uniform. Among them was the regiment's pipe major, complete with bagpipes, with which he provided some entertainment not usually heard in the pub. Not that my father had anything special against bagpipes, but his was a drinking and talking pub where sing-songs or the production of musical instruments generally resulted in immediate expulsion. The only known exception he made was that unusual day.

I was at that time working as a volunteer at the headquarters of the Central Citizens' Defence Committee (CCDC), a non-violent civil society initiative begun in 1969 and strongly supported by my father, in whose premises the main protagonists met in the early days. They were men of peace, like the businessman Tom Conaty and the nationalist socialist politician Paddy Devlin, both close friends of my father. They met senior police and army officers and British government politicians including Jim Callaghan, then the British Home Secretary, who had taken the decision to deploy the army to Northern Ireland. My father was involved in some of the high-level delegations that tried to advise the authorities on how to calm the situation. They could see from their everyday lives on the ground that cool heads were losing influence within an increasingly angry and frustrated Catholic community.

The CCDC was excoriated by both republicans and union-ists: by the former for not advocating taking a stronger course of action, and by the latter for daring to accuse them of acting unjustly. Into the vacuum of moderate politics flooded a ser-ies of actors and radical ideas that vied for the hearts and minds of nationalists. The Long Bar, and in particular the club rooms above, was now a locus of a revitalised, and rap-idly evolving, republican movement.

Old-timers from past campaigns appeared on the scene. New faces materialised. I, the pint-puller, observed and lis-tened. Nothing I heard impressed me. I was a constitutional nationalist raised in the Daniel O'Connell tradition. O'Connell had, in the early decades of the nineteenth century, cham-pioned the emancipation of Catholics and Presbyterians in the United Kingdom, of Jews in Russia and of slaves in the United States. Importantly, he was a staunch opponent of the use of violence to achieve political ends. As a young man he had been in Paris at the outbreak of the 1789 Revolution, and the memory of its cruelty and its uncontrollability never left him.

O'Connell was a great favourite of my father's, and I was mesmerised by his faith in the power of persuasion through words and the use of the law. His desire to reconcile the two nationalist traditions in Ireland, one wedded to constitutional politics and the other to rebellion, was not realised in his life-time; and I, like many nationalists, saw in John Hume the man who might (as he eventually did) accomplish that ambition. Both men were revered in our home (and when Martin and I married, in 1976, we made a pilgrimage to O'Connell's Kerry home on the first day of our honeymoon). I was thus deeply unimpressed by the recent recruits to violent Marxist republi-canism who sought to establish an Irish republic. Equally, the self-styled Trotskyists who argued for a two-nation solution seemed swaggering and ludicrous. There were Maoists, communists, republican socialists, old IRA, new IRA – the various groupings could not abide each other, but they were part of a fast-moving political foment that soon produced a reconstituted IRA. With so many old and new voices vying to lead it in different directions, it split in 1969 into the Provisional IRA and the Official IRA. The latter was initially the bigger of the two, but that was not the case for long.

I could not abide any of them, seeing in them little more than macho shape-throwers bent on using the volatility of the moment to insert their own inchoate agendas, which I could already see would further imperil the Catholic community and render conciliation impossible. I had been completely persuaded by the principled non-violent, non-sectarian activism of Gerry Fitt, Paddy Devlin and John Hume among others. My father, for his part, trusted very few of the new pub clientele, often complaining that at least half were MI5 or RUC Special Branch – which given the pub's growing reputation as a gathering place of republican thinkers and activists seems very likely.

The crunch came with the Falls Curfew in early July 1970. I was the only person on duty in the CCDC headquarters, on the front of the Falls Road, on the afternoon of 3 July, when the army entered the Lower Falls in search of an IRA weapons dump, and not with notable respect for people or property. Martin had walked over with me from Ardoyne, leaving me there around five o'clock to return home to east Belfast – an inadvisable journey, for there were now street battles ongoing between the army and groups of youths, and CS gas had been discharged. The tension on the road was palpable and I was not entirely happy to be on my own. Groups gathered. I went to the door to investigate a sudden intensification of the noise;

a few yards away someone was digging up the road with a pneumatic drill. Down the street outside Burns's shop a couple of people were chatting. A shot rang out and they scarpered into the shop, as I too rapidly retreated into the CCDC headquarters. It was a few minutes later that word came to the door that William Burns, the shop's owner, had been shot by the army. The pathologist later said it was a ricochet bullet. William was a well-known business owner and community volunteer, and a friend of my father's.

Now I was really scared. Venturing out to the door for an update on the chaos, I was delighted to see a very white Martin McAleese picking his way through the rubble, having decided I needed company. With the shooting and the rioting, I felt the nationalist politicians and community leaders associated with the CCDC needed to be there too. I phoned Paddy Devlin, Gerry Fitt, and the leaders of the CCDC. The place began to fill up with politicians, journalists, CCDC activists, the injured and the irate, just in ahead of the curfew, which was announced at 10 p.m., or chancing a bullet to get there. I became the tea lady by default, being the only female present. Ironically I was never once asked for my eyewitness account of what happened in those hours, even when the CCDC later published its report. Women were invisible makers of sandwiches and answerers of phones.

I kept the lot of them fed during the night, raiding the cupboard of the priests on whose property the CCDC headquarters was billeted. It was a loaves and fishes operation, for the CCDC budget did not run even to a packet of biscuits. The priests, who were absent throughout the curfew, later complained that I had used their food. Given that the curfew trapped people for three days and that the British Army were not exactly handing out picnic baskets, their complaints seemed puny and mean. We were talking about a few tea bags, a lot of coffee, a jar of beetroot, a pan loaf and a half-pound of butter.

At one point, rather foolishly, Martin and I decided to try to escape back to Ardoyne by climbing over the building's back wall. A shot rang out above my head as I stuck it over the top of the wall and an irate English voice commanded us in very unparliamentary language to go back where we'd come from. He did not need to repeat the instructions. During the night, the relentless shooting forced us onto the floor.

My father had been at home in Ardoyne when the curfew was announced, and now his worry was for me and my safety. He talked on the phone to Paddy Devlin, who assured him that he would look out for me, though in truth there was little any of us could do that night of the miserable beetroot sandwiches.

The curfew resulted in enormous physical damage, but it was the psychological damage which reset the political landscape. The army was now emphatically not trusted by the nationalist population. The Unionist government was already not trusted by the nationalist population. And the British government was not trusted by the nationalist population.

A few months later, in November 1970, the CCDC published an advert calling for restraint and non-violence from the nationalist community, even in the face of acknowledged government injustices and army heavy-handedness. But it was already too late.

My maternal grandparents, Cassie and John McManus, lived nearby in the Glenard estate and were a big part of our lives. Although Granda had been in the old IRA during the War of Independence, he was a gently spoken man of very modest views, and Granny was the undisputed boss of the house. She quietly decreed, he quietly agreed. She baked fresh griddle bread every single day in a kitchen barely the size of a modest armchair and would not permit bought bakery bread over the door – even though he worked for Barney Hughes's bakery! His favourite trick was to pick her up, swing her around and quote from Yeats's *Cathleen ni Houlihan*: 'Did you see an old woman going down the path? I did not, but I saw a young girl and she had the walk of a queen.' She protested – 'Och, John!' – but was never convincing. He never mentioned his days in the IRA, and if he had strong political opinions we never heard them.

One day, a Protestant friend of mine who was regularly in our house got talking to him, and somehow prised from him a fact his own children and grandchildren did not know: that in a box in a press in his house there were medals for his IRA activity. This in 1970, with the British Army at the front door, loyalist gangs marauding the parish and the IRA getting set for a thirty-year war. Granda disappeared off home to Glenard and then reappeared fifteen minutes later, having brought the medals for her to see. She was enthralled. But my mother, who had just sent a couple of apple tarts to the British soldiers who regularly patrolled our area, was borderline patricidal: 'Sweet suffering Jesus,' she muttered, 'fifty years he has had those bloody yokes hidden away and he chooses now to produce them! He'll get us all murdered in our beds.'

Granda died in 1973, and I never saw the medals again until many years later, when I was President and my Uncle John, who had become their custodian, sent them to me at Áras an Uachtaráin. I wore them on the one hundredth anniversary of the Easter Rising, figuring that by then the trigger mechanisms had been long defused and I owed him something. I alerted his children to look out for them. All bar two – my mother and Uncle John – had never heard of their existence until then.

Like his wife, Granda seldom sat down during the day, mostly gardening or mending shoes in the minuscule yard at the back of the house, where he kept an ancient collection of cobbler's tools. These he put to daily use on a rough-hewn workbench attached to the wall that gave onto the lane running along the rear of the terrace of houses. With so many children and grandchildren and neighbours' children, there was always a pair of shoes to be mended, usually with old car tyres, offcuts of leather, and steel toecaps for the boys. The high walls around his little empire were covered in hook holds for his eccentric array of gardening implements, and he was much in demand as a volunteer gardener – especially in our house, where my father was useless at anything vaguely concerned with gardening or DIY and my mother had enough to be doing. Granda was always on hand, often seen strolling through Ardoyne with implements more suited to a Dromara farm than a Belfast garden: an axe for chopping logs, a billhook, a sickle and a scary-looking scythe. He was frequently to be seen and heard sitting on a stool honing these tools to dangerous perfection. One of my recurring nightmares is of the awkward-looking scythe falling from its wall cradle and taking my head off as it hits the coal pile below, possibly because almost every time I entered that diminutive yard, one or other grandparent would warn against that very possibility.

My grandparents' yard was also home to the standard-issue Belfast Corporation dustbin, on which was painted the house number, 23. It was probably not the Corporation's intention that the metal lids of such bins would be repurposed as percussion instruments during the Troubles, when their repetitive banging became the WhatsApp red-alert system of its day, to warn of the approach of army patrols in the neighbourhood or initiate a noisy protest after the soldiers had done whatever they came to do, or indeed while they were doing it. Once a week, the wheelless metal dustbin was dragged out through the door from the yard onto the entry, to be emptied by the dustmen. When we were visiting my grandparents, the sound of bins being scraped along concrete was a galvanising one, for a regular and dreaded scenario was to set out from the yard into the narrow entry wheeling a pram or buggy (then referred to as a 'tansad') and to encounter the bin lorry coming the opposite way with about six inches to spare on each side. Pushing past it was not an option. The only course of action was to retreat back into the yard (assuming there was still someone inside who could hear the frantic knocks on the door) or pray someone else's door would open to let you in.

My grandparents' house was heated by an open coal fire in the living room, behind which there was a Baxi boiler for heating water. The coal pile in the yard was replenished each week by the coalman on his low-loader, which, like the bin lorry, filled the entire entry. There was no nerve-jangling scraping noise to signal his presence; the coalman just roared, 'Coal!' and hoped to be heard over the internal din. The full coal sacks sat upright in serried ranks on the lorry. A helper hauled the sack onto the soot-covered shoulders of the coalman, who carried it into the yard and heaved it in such a way as to send the coal clattering roughly into place. Dust flew up in all directions, and since the three strands of the washing line shared the airspace over the coal pile, the weekly wash had to be judiciously timed.

My grandmother had a deep ceramic Belfast sink that sat under the mean kitchen window. Standing at that sink, one was afforded a view of the backyard door, the coal pile, granda's workbench, the bin and the washing line. Not exactly the Dromara Hills! Underneath the sink lived the wooden scrubbing board used to make stains disappear with the help of brute force and large bars of Sunlight soap, both of which Granny seemed to have in abundance. In the yard up against the coal scuttle was the hand-cranked cast-iron mangle with its two wooden rollers through which the sodden clothes were passed to wring the water out of them and notionally make drying easier. Volunteers for that shoulder-dislocating job were rare, and we avoided Granny's house on certain days of the week, for she was a creature of habit. Her children collaborated towards the end of her life in the purchase of a non-automatic top-loading and extremely slimline washing machine, which she stored with lavish care under cover in the yard when it was not in use. After the arrival of the washing machine, the manoeuvring of prams or buggies through the yard to the lane became impossible.

Granda's evenings were spent attending wakes or whist drives. He loved a good wake, regardless of the religion of the deceased or the extent of his acquaintance with them. Each day, the *Irish News* (Catholic) and the *Belfast Telegraph* (Protestant) were delivered to the house, and he carefully scanned the death notices in both. That done, he would map out his itinerary of the day's available wakes, always careful to dovetail them with scheduled whist drives. He had neither a car nor a bike, so his wake-and-whist agenda was governed by available bus routes and proximity to Ardoyne. Not surprisingly, his own wake was a large affair at which at least twenty Barney Hughes pan loaves of ham sandwiches were devoured by other serial wake-goers, most of them strangers to us. He memorably once mistakenly spent two hours in a wake house extolling the virtues of the dead man, only to discover the intended house was in the next street. No matter: he made a bunch of new friends.

Of the eighteen violent deaths in 1969, eight had been caused by police action, five by republican paramilitaries, three by loyalist paramilitaries and two by the British Army. A year later, of twenty-eight people killed, twenty were the victims of republican paramilitaries. Another year later, 1971, and one hundred and eighty people were killed, of whom one hundred and seven died at the hands of republican paramilitaries, forty-five at the hands of the army, twenty-two at the hands of loyalist paramilitaries, one death was caused by the police and six paramilitary bomb-makers were killed by their own bombs.

By now, the demagogues on both sides were whipping up their camp followers. Hooded squadrons of the loyalist Ulster Defence Association marched in menacing military formation. In December of that year, fifteen people died in the loyalist bombing of the pub and home of my father's friend Paddy McGurk. There were scurrilous official attempts to insinuate that the McGurks were the victims of an IRA bomb that had been intended for use elsewhere but had exploded prematurely. The naked opportunism and deceitfulness of these allegations made a dreadful situation even worse, and of course it was grist to the IRA recruitment mill. Now so-called touts were being killed, and all around us there were street confrontations between Protestants and Catholics. The first soldier to die in the conflict was murdered that year by republican paramilitaries.

But 1972 was the grimmest year. It began with the murder of thirteen innocent Catholic civilians by the British Army in Derry during a peaceful protest march. The British government moved to cover up the truth of Bloody Sunday, and in so doing pushed the conflict up another level or ten. Within the month, republican paramilitaries had tried to kill Ulster Unionist politician John Taylor (now Baron Kilclooney). He was badly wounded, but survived, requiring considerable facial surgery in the process. In early March, the Abercorn café in the city centre, where Martin and I met once a week for a toasted bacon and mushroom sandwich, was bombed by the IRA, killing two young women and injuring over a hundred, leaving many with appalling, life-changing injuries. The era of IRA bombings was upon us, as was the era of loyalist murders of randomly selected Catholics. Two weeks later, William Craig, the head of an extremist offshoot of the Ulster Unionist Party, told his supporters that 'We must build up the dossiers on the men and women who are a menace to this country, because one day, ladies and gentlemen, if the politicians fail, it may be our job to liquidate the enemy.' He specified that by 'the enemy' he meant 'terrorists', but in the climate of the time, Catholics did not feel confident that loyalists would observe the distinction.

Four hundred and ninety-six people were killed in 1972. Half were civilians, a quarter were army or police personnel, seventy-four were republican paramilitaries and eleven were loyalist paramilitaries. Over half the deaths were caused by republican paramilitaries. A quarter were caused by loyalist paramilitaries. It was not hard to see that the nature and shape of the conflict had changed radically.

In the teeth of that tempest, politics failed abysmally. There were no cool heads, just angry people thumping the sides of tribal bunkers. My father, who was Grand Knight of the Belfast Council of the Knights of Columbanus in 1971–2, tried to do what he could. He travelled with a Knights delegation to London, where they met Cardinal Heenan and the Secretary of State for Northern Ireland, William Whitelaw. Along with knights south of the border, he tried to get groups of impressionable young people from flashpoint areas out of the North over the summer months. My mother's way of handling the menacing events to which we woke up each day, and which threatened her family, was to pray and knit and sew and bake and dust and polish. She and my father often brought every one of us breakfast in bed of sweet tea, toast and oranges. It was their way of trying to create a nurturing atmosphere in a world they no longer understood, but which we looked to them to interpret for us.

# 5

Ardoyne, that small suburban area, has the distinction of accounting for one in five violent deaths in Belfast during the Troubles. There was a shocking toll of murders of friends and neighbours, civilians and security force members, victims of both sides.

Beyond the awful death toll, we lived with a constant, nagging, physically debilitating anxiety that accompanied the simplest things, like going to the shops, getting the bus into town, coming home from school in a particular school uniform, walking home after a night out. To live in a place where your streets are not yours is to live in a nightmare. Yet every day we woke up and got on with the ordinary things of life, unobtrusively adapting to the abnormality that was now routine: street riots, CS gas, choking eyes and throats, petrol bombs, barricades, burning buses, hijacked cars, vans, petrol tankers, car bombs, van bombs, tanker bombs, law-abiding delivery men forced to deliver bombs, drive-by shootings, armed police and soldiers on street patrols, armoured tanks, random identity checks, checkpoints, bag inspections, pipe bombs, sudden bangs, plumes of smoke, bomb scares, false alarms, evacuations, running for cover, the rat-a-tat-tat of gunfire through the nights, the crying for the peace of sleep, the litany of violent death, malicious injury and untold heartache on the news each morning, the murder of the innocent by both military and paramilitary forces, the funerals, the incendiary politics, the official cover-ups, the paramilitaries' fig-leaf justifications, the arrests, trials, internment without trial, the plaintive pleas of the few courageous peacemakers, the retreat into renewed ghettoisation, the ethnic cleansing of whole streets, the wrecked nerves and the complete demolition of peace of mind.

We were vacuum-packed so tight that the fresh air of possibility was shut out. As the streets of my childhood became bloodstained battlegrounds, a sense of dread and horror took hold. I longed for quiet enjoyment of the earth and our earthly lives. I longed to live in a peaceful place where equality, tolerance and acceptance of diversity were normal. I wanted to be able to open the front door, walk to the park or the shops or take a bus into town without running the gauntlet of death squads.

The road in front of our house was a daily battleground. Why we stayed as long as we did perplexed me until marriage, kids and a mortgage taught me that there are few places to go with nine children – and few buyers for a house that is in a murder zone. The compensation my parents eventually received for the home they lost was a pittance: about one tenth of the value of the house before the Troubles took hold.

I remember the day in May of 1972 when Benny Moane was abducted and shot by loyalists as he went about his work in the Shankill area. A Catholic father of six, he was a sales representative for a drinks company that my father had once worked for, the Irish Bonding Company. My father had helped him get the job. Benny's death hit him hard. It hit all of us, reinforcing the surreal vulnerability we inhabited as normal life.

The road on which we lived, the main arterial route from the city centre to the airport and the aptly named Nutts Corner, had become a stage for belligerent shape-throwing and worse by the loyalist paramilitaries. A few days after Benny's death, they killed a local Protestant civilian in a botched attempt at a hijacking a short distance from where we lived. A week later, a twelve-year-old Protestant girl was killed nearby in crossfire between the IRA and security forces. Another week and a Catholic shopkeeper was shot by loyalists outside his record shop. A week later it was the turn of a local Catholic greengrocer. Two teenagers also died that day in gun battles, one a Catholic and member of the IRA and the other, also shot by security forces, a young Protestant.

Visiting or being visited by my grandparents was a dangerous activity. Two streets away from them in Glenard, a woman putting her dustbin out was hit by an IRA bullet. She survived. A British soldier they aimed at was not so lucky. He was the father of three-month-old twins. Loyalist drive-by shootings were commonplace. On one evening, a group of us were enjoying tea and currant buns in our schoolfriend Kathleen Boyle's house while her brother Thomas was getting ready to go out and meet his friends. We were bemused by Mrs Boyle's refusal to let him leave the house until she had recited a prayer to St Joseph the Worker to preserve him from death or injury by gunshot. The prayer leaflet could not be found, and he was apoplectic until it was finally retrieved from under the cushion of an armchair and duly recited. Two hours later we were sitting with him as he shook uncontrollably in the Accident and Emergency department of the Mater Hospital, having survived a shooting that claimed the life of one of his friends. I made a special trip to a religious-objects shop in Chapel Lane the next day to buy multiple copies of that prayer leaflet.

In early June, I went to San Francisco on a student working visa with a group of friends from university. Martin stayed behind and wrote every day, reminding me of what was happening back home. A week after I left, he was telling me how he had helped my parents move stuff to Dromara for safety. He was particularly pleased to have moved a portrait of me by the County Down artist Kieran McGoran, which he had commissioned for my twenty-first birthday and which still adorns our bedroom wall. It was supposed to be a summer of escape, but the grim news from home tormented me, and during that first month it was so awful I could not settle and just wanted to come home. Martin was enthusiastic in his efforts to persuade me to return, but I stuck it out until the end of August. My parents and siblings, however, were in the thick of it.

My twenty-first birthday, 27 June, was the last day on earth of a young Protestant shot in a sectarian gun battle in nearby Duncairn. A few days later, two Protestant men were murdered by republicans even though the IRA were supposed to be on ceasefire. The UVF retaliated next day, killing a Catholic father of six who had ventured out onto our insanely dangerous road to buy chips.

In that sickening world of inexorable tit-for-tat killings, a Protestant man who suffered from epilepsy became the next victim, likely killed by republicans. On 11 July, loyalist paramilitaries kidnapped and murdered a Catholic man on his way home from having a drink in a hotel. On the same night, a short distance away, loyalist paramilitaries murdered a fourteen-year-old Catholic boy at his home and raped his mother with what a judge later described as 'the lowest level of human depravity'. Two days later, a Catholic father of four and former member of the Royal Navy was shot in error by the security services. Over the next couple of days, a short distance from our home, the IRA shot dead three British soldiers and a police officer in separate incidents around the area. Soldiers, also in separate incidents, shot dead four civilians. Two of them were members of the IRA. The others were alleged to have been armed, but were said by their families to have been entirely innocent. On 21 July, a short distance away on the Cavehill Road, the IRA killed two Catholic women and the young son of a Protestant pastor and well-known peacemaker, the Reverend Joseph Parker. Stephen Parker had told his mother earlier that day of his sense of dread that something bad was going to happen. He was not alone in that feeling. The gathering death toll, the daily litany of gun battles and street battles in the area meant that many of its inhabitants – myself included, even in San Francisco – carried with them an unshakeable sense of foreboding. And yet my family stayed.

That summer, I lived in two dizzyingly different spheres. I was physically in America but emotionally in Ardoyne. I stayed with my father's brother Dan, his wife Dorothy and their six children in the San Francisco suburb of Pacifica. My uncle worked for TWA and got me a job with a small company that produced food for airlines. Club Catering practically sat on the runway at San Francisco airport. It was owned by a marvellous Jewish man called Walter Seelos, who had extricated himself from childhood poverty by selling newspapers on Sunday outside the Catholic cathedral in Chicago. He loved the Irish with a passion, he had a natural instinct for empathy when people were hurting, and he was exceptionally kind to a very subdued and often distracted me.

My line manager was a gentle gay man who was nursing rejection by his family, and Wally became his surrogate father. We made a nine-tier cake for Wally's daughter's wedding, and true to form, on the day of the wedding, he laid on a celebration for his staff. I promised to myself that if ever I became a boss, I would want my staff to be as happy as we were working for Wally. There was banter, practical jokes, coffee breaks with iced doughnuts – and the work always got done.

I arrived back from the United States, my suitcase full of exciting presents from civilised, sunny San Francisco, to find the army blocking the road right at our gate. A gun battle was going on further down the street. I had to crawl on my hands and knees from the roadblock to the house, dragging my red suitcase behind me, knowing that my siblings would be wanting their presents, battle or no battle. I also was anxious to cross-examine Nora about how the brand-new navy military-style coat I had bought before leaving for the States, and carefully locked away, had come to be in a photo I had seen of a family wedding I had missed. Months of saving had gone into its purchase and I was insanely protective of it. I had stayed with relatives in Philadelphia before coming home, and they had been back in Ireland for the wedding. They had the photos, and there was my coat in the front row and Nora wearing it, a grin the size of Belfast Lough on her face: I had taken the wardrobe key with me, but she had found the spare. Lucky for her, my mother had a welcome-home lunch of sausage, beans and chips and lemon meringue pie – my favourite – sufficient to distract me from my Columbo moment of truth. The coat was back in the locked wardrobe in pristine condition and Nora was sure she had pulled a fast one until I produced the photograph.

Outside, the madness just went on and on. The news that day was of a Catholic woman killed by a loyalist bomb in north Belfast. A week later another loyalist bomb killed a Protestant neighbour, an elderly Protestant lady in her nineties and a Catholic mother. Four days after that, an IRA gunman was shot by the army near our house. The following week, the IRA killed a Protestant man just up the road from us at Ligoniel. The end of September brought a spate of killings, a Catholic shot by the army and a soldier killed by the IRA.

My father was soon no longer able to get safely home at night from his pub on the Falls Road, so he stayed with his cousin May Fitzpatrick (Cassidy) and came home only for dinner in the early evening before returning to the pub. On the last night he had come home after pub closing, he had been attacked at our door by four apparently unarmed loyalists who lay in wait for him in the bushes to the side of the house. He managed to escape, for the first time ever finding the front door key straight away from the enormous bunch of keys he always had with him. Many a time we had stood for ten minutes at that door as he fished and foostered around to find the right key. Not that night, luckily.

From my bedroom window I had heard the four would-be attackers talking among themselves before my father's car had arrived. In my innocence I just thought it was a group of men wending their way home from a club. It never occurred to me that anything untoward was about to occur until shouts and the sound of scuffling had me taking the stairs at a gallop and arriving just as my father fell in the door. He and I pushed against it to stop his attackers from entering the house. Luckily for us, they disappeared into the night. But now my father knew he was likely on someone's liquidation list. He stood out in our predominantly loyalist area – a Catholic, a Southerner, the owner of a pub in a republican area, not to mention the father of nine Catholic children. Put it all together and it was enough to justify his elimination in the minds of local bigots.

Ridiculous as it must seem, some vestige of normal life was made to continue. My brother John, profoundly deaf from birth, was now in his mid teens, and went the odd evening to a city-centre deaf club on his own. He caught the bus fifty yards from our front door, and the return bus left him just across the road from home. One hundred yards up the road, St Gabriel's youth club for Catholic teenagers continued to operate as if that stretch of road was Disneyland and not a killing field.

My mother and I were watching television one night when we heard strange screams from outside. At first we thought it was kids from the youth club acting the eejit. But the timbre of the sole voice was haunting – and even now, I often hear it in my dreams. In an instant of ghastly clarity, I realised the voice was John's. I had never heard him scream. We rushed to the front door, where an old man stood, blood dripping from his hands, unable to speak and pointing to the gate where John now lay unconscious, an artery severed by the four teenage attackers who had followed him off the bus, broken a beer bottle over his head and stabbed him repeatedly in the neck and face with its remnants. I went with him in the ambulance that took him to the Mater Hospital a mile away on the same road, screaming, screaming, praying, praying. My mother followed behind in her Mini-Minor, seven children (most in pyjamas) packed into it, for she was not allowing any other child out of her sight. My father looked so grey and old when he later reached the hospital I thought he would have a heart attack.

John survived physically, but the attack and its aftermath were to make his life unbearable, for his main attacker, whom he recognised, lived a couple of streets away and was the son of a local Orangeman.

When he had recovered a little, my parents took him to Dublin for a couple of days' recreation. Nora and I were in charge, helped by our grandparents. I had taken the Mini-Minor to attend the parish mission and was driving the short distance home, just passing the next-door Protestant school, when I spotted my eleven-year-old sister Catherine, in her St Dominic's school uniform, being followed by a group of teenage girls from the neighbouring loyalist estate. Suddenly they were on top of her, pushing and kicking as I went by. I parked at the house and shouted to Nora to come and help. An anger took hold of both of us that is impossible to describe but that undoubtedly helped us knock the living melt out of our wee sister's assailants. I am morally certain that the imprint of Everton School railings is still visible on at least two of them.

Within days, a very shaken Catherine was sent to board at the St Louis Convent in Kilkeel. Our brother Damien was already boarding at St Colman's College in Newry, sent there for fear that he too would fall victim to the sectarian lunatics who stalked our road. Patrick followed Damien to Colman's for safety too. My father was not earning the kind of money that paid boarding fees, but somehow the fees were paid. At home, the unease was palpable and inescapable. And still life continued, for I travelled across the city each day to the university, and Martin, who lived in a loyalist stronghold in east Belfast, regularly risked life and limb to leave me home and then walk back to his own house through the most dangerous streets in Europe. If he was extremely lucky, there might be an unburnt bus still running into the city. More often than not he walked the whole way.

Walking was dangerous. Shortly after I came home from America, a young Protestant leaving his girlfriend home was shot dead by republicans as he walked through Ardoyne; and one by one there was a run of Catholic victims of what one newspaper described as a loyalist execution squad operating in north Belfast. As if to underline the barely concealed jitteriness that invaded all our hearts, two soldiers in separate events in the same week were mistakenly killed by fellow soldiers.

Then came the murder of a dear family friend and fellow Queen's student, Peter Lane. I can see him still: the handsome young medical student with the long hair and the guitar. He lived up the road from us. His Cork-born father, Paddy, was a famous surgeon and sculptor who had worked most of his life in the British Army Medical Corps and the British Colonial Service before bringing his family from Tanganyika to north Belfast, where, in their ignorance of local politics, they bought a house in a loyalist stronghold. Peter, one of five hugely talented children used to running wild in the African bush, had gone out to buy milk. The loyalist death squad kidnapped him and tortured him to death.

His mother Eileen, an English Protestant who converted to Catholicism, never once responded in anger or bitterness, but Paddy's anxiety tore right into him. With his own hands he built a small house in the foothills of the Mournes, in the village of Rostrevor, and moved there for solace. He handcarved every stick of furniture for the house as if some fury was driving him. Paddy died young of a heart attack. Eileen would live to be over one hundred, sitting noiselessly embroidering or knitting or praying the Divine Office, not a word of anger, not a word of vengeance. I loved to sit with her and just draw consolation from the grief-stricken calm that came from the very depths of her being.

After my parents moved to Rostrevor a couple of years later, they brought Eileen to Mass or to the shops. And after

Martin and I moved there ourselves, in the late 1980s, we often rambled into her house, and she came to us each Christmas morning after Mass for a clan gathering and the first course of Christmas dinner before all scattered to their own homes. She made the most delicious bread rolls for that annual event, and beautiful hand-made gifts. Nudging our kitchen window was a Japanese winter-flowering cherry tree, which she knew I loved. Shortly after I became President, she gave me a little framed piece of embroidery showing the tree and the date of my election. I could never look at it without a shadow of homesickness overcoming me, both for Rostrevor and for our broken Ardoyne lives.

A week after the loyalists murdered Peter Lane, they came for my father. They had announced on their illegal radio station that he was a particular target because of his association with the Long Bar. That is the kind of mad place we inhabited, where criminals believed with some justification that they could act with impunity and felt empowered to name their victims in advance. On 7 October 1972, they drove a car loaded with a bomb to the door of the Long Bar and ran off, leaving the car rolling forward to stop just beyond their intended target. A local man alerted the neighbours and ran into the pub to shout a warning. My father got all his customers out through the back door and went to check there was no one left at the front. The car bomb exploded as a young woman, Olive McConnell, ran across the street to find her little child. The keys of the exploding car broke her neck. My father ran to catch her as she fell. An RTÉ cameraman who arrived on the scene shortly after remembers that my dazed father thought she had just fainted; but she was dead.

By some miracle, my father was physically unhurt. But when he came home that evening, he was not the man he had been that morning. Something in him had disintegrated, and he was overtaken by what we now know was catatonic depression. It would be several years before he returned to any semblance of life.

On and on it went, and loyalist paramilitaries were not finished with us yet. But first they turned their fire on Gerry Kelly, our neighbour on the Crumlin Road, in his little sweet shop and newsagency. It had been bombed and daubed before, but he kept on going. In the weeks before they entered the shop that November day and sprayed him with bullets in front of his young daughter, we who regularly bought sweets and comics from him had, with some sixth sense, stopped going there. It should have been obvious to anyone, for example us, and possibly the police, that there was a cleaning-out of Catholics going on, that extra surveillance and protection were needed – but no such measures were provided. Still we stayed. Why on God's earth did we stay?

They came with bricks on Hallowe'en night – a baying and braying mob gathered outside our gate, led by a thug we knew who lived in a nearby loyalist estate. They broke every window in the house. It was terrifying. We phoned the police, pleading and crying; it was four hours before they turned up. Meanwhile the mob had been run off by the occupants of a white car, whom we later learned were members of the IRA who had heard of our plight on the police radio. I never wanted to be grateful to the IRA, but that night they did save lives. Ours. We had to persuade my father to stay put on the Falls Road in case members of the mob were lying in wait for him. Still we stayed.

A month later, fourteen-year-old Rory Gormley was shot dead by the UVF while wearing his Catholic school uniform. His father – a Mater Hospital colleague of the late Paddy

Lane – and his brother were shot as well, but survived. In the febrile climate of that time, children toing and froing in a Protestant area, dressed in Catholic school uniforms, raised old hackles and fears of being outbred by Papists, thus weakening the Protestant hegemony that God apparently had intended in perpetuity for Northern Ireland.

They wanted us gone and soon succeeded. In the dark early morning of the Feast of the Immaculate Conception, 8 December 1972, loyalist terrorists fired the contents of two machine guns through every window of 657 Crumlin Road from which a light shone. Nora's bed was riddled like a colander.

We weren't home. Clement, then aged three, was enchanted to find the bullet casings strewn all over the garden on his return from first Mass with my mother and six of our siblings. It was a Catholic feast day, and Mass (which the terrorists luckily hadn't reckoned with) was obligatory. Nora and I, for our parts, had gone to a party the night before on the university side of the city, and stayed over because of the perils of travelling back into Ardoyne late at night.

No one among us was hurt, thanks to the strict ecclesiastical and early-rising discipline imposed by our mother. But there was no question of us ever living there again.

Our parents distributed the nine of us around relatives and friends. By the time my father returned later that day, the house had been thoroughly ransacked. A police and army patrol watched as he entered the house, later advising him to leave immediately, as a sniper was attempting to kill him from the roof of Everton School – and, by the way, the tax on his car was several days out of date. Such was the ugliness of life back then.

The police described it as the worst attack to date on a Catholic family. They were wrong. No one died or was injured in our house. There had been much worse, and there was much worse to come, as Catholics and Protestants, civilians, police, military, judges, lawyers, prison officers fell victim to a savage war of tit-for-tat attrition.

Years later, when trying to cajole my then seven-year-old daughter Sara to get up for Mass on the anniversary of our non-liquidation, I foolishly told her that since Our Blessed Lady had given us her protection on the Feast of her Immaculate Conception, the least we could do was turn up and say thank you. She pulled the duvet over her head, defiantly saying, 'Huh – sounds more like Immaculate Coincidence to me.' She is lucky she wasn't liquidated there and then. We were living in the centre of the beautiful, peaceful village of Rostrevor, County Down, on the shores of Carlingford Lough and in the foothills of the Mourne Mountains, enjoying the happy, carefree life we should all have lived in the once lovely urban village of Ardoyne but for the festering sectarian hatreds and injustices left unresolved for generations and ruinously exploited for political ends.

No one was ever prosecuted for any of the offences visited on my family. The same young loyalist paramilitary who had led the brick attack was one of those who later returned with a machine gun. He lived five minutes away. His brother was friends with one of my brothers and had been a regular visitor to our home.

It would be two years after the attack on 657 Crumlin Road before we owned our own home again, miles away from Ardoyne. Meanwhile we were distributed among relatives, until we were offered the chance to rent a house in Andersonstown and were all assembled under one roof once again. The house was scheduled for demolition, but the order of nuns who owned it let us have it while the planning process for a nursing home took its course.

Money was scarce, and there was an ominous sense that the things that had been strong and central to our lives were now fragile. We had a machine-gunned home we could not live in and which was not sellable. We had a business that had been bombed, friends who had been murdered, children who had been assaulted, and there was no clear way out of our financially parlous situation. Worse still, it became obvious that the rented house we were now camped in, which had previously been lying derelict, had been used by the IRA for the storage of weapons, and the very large wild, wooded garden had been employed for training purposes. Organised attempts were made by gangs of young thugs to intimidate us out. Windows were smashed, car tyres slashed, even our dog was stoned. In desperation, my father wrote to the *Andersonstown News* pointing out the irony that as Catholics we had been violently driven from our home by loyalists, and now here we were in a Catholic ghetto that was just as unsafe. Why?

The response was swift. Sentries appeared at our gate while unknown men came to tell us that the intimidation would stop. It did, and by means we were not directly privy to, though indirectly it became clear that threats of violence were involved. An anxious mother came to our door begging us to tell the unnamed men that her son was not one of the offending thugs. He was home every evening doing his homework, she said. He stood there in a school shirt and tie, hair neatly combed and an angelic expression on his scrubbed visage. I asked her to wait a minute and went to the cloakroom, where I retrieved the jacket I had pulled from his retreating back as I chased him after he had injured my mother and our dog with half-inch steel staples launched from his catapult. I had also collected some of the offending ammunition, and brought it to show Mama for good measure. Her tone changed once this evidence had been presented, and she went back up the garden in entirely different humour. Judging by the howls that emanated from our studious hero, she definitely did to him what I would have done if I had got the chance the day he attacked my mother.

In 1971, my father had bought a half-share in a city-centre pub comprising three integrated venues: the Rosemary Rooms, which was a cocktail bar; the Red Barn; and the Star and Garter. The customers were office workers, professionals of all sorts, groups of friends out for a night, shoppers, journalists and a large cohort of horse-racing enthusiasts. People of all politics, perspectives and faiths assembled there: it was neutral territory.

My father's partner in the venture was a fellow Roscommon man, Tommy Hunt. He was the uncle of the internationally renowned musicians Fionnuala and Una Hunt, whose father Paddy was a friend of my father's. The plan was to grow that business, with my father doing the everyday management in the hope that he would eventually be able to move on from the increasingly difficult atmosphere on the Falls Road, including pressure from republican paramilitaries for protection money. Initially he toggled between the city-centre pub and the Long Barn, and I helped out in both at weekends. But city-centre businesses were badly hit as the Troubles ratcheted up, and there was none of the usual night-time trade on which pubs depend. Then came the loyalist bombing of the Long Bar and the loss of our home, which caused my father a serious loss of confidence.

One night in November 1974, the IRA left two parcel

bombs in the Star and Garter. No one was on the premises, but my father was called to the scene by the police. The building was well on fire by the time he arrived with the keys to the massive steel doors the firefighters needed to open. He was given protective clothing and guided the firemen through the burning building. By the time he got the last door open, flaming debris was falling all around. Back out on the street, the fire alarm on the outside wall was still screeching and eventually had to be attacked with an axe to silence it. It was the only comic moment in a night that piled trauma upon trauma and gave my father the distinction of having businesses destroyed by both loyalist and republican paramilitaries.

I discovered something new about our Andersonstown house the morning after I was called to the Northern Ireland Bar, at the end of 1974. I was carrying my wig and gown in the traditional blue barrister's bag and aiming for my desk in the Bar Library, contemplating my first day of professional unemployment, when I heard my name called by the man exiting through the same revolving door through which I was entering. It was Anthony Campbell, then an eminent Queen's Counsel and, as I discovered over many years of later working with him, as pleasant and clever a human being as God ever gave a completely rounded personality to. I did not know him on that fateful morning. 'I have been looking for you,' he said. 'You are with me at the Crumlin Road courthouse.' It emerged that he had been my master Peter Smith's master at the Bar, and needed a junior barrister. The Northern Ireland Bar was small in number, with fewer than a hundred practitioners – all male, until I arrived with two other females.

This was my first ever case. I thought of hiding inside the

large bag I was carrying. Anthony saw the stricken look on my face and brightly reassured me: 'You won't have to say a word. Just sit beside me and pass me papers.' He handed me a set of documents about which I knew absolutely nothing, and suddenly I was in his car. I opened the file. It was a criminal injuries compensation claim on behalf of soldiers who had been killed and injured when the tail fin of a rocket launcher exploded at Fort Monagh barracks. They had found the device at a derelict house, number 20 Fruithill Park in Andersonstown – our home – shortly before we moved in.

Because of the irregular uses to which that house's garden had been put, soldiers sometimes patrolled through it, using it as a shortcut from the periphery into the heart of Andersonstown. There was an old air-raid shelter in the garden and they naturally checked it. That was where the tail fin of the rocket launcher was found. We knew none of this, not when it happened, not when we moved in, not until now. As I read the file for my first case as a barrister, I was hit with the realisation that these claims could just as easily have related to me or my brothers or sisters, but for the fate that sent the soldiers – members of the first battalion of the King's Own Scottish Borderers – on patrol to that garden in the days before we arrived with nine children who would just love to have drop-kicked a weird-looking piece of metal found in the air-raid shelter of their new and strange home.

The tail fin of the rocket launcher, part of a long-out-of-date weapon originally made in Britain, was deemed harmless by the soldiers. They bore their trophy back to their barracks at Fort Monagh and were having a photograph taken with it when the device exploded, killing Colour Sergeant Henry Middlemass and injuring two of his fellow soldiers. Newspaper reports simply said the weapon was found in a derelict house in the area. It was reported that the device was not booby-trapped, as originally thought, but had merely been abandoned as useless by the IRA.

Eventually, as we got closer to the courthouse, I was able to explain the coincidence to Anthony. We both arrived there shaken. Anthony did a superb job on a delicate and dreadfully sad case.

That was day one in my career as a barrister. The next days were no better. I found a well-known solicitor, Paschal O'Hare, waiting for me at the Bar Library. He shoved a fist-ful of papers at me and told me my client was waiting at Number Two Court across the road. He had been charged with assault and intimidation of a family a street up from the Ardoyne home we had fled. The client claimed he had been at home with his wife at the time of the alleged offence. He obviously did not recognise me, for the last time I had seen him he had been on the far end of a brick being heaved through our windows on Hallowe'en night 1972.

His victims this time were a Catholic family we had grown up with and knew as friends, one of whom was now a police officer. I had to cross-examine the police officer and suggest that the man with the brick and the baseball bat he had eye-balled at his door and had drawn his police weapon on was not the man in the dock but some other person. His answer flummoxed the magistrate: 'Sure you know him as well as I do, Mary.' My client got six months' imprisonment, but as it was my first appearance in the magistrates' court and the first appearance there by a female barrister in the experience of the magistrate, and since the magistrate's daughter and I had been best friends at school and he was charmed at how I had turned out, he declared that I had made the best case I could in the circumstances and suspended the sentence. My client was thrilled, despite having had misgivings at the outset when it looked as if I did not know where to sit.

Worse was to come. The *Belfast Telegraph* carried the story of my first criminal case on its front page. The evening edition arrived in our house. I rang my mother to tell her the events of the day. She told me not to come home any time soon, and, in the name of all that was holy, was that what she and my father had brought me into the world and educated me for?

My client, it turned out, was even more sinister than any of us had imagined. According to what we later discovered from the police, he was one of two members of the UDA who had launched the machine-gun attack on our home. He was part of a death squad, but it seems he later had a falling-out with his fellow murderers in the UDA. First they punished him by kneecapping him: that is to say, they maimed him by shooting him through his kneecaps. A year later, two of them took an evening off from sectarian murders and killed him at his front door, five minutes from our old Ardoyne home. According to the judge who convicted his killers, he was murdered 'simply because he was not liked'. I very much doubt that assessment. He was a notoriously out-of-control psychopath, though that may of course explain why he was 'not liked'.

A few days after my magnificent performance in my first criminal case, I was asked to do a bail application on behalf of a man who belonged to the UDA/UFF and who was charged with five murders. He had spontaneously confessed to killing four random Catholics in retaliation for murders carried out by the IRA, including the Birmingham bombings; but he had concluded his statement by offering an apology to the family of the good Christian Protestant man he had shot in the back outside Ardoyne chapel in the mistaken assumption he was a Catholic.

The murderer was John Shaw, my old neighbour and family friend. He shot the Protestant, John Ramsay, another neighbour of ours, a few feet from my cousin Paddy Cassidy's shop. Paddy tried to help and comfort John Ramsay as he died. The trauma overwhelmed him.

John Shaw did not want me as his lawyer, and I gratefully handed over his papers to a fellow rookie. Among the other people he had murdered was a twenty-year-old Catholic girl, killed on 22 November 1974 while working at a filling station in a Catholic area. Next day, in retaliation, the IRA killed two Protestants who worked in a filling station in Ardoyne, one a teenage girl, the other the young manager. Two days later, just in case their point had been missed, they shot a Protestant man on his way to work near Ardoyne. It was the day after that killing that John Shaw, on behalf of the UDA/UFF, shot John Ramsay. We were living in some kind of hell, and no one, it seemed, could stop the madness.

Walking back to the Bar Library one day after another depressing hearing, I was stopped by a young bearded police officer, who said hello. I did not recognise him, but he recognised me from when he had come to our house after my brother John was seriously assaulted. He had been with John the day John identified one of his attackers as he walked out of his workplace at Mackie's foundry. The name of the gang leader was already known to us. He lived on a street where we had once lived. John had recognised him, and our old neighbours had identified him immediately from the photofit John put together. Some of them had wanted to do to him what he did to John, but were roundly turned on by my father and mother, who wanted no more violence.

The young police officer had been helpful and kindly, but in the end there had been no prosecution and no explanation had been offered. Now, however, he volunteered a story. By coincidence, John's attacker was that very day being arraigned for the murder of the Catholic manager of the branch of the Ulster Bank nearest Ardoyne. The police officer said my family had been very much on his mind, for if only John's attacker had been convicted, perhaps the man he had murdered might still be alive. I asked did he know why the prosecution for John's attack had never materialised. He told me, and with a little anger, that the offender had a relative who was high up in the Orange Order. This relative had provided a cast-iron alibi. End of story.

Over Christmas 1974, my parents had moved to the village of Rostrevor, to a pub in the main square called the Old Corner House. It had living accommodation attached, which could not be described as spacious, to put it mildly; but it was a fresh start, and in a magical village that was the inspiration for C. S. Lewis's Narnia. Its beauty, its normalcy, its kindly people and decent community relations were like a balm to addled minds and stressed-out bodies. It was not enough, though, for my father. Within the year he had his first massive heart attack, and his full-strength working days were numbered.

His health declined until he was rescued from death's door sixteen difficult years later by a quadruple bypass – an operation that he got only because, as he lay in hospital waiting to die, a space opened up on the surgery list and his terrific cardiologist, Michael Scott, pleaded for him to have it. Amazingly, the operation gave him twenty-two more years, though he coped with serious ill-health for most of it: Parkinson's, epilepsy, dementia. In Rostrevor there was peace and a kind of normality, but there was also the financial pressure that came with raising a large family and starting over again with a large mortgage at almost fifty. He must often have wished he had stayed in Roscommon.

Martin and I married on 9 March 1976 in St Mary's Star of the Sea Church in Rostrevor. Our dog Fox – whom my father had acquired after an explosion in Belfast had disoriented him so that he wandered off from his original owners – was notoriously friendly. He jumped up on my wedding dress with mucky paws as I emerged from the kitchen door to go the one hundred yards to the chapel. The paw marks are still visible all these years later. I thought then that was the worst thing that could happen on my wedding day. It wasn't.

Our dear friends and mates Tony and Myles O'Reilly, with whom we had discussed our wedding arrangements backwards and forwards, were murdered that morning by loyalists: first shot and then set fire to. I don't remember much about that day: just how the atmosphere at our wedding reception suddenly collapsed as the news of their deaths reached the guests – though not Martin and me. A conspiracy of silence saw us off on the road south on our honeymoon, en route to Kerry via Dublin. We were to spend the night at Sachs Hotel in Donnybrook as guests of the businessman Hugh Tunney, a friend of Martin's. I remember our happy dinner, and then phoning home from our room. I remember how, on hearing the news, I shrank into a foetal ball on my honeymoon night, sobbing, sobbing, thinking of their wives, Tony's seven children, their eleven siblings . . . Sobbing, sobbing.

# 6

Martin had moved to Dublin for work in 1972. He had just graduated in physics from Queen's, but decided on a career in accountancy and a break from Belfast, and so took a job with Stokes Kennedy Crowley. He lived in an eclectic series of shared lodgings, which I experienced as an occasional visitor from Belfast, where I had two more years of legal studies still ahead of me.

Early on, he stayed in the grand and rather old-world home on Sydney Parade Avenue of a very engaging female descendant of Michael Davitt. The fact that the oft-discussed political hero's death from septicaemia resulted from a dental extraction probably played no prominent role in Martin's subsequent switch to a dental career, but the idea was possibly implanted during those gory discussions. His housemates were friends from Queen's at first: John McCrory from Belfast and Derry footballer Seamus Mullan, fellow accountancy students with little time for socialising and even less money. I had undergraduate law finals in 1973 and then Bar finals in 1974, not to mention a catalogue of Troubles-related family problems, so my visits south were rare enough; but when Martin moved into a madhouse in Garville Avenue with Moss Keane, an old pal from Sigerson Cup days (and future rugby legend), the fun really started.

Of the four who shared that unique Petri dish, Martin and the three Kerrymen (Moss, Denis Coffey and Jim Coughlan), only Martin survived to collect the free bus pass. But if the lives of the others were tragically short, they were overloaded with entertainment, for never did a trio have such a gargantuan and exuberant appetite for life. I was the hapless butt of many of their jokes, apparently, but since I could not understand a word they said, no damage was done. In fairness, they had as much difficulty with my Northern accent as I had with their rich Kerry *blas*. Their zest for life and the relaxed normality of Dublin planted the idea in my own mind of moving there – though with very imperfect timing I had no sooner put in my application to Trinity College for a job than Martin was moved back to Belfast with Seamus Mullan to help set up the new Peat Marwick Mitchell (later KPMG) office there. Martin and I also had a falling-out that was to last for the best part of 1975.

The job I had applied for at Trinity was a junior lecturer's post. In reply, I received an intriguing letter from the head of the Law School, Regius Professor Robert Heuston, a famous tort scholar and debating stalwart of the College Historical Society. He suggested I apply instead for the post of Reid Professor of Criminal Law, Criminology and Penology, which had just been vacated by Mary Robinson and was due to be advertised. I did that, and had a very agreeable job interview followed by lunch with Professor Heuston in the Common Room, where, thanks to his recommendation, I had my first introduction to its famous lemon posset with shortbread. I reckoned if I did not get the job at least I could try to acquire the recipe for that unequalled delight.

We were joined at lunch by two Northerners, Professors Dan Bradley and Vincent McBrierty: both former students of my cousin Brother Bede McGreevy, and the latter a close friend from Ardoyne. None of this background, it seems, was known to Professor Heuston, who had merely thought to make me feel at home by recruiting two nearby Northerners to tell me of their lives at Trinity. He listened in growing bemusement as we eagerly unpacked all the many points of intersection in our lives, including the fact that Dan's father and my grandfather had worked together in Derry, not to mention that Vincent's mother, the local Ardoyne district midwife, had delivered several of my siblings. I was told a short time later that the post was mine, leaving me to conclude that my brief and undistinguished career at the criminal Bar in Belfast, plus the fact that I had opted for every option associated with criminal law as an undergraduate, was regarded as a tolerable body of qualifications. Back then a doctorate was not a requirement for academic appointments, but my performance in my undergraduate and postgraduate studies was sufficient unto the day, thankfully.

The Reid post was particularly suited to a lawyer at the start of an academic career. Up until my appointment, it had been designed as a part-time role for someone who also wished to practise at the Bar, which is why it had suited Mary Robinson. It was a measure of the changes taking place in legal education that Trinity now insisted it become a full-time post, which was exactly what I wanted. That seemed to impress my interviewers, and I knew before the lemon posset was finished that the job was mine if I had a mind to take it.

I was duly appointed in the summer of 1975, by which time my parents and most of my siblings were resettled in Rostrevor. That is where I went at weekends, to keep a weather eye on a still fragile family and to revel in the walks in the oak forest that had inspired C. S. Lewis, to ramble up the Fairy Glen, to climb Sliabh Martin or just sit on the sea wall looking out over Carlingford Lough. After Belfast, Rostrevor seemed like nirvana. But now Dublin was to become the centre of my professional life.

Home was a bedsit on Waterloo Road, a floor down from those of my sister Nora and an ex-nun friend from Cork, Frances Lynch. It was just up the road from Mary Robinson's home, and she was very helpful and encouraging when I visited her that summer looking for advice on what my new role entailed. I had never taught a class before, unless you count an unsuccessful stint as a hastily drafted junior infants substitute teacher in a Dominican primary school during a flu epidemic while I was at Queen's. The children had the cherubic faces of the five-year-olds they were, but their capacity for brilliantly organised collective mischief-making was impressive. There was a class pet, a gerbil in a cage. I had never really warmed to David Attenborough's easy facility with bugs and rodents, and the children intuitively knew that I was not a gerbil fan. They opened the cage and sat back to watch and scream as hell on an epic scale broke loose. The headmistress was not impressed to find me marooned on a table and shrieking for help while thirty children looked like they might actually die laughing.

So I was a bit lacking in experience when I sauntered through Trinity's Front Gate, into Front Square, past the Campanile and into number 38 New Square to begin my stint as a professor of law. Luckily, help was forthcoming. An old friend at the Northern Bar, John Maxwell, had been through the Trinity Law School a few years before, and he bequeathed to me his set of meticulous lecture notes: a little out of date, but a start nonetheless. I took up almost permanent residence in the small departmental library and the considerably larger Berkeley Library, a 1960s 'brutalist gem' that I eventually came to like if not exactly love.

Trinity's tradition of staff wearing academic gowns was still alive when I arrived, so I put my expensive and little-worn Ede & Ravenscroft barrister's gown to use instead of buying a new black academic gown. One of my new colleagues was Sydney Cole, an elderly barrister and senior lecturer who normally wore morning dress to College but changed religiously to cricket whites as soon as term ended and for as long as the summer holidays endured. He was a stickler for rules and rituals, and quietly suggested to me that wearing my barrister's gown, with its pouch on the back for discreet payment by clients, was not the done thing. I pondered his advice and then joined the growing group of staff who were developing a new fashion that Sydney detested even more: no gown at all. He pleaded with me to revert to the barrister's gown, which was better than nothing, but in the end the gown-wearing culture evaporated more or less across all of College, much to Sydney's dismay. He and a few others of the unwavering old school continued to wear their gowns to class, and the sight of them so clad walking across the Front Square, black serge billowing in the breeze, often made me nostalgic for the times they remembered and I did not.

During our regular encounters, Sydney and I became good colleagues. He was invariably jolly, except on the subject of disappearing traditions; and as well as very generously giving me a copy of the only existing text on Irish criminal law, a very slim volume written by Sydney himself, he introduced me to his great passion, the tragic Trinity 'Pals' who had died during the Great War. At the drop of a tea bag into a mug of boiled water and the production of a ginger snap biscuit, he was off.

There being no staff room, we Law School staff members either met in each other's rooms or drove the Law School secretary insane by propping ourselves on either side of her ancient filing cabinet and yakking until she barked at us to go away. It was a performance often repeated with colleagues Kader Asmal, William Duncan, Gerard Hogan, Brian Lenihan, Fidelma Macken, Paul O'Higgins, Niall Osborough, Mary Robinson, Yvonne Scannell, Alex Schuster, Patrick Usher, and Gerry Whyte – individually and collectively brilliant, fascinating and absorbing company. Between us clogging up the narrow room and a tribe of students coming in and out with queries, it is hard to credit that the poor secretary got any work done at all. She was gone (and who could blame her) before I really got to know her well, but her successor Margot Aspell, who plied us with invective and home-made lemonade in equal measure, became the closest family friend I made during my Trinity days. Departmental secretaries, who were shared between demanding academics and armed with ancient typewriters and Tippex, were the hardest-working people in College in those times.

The Law School atmosphere was collegial, eccentric and fascinating. A goodly proportion of the students were from Northern Ireland, and some were from further afield. The school catered not just to students doing full-time law degrees but to people from other disciplines and from outside College who were doing a variety of other degrees and professional courses. It made for a slightly more heterogeneous environment than I had experienced at Queen's, and sometimes it was difficult to know how to pitch lectures. A big advantage was that, unlike in Belfast, classes and studies in the library were never, ever interrupted by bomb scares. That took some getting used to.

Advice about the subjects I was to teach came from Supreme Court justice John Kenny, who in sessions at his home on Nutley Lane helped me understand the ins and outs of the Irish Constitution – a subject that had not merited a mention in law school in Belfast. He brought me up to speed on the dissimilarities between Irish and UK criminal law, which were then still relatively few. Judge Kenny was also an expert on the Reid chair, whose dramatic history he introduced me to.

The chair dated back to 1888, a period when university studies in law were becoming more systematised – a process still ongoing when I arrived in Trinity in 1975. Killarney-born barrister Richard Touhill Reid, who had had a successful career in Bombay, died in Rome in 1883 and left a substantial sum of money that eventually went to fund the chair and a number of scholarships. Even today, Reid's bequest funds five entrance exhibition scholarships for students from Kerry. Happily, the Reid chair was not limited to denizens of the Kingdom, otherwise who knows where I might have wound up. Despite its elevated title, I started on a junior lecturer's salary.

From Sydney Cole and John Kenny I learned that among my predecessors as Reid Professor was Ernest Julian, who as a young lieutenant in the 7th Royal Dublin Fusiliers had died with tens of his Trinity comrades at Suvla Bay in August 1915 during the annihilation that was the Gallipoli campaign. His story always moved me to tears, as it did when I called him to mind on an official visit to Gallipoli in March 2010 to commemorate those who died on all sides during that awful campaign.

The Law School house at 38 New Square was too small to have a room for me, which is how I came to be billeted in a dark, miserable building in Pearse Street. John Horne, Professor of Modern European History and later director of the Trinity Centre for War Studies, was based downstairs. I was up in the attic, in a low-roofed room the size of a respectable dog basket. I was always happy to be detained in animated conversation with John at the door of his downstairs study before ascending to what was nothing like Mount Olympus except to the extent that it required Herculean effort on my part to reach it. His quiet and superb scholarship helped Ireland rediscover its legacy of Great War dead, and would later inform my efforts as President to help redeem the lost memory of the Great War and to reveal in it a hidden platform of shared memory capable of reconciling North and South, Protestant and Catholic.

Eventually I got a room to share in New Square with another historian, Dr Bill Vaughan. His research interest in nineteenth-century Ireland extended to crime, police and criminal trials, so he was a very well-chosen roommate for a professor of criminal law. His research assistant was a wonderfully energetic and funny older woman, Sheelagh Harbison, who was doing a doctorate in medieval history. She had enough personality for three extroverts.

Talking with Bill and Sheelagh was an enjoyable diversion from getting to grips with the Republic's law of larceny, which was still based on the pre-independence Larceny Act of 1916. The Act had applied throughout the United Kingdom until updated and reformed in 1969, the year I started studying law as an undergraduate. So the old law was new to me. John Maxwell's notes proved their worth! It would be quite a few years before the old British Larceny Act ceased to apply in the independent Irish Republic. Luckily for me, the vast Trinity Library collection held any amount of old British criminal law texts, the content of which, with little or no adaptation, continued to be relevant to modern Ireland. I soon discovered why Sydney's book was so slim.

I had to teach penology and criminology as well as criminal law. These were not standard elements of law degrees elsewhere, but it was just my luck that criminology especially was becoming an area of febrile academic debate, with many new scholars churning out publications, some highly political and many impenetrable. Both subjects were ideal territory for law students who wanted to dabble in sociology, psychology, forensic science, political science, history, philosophy, phenomenology and statistics. It would be accurate to describe both subjects as being seriously underdeveloped in an Irish context, but as my own interest in them grew, I became involved in research into the Irish penal system, and in international research on children in custody and women in prison.

I was excited by the fact that these research projects were treading new ground, as well as by the calibre of the people I collaborated, researched and wrote with. A collaboration on the Irish penal system with (among others) the recent Nobel peace laureate Dr Sean MacBride SC, Professor Father Micheál MacGréil SJ, my future successor as President of Ireland Michael D. Higgins, and Professor Louk Hulsman, initially in an unofficial commission of enquiry, produced a substantial and influential report, later published as a book. With Maynooth's Séamus Ó Cinnéide, and British scholars Professor Norman Tutt, Gillian Stewart and a number of others, I undertook Carnegie and Rowntree Trust-funded research into children in custody across England, Ireland, Scotland, Wales and Northern Ireland. I also worked with social scientist Dr Francesca Lundström on victims of crime and criminal sanctions, and began my own personal research on women in prison to help fuel debate in penology classes.

For the students who chose penology and criminology there was a rare opportunity to engage in original research at undergraduate level, since there was little in Ireland by way of academic study on either subject. My friendship with the redoubtable Sheelagh Harbison emboldened me to ask her son John, the state pathologist, to contribute to my criminology course. He agreed with the alacrity of a man who knows what is coming next. His account of the gruesome details of the work of a forensic pathologist and his graphic slides of the bodies of murder victims were generally too strong for the stomachs of mere aspiring lawyers. But he already knew that. He obligingly brought a supply of sick bags!

It was easy to get to know the law students, for Trinity's collegiate structure, with so many students living in, meant we were always running across one another. But there were also opportunities to get to know people from other spheres. Coming from a background in school and college debating, I soon found my way to discussions and debates in both the Philosophical Society and the College Historical Society. By late 1975, I had already lambasted the denizens of the Hist for their baleful ignorance of what was happening in Northern Ireland, and a short time later I was chairing (refereeing) a debate on the proposition that 'Gay rights are human rights'. The Hist was an unmerciful bearpit, wickedly worse than anything I had experienced in the more sedate debating circles in the North. Whether one was chairing a debate or speaking to the motion, control of the baying crowd was a regular problem; but it was a very useful if painful way for any new lecturer to develop a thick skin. One of the Hist's eminent auditors, the poet Micheal O'Siadhail, describes it as 'this arena where we found our feet', echoing Marianne Elliott's view in her opus on Wolfe Tone that historically it was the training ground 'for almost all the leading political figures in the age of Grattan's Parliament'. And not just that age! Pick an age, any age in the last two and a half centuries: Tone, Davis, Carson, Wilde, Yeats . . .

The student cohort was bright and sharp to a testing degree. They were a terrific bunch to teach and their intellectual acuity was a great source of energy. It was essential for sanity's sake to be one step ahead of them. For students who came up to Trinity from small schools where they had always been top of the class, adapting to an environment with similarly able students was not always easy, as I found out quickly in my work as a tutor. Trinity has a great tutoring system whereby students are assigned to certain members of staff to be individually mentored and generally helped on their journey through College. It was the part of the job I loved best.

One young man arrived for his first interview with me just before commencing his four years at Trinity, hair cropped pudding-bowl style, wearing short pants (not then fashionable in the least!) and accompanied by his father. Every question directed to the student was answered by the father. They were farming people from a remote country area and the young man was the first of his clan to go to college. He was petrified. What was more, he was just sixteen. I was worried that his peers would eat him without salt and suggested that he take a gap year – maybe abroad, to brush up on a language – and then come back to College when everyone in his class would be the same biological age. Both seemed relieved at the suggestion, and the arrangements for deferral were made. The student turned up a year later in a cropped leather jacket, torn designer jeans, long hair, and earrings in both ears – and fluent in French. He was a delight to teach and College was no bother to him. It was graduation before I set eyes on his father again, and both parents seemed suitably in awe of their transformed son, who managed to turn out perfectly clad and groomed for the ceremony. He made a very fine country solicitor.

Each lunchtime I sprinted from class, tripping inelegantly across the dangerous cobbles in Front Square to Mass at five past one in the College chapel. My old Ardoyne pal Vincent McBrierty and I generally collided in the doorway, though in fairness he had a longer sprint than me from the physics department at the farthest end of College. We were both members of the College Catholic chaplaincy chapel team, which meant we acted as Ministers of the Eucharist betimes and turned up for theological discussions at chaplaincy get-togethers, where I first befriended Dermot McCarthy (later Secretary General to the Government) and Rosemary Grant, his future wife.

Another very pleasant way of meeting non-law people was taking morning tea in the Common Room, where there were memorable encounters with the altogether forbidding medieval historian (and rare female College Fellow) Professor Otway Ruthven, known to all and sundry as the Ott, though she had the charming birth name of Annette Jocelyn, as I learned only when reading her death notice. She frightened the living daylights out of me until I got to know the sheer kindness, humour and desire to encourage college women that lay behind her rattling chain mail. There too I first met and got to know wonderful College women like Trinity's first female Fellow, Professor Barbara Wright; the elegant and thoughtful Professor of Italian Corinna Lonergan; Noreen Kearney, a brilliant social scientist with whom I often collaborated; and some of Trinity's many geniuses, among them the gentlemanly mathematician Petros Florides, the economist

Sean Barrett, medic John Arbuthnot, and the legendary R. B. McDowell. Over and above the Senior Common Room, however, I preferred a convivial scone in the upstairs café in Kilkenny Design. Between 10.30 and 11 most weekday mornings it was commandeered by a random selection of TCD staff, including many of my Law School colleagues and friends from the expanding circle I was gathering in areas of interest from homelessness to juvenile justice.

Martin moved back to Dublin in January 1977 to work as financial controller of Blueskies, an Aer Lingus subsidiary. He and I made good lives and good friends in Dublin, but while I developed a deep interest in the politics of the Republic, we were both perplexed by the general lack of interest in events across the border. The grisly sectarian reality of the IRA campaign no doubt seriously dulled any sense of empathy with the place. There was a fear that the Republic would be seen to condone the IRA, which was already long past any claim to being a hastily mustered corps for the protection of beleaguered Catholics, and was instead contributing to their endangerment and that of many others. It was also postponing any hope of realising the ambition of a united Ireland by making the mere mention of it toxically associated with sectarian murder, economic destruction and mayhem. Even so, we were struck by the almost dismissive distaste we encountered towards conversations about the North.

I became deeply involved in a number of civil rights and legal issues of the day, speaking at conferences on penal reform, sentencing policy, juvenile justice, the Prevention of Terrorism Act in the UK, and on new laws on the admissibility of confession statements in the Republic. I became an active member of the Irish Council for Civil Liberties and a co-founder, with David Norris and others, of the Campaign for Homosexual Law Reform.

As a result, I was asked to do interviews from time to time for RTÉ radio and television. On one occasion I was asked to do an informal preview of a current affairs programme to see if it was likely to run into any legal difficulties, and that was how I came to hear that the station was recruiting new current affairs journalists. I wondered if a role in current affairs journalism might be a way of getting to understand the complexities of the Republic better. Muiris MacConghail, a former senior government adviser who worked at RTÉ (and would later be its Director General), encouraged me to apply. I had a benign interview, which led to the offer of a job, and got off to a very lawyerly start when I sent back the initial contract and asked RTÉ to consider revising the proposed salary upwards. The positive if exasperated reply came back: 'The question of your starting salary has been further considered . . . Perhaps you will now let me know if you accept the offer.'

At the end of the academic year in 1979, I started work as 'Reporter/Presenter in Current Affairs (TV)'. The new career began with a brief training scheme on which were a group of other trainee newcomers, Colum Kenny, Joe Little and Colm Keane. I could not have hand-picked better people to start out with.

I did not talk the change of career over with Robert Heuston before I had my mind made up. That was a mistake, for he was visibly upset when I told him and immediately felt that he was in some way to blame. He was not. I explained my restlessness to get to grips with the fullness of life in the South. He understood, but was fairly scathing about the merits of a career in journalism as opposed to academia. He insisted that if the move did not work out then I must consider returning to the Law School. He was, as usual, prescient to a rare degree.

My first appointment in RTÉ was to the main current affairs programme, *Frontline*. The programme was headed by Peter Feeney, a thoughtful, reflective Dubliner who had lived and lectured in politics in Northern Ireland (the latter a rare enough if not unique phenomenon in RTÉ Current Affairs). I developed the highest regard for him. He was always courteous, affirming, and respectful of others' opinions. There were no cliques, no favourites, no panderers or flatterers, no high-wire theatrics, no craving for recognition and no exaggerated spinning of *Frontline* as the programme from current affairs heaven. There was simply an honest job to be done. The programme team worked exceptionally well under his direction.

Peter knew Northern Ireland and its political vanities intimately. His gentlemanly, unflappable manner belied a studied and sensitive approach to all subjects, no matter what the pressures, and he brought those characteristics and skills to bear on Northern Ireland's daily diet of tragedy and political drama. I got good training at *Frontline* and worked on a catalogue of excellent programmes dealing with subjects including abortion, fire services, deaf education and the Whiddy Island disaster. But for reasons never explained to those of us on the staff, the decision was taken in 1980 to cancel *Frontline*. When we left for our summer holiday break, none of us had a clue what was coming next.

It was not until the autumn that I learned from press reports that I was to be working on a new current affairs programme, entitled *Today Tonight*. Its editor, Joe Mulholland, said that it was to be 'an authoritative current affairs programme with a distinctive style'. Certainly the style of leadership and the working culture were very different from what I'd experienced at *Frontline*. In my first personal encounter with Dr Joe, whom I had never met before, he was not pleasant, telling me that if my Irish had been better I would have been shunted off to the Irish-language programmes. I would come to wish I had been reassigned there myself, for first-rate journalists and colleagues like Mick McCarthy and Eamonn Ó Muiri, working on the Irish-language current affairs programme *Feach*, were to provide far more insightful commentary on Northern affairs than *Today Tonight*. It was made clear by Joe on that first occasion that my knowledge of the North would not be required, as others with more credible experience – among whom he appeared to count himself – were available. Certainly a lot of effort went into publicising and talking up the new programme before it was tried and tested, rather like the reverential hagiographies that greet the appointment of new popes.

There were staff who were in favour with Joe and staff who were not. I was in the latter category. It turned out that while Joe was not particularly well versed in Northern politics, in other respects he could rightly claim that *Today Tonight* had a respectable team that produced respected programmes. It started winning gongs for its general current affairs coverage, and when away from the maelstrom of coverage of Northern Ireland it was capable of decent work that I was usually happy to be associated with. Its coverage of the deadly Stardust nightclub fire, in February 1981, comes to mind as an example of particularly thorough public-service broadcasting.

But it was unfortunate that within weeks of *Today Tonight* beginning its first run, republican prisoners in the North's jails launched a hunger strike, and from then on the programme's weaknesses on Northern issues would become more and more evident. The programme became known in some quarters as 'Today Tonight the Workers Programme' – a reference to Sinn Féin the Workers Party, whose members, also known as 'Stickies', had morphed from being anti-British, anti-partition Irish republicans into Marxist, quasi-unionist partitionists. For a short while they had a disproportionate influence in the media, and Workers Party tracts were regularly left on our desks anonymously.

Programme meetings, at which projects and plans were discussed, became tense affairs when the North was raised. No effort was made to lay down ground rules for a respectful atmosphere. It was commonplace to hear personalised comments made against those who argued for greater balance, insight and accuracy in our Northern coverage, which was visibly slanted away not simply from Irish republicanism (understandable given the violence of the time) but from moderate Irish nationalist views (unforgivable given the violence of the time).

Meetings could involve hours of long-winded and often pointless discussion. The programme was deeply polarised, between those who wanted to tell the story as it was and those who wanted to shoot the messengers. It came to a head when one of the finest and most experienced journalists on the programme, the Scotsman Forbes McFall, was lambasted in scathingly defamatory terms by a particularly obnoxious colleague for his factual and fair coverage of a story from Belfast. As Forbes tried to defend his broadcast, he was shouted down and finally accused of being 'a fucking Provo'. The accusation was beyond risible; it was defamation pure and simple.

Forbes, a gentleman to his fingertips and the most scrupulous of journalists, was eventually rendered speechless. Joe stayed silent. In fact everyone stayed silent until I asked: 'Is no member of senior management willing to say that calling a colleague an effing Provo is highly libellous and is creating a hostile working environment?' No one answered. That was when something broke inside me. I, like Forbes and several others, had put up for months with the insults, the name-calling and the backbiting. I laid it out plain and simple. There were journalists on the programme who were diligent professionals, and who took seriously their obligation under the law to be objective and fair to all the parties on any issue on which we broadcast. We were tired of being scapegoated by others who thought and behaved differently. I made it clear that such comments were unacceptable among professionals. I also made it clear that if at any time such personalised comments were ever made about me, I would sue. A few courageous colleagues then began to speak in defence of Forbes, but it was an ignominious episode, the rawness of which left me beyond hurt and frustrated. It was the beginning of the end for Forbes too. We both, along with a few others, began to discuss leaving RTÉ while we still had our sanity.

Training for people management, and concepts like workplace harassment, were still quite undeveloped in RTÉ at that time. And the station's branch at the National Union of Journalists was of little help. Joe simply let wounds fester and was allowed to do so. The sourness came to a head in the spring of 1981, when Bobby Sands, an IRA prisoner on hunger strike, stood in the Fermanagh and South Tyrone by-election.

Sands's only significant opponent was the veteran unionist politician Harry West. The SDLP, which had contested previous elections, stood aside. I checked the numbers on the voting register in advance of the programme meeting, and offered the view that since it was likely to be a straight sectarian fight, Sands could possibly win. A verbal war ensued. The dominant editorial view was that SDLP voters were not likely to vote for Sands. I explained it was at least feasible that there would be enough republican/nationalist votes to get him across the line. I also felt that whether Sands won or lost, the by-election was likely to be a story of national and international import, given the gathering interest in the hunger strike at home and abroad. I suggested that as the major national current affairs programme, we should at least plan to have a crew at the count and a broadcasting slot on the day. *Today Tonight* did not broadcast on Fridays at that time – and the election results were due on a Friday. If we were to honour Joe's belief that people depended on us for development of news of the day, then we should be ready for the news of that day. We would need permission from higher up in RTÉ to get a special broadcasting slot.

Joe's reaction to this suggestion was negative. It was the firm view of the senior editorial team that there was no chance Sands could win, and that win or lose it was a non-story; and so no plans were made for the major national publicly funded Irish broadcaster to cover what turned out to be one of the biggest and most significant political stories of the Troubles. The main UK broadcasters and many foreign broadcasters were at the count, as was *Feach*, but *Today Tonight* was not.

Before lunchtime on the Friday, I was at my desk in the *Today Tonight* office when the news broke via a newspaper stringer at the count that, according to the tallymen, Sands had won the by-election. When the final count came in, the winning margin was nearly 1,500 votes. Joe came thundering from his office, past other colleagues working at their desks and straight to mine, to announce to me that 'your man won'. I was outraged by the personalised nature of his comment, and I decided I had had enough. I left him (and anyone else listening) in no doubt that Sands was not my man. I was not then and never had been a supporter of paramilitary violence. I was no supporter of the hunger strikes. My political views were in any case irrelevant, for I was under a legal obligation to be objective and fair to all the parties as per the Broadcasting Act of 1965, and I took that obligation seriously. I told him that I was merely a journalist who was numerate and had done her homework, which was after all the job the public paid me to do. I asked Joe if, by his twisted logic, Harry West was 'his man'.

He stalked off without apology, only to return a while later, when the office had emptied for the weekend. He was now in a visible panic and instructed me that I was to go immediately to the count in Fermanagh. I had hung around for just this inevitable moment and took great pleasure in telling him that I had made other plans, though possibly not as politely as that. I went shopping and then headed home early to watch the BBC. Joe had to suffer the embarrassment of hastily organising a programme slot borrowed from *Feach* (thanks to the generosity, and much to the bemusement, of Mick McCarthy – probably the cleverest and certainly the wittiest colleague from my time in RTÉ). The crew he hastily sent north arrived too late to get much in the way of useable coverage, and so he was reduced to showing film footage of the election count borrowed from an equally bemused BBC. The story is still told and retold wherever two or more BBC and RTÉ old-timers are gathered.

Heads of course did not roll, and so nothing was learned by the time Bobby Sands died a month after the election. His funeral was to take place on 7 May. At the programme meeting, I asked: would *Today Tonight* cover that event? Joe agreed with the view of Barry Cowan, an experienced and respected journalist from Northern Ireland, who remarkably thought the funeral not worth covering since in his words 'there would be more cameras than mourners'. Having spent endless hours in the North in the interim trying to read the nationalist mood, I was sure that the hunger strike and the British government's reaction to it had stirred moderate nationalist sentiment in a radical new political direction, and that the funeral was likely to indicate that. Once again my views were dismissed out of hand, and in a hostile way that carried the same offensive innuendo that I was advocating for what I *wished* to happen as opposed to what any objective, self-respecting journalist could see might very well happen. I shrugged off the groundless insult, simply saying that on the day of the funeral the numbers would tell their own tale and someone on the programme would be wrong and someone would be right. I was happy to wait and see. There were an estimated seventy thousand to one hundred thousand people at the funeral. Like the by-election, it was an important political signpost, which *Today Tonight* was unprepared for and incapable of comprehending, never mind explaining to a national audience.

Disturbing events a week before the Sands funeral had already helped me make up my mind that it was time to resign. I was usually kept well away from broadcasts involving Northern Ireland, but to my surprise I had been sent to Belfast to do a live studio interview on the ongoing political chaos being churned up by the hunger strike. The production team was not particularly North-savvy. I learned late on the day of the broadcast that one of the people I was to interview was to be Glenn Barr, a man closely associated with the UDA. I pointed out to the programme producer that interviewing a member of, or apologist for, a paramilitary group would very likely put us in breach of the government directive under Section 31 of the Broadcasting Act of 1960. Bear in mind that at that time, under the same law, we could not have interviewed Gerry Adams or Martin McGuinness because of their association with republican paramilitarism. The law prohibited RTÉ from broadcasting anything that could be interpreted as supporting the aims or activities of organisations that 'engage in, promote, encourage, or advocate the attaining of any political objective by violent means'. It clearly excluded members or supporters of both republican and loyalist paramilitary groupings.

I also mentioned that I had overheard conversations within the programme team as a result of which I understood that Andy Tyrie, a loyalist paramilitary leader, had been involved in securing Barr's participation. The programme producer, however, insisted the interview was to go ahead as planned. I was incredulous and remained adamant that it should be dropped. There followed some frenzied toing and froing on the phone between the producer in Belfast and Joe behind his desk in Dublin. The upshot was that I was firmly told that Barr was to be on the programme, and was to be identified solely as 'Chair of the Ulster Political Research Group'. The live programme began, and almost immediately, and without any prompting from me, Barr openly acknowledged his closeness to the paramilitary UDA. I was therefore sitting in a Belfast studio with a live broadcast that was manifestly in breach of Section 31 – a fact immediately pointed out, not unreasonably, by the other studio guests. None of the mess was Barr's fault. It all belonged to *Today Tonight*.

Had I been set up? The question was definitely in my mind. I will never know, but one thing I was determined on was that if there was to be any blame cast, it would miss me by a mile. I wrote to Joe that night (and on reflection should have copied it to a higher authority, though it would likely have made not a bit of difference). On his desk next morning I left a comprehensive account of the events and discussions before and during the programme. He replied immediately, admitting that there was a clear breach of Section 31; that it was 'unfortunate and must exclude him [Barr] from broadcasts forthwith'. He accepted that the decision to have Barr on the programme must be laid at his door and that 'the buck stopped' with him, but he took pains to point out that he had not been involved in conversations with Andy Tyrie before the broadcast and said he was surprised when Barr 'identified himself as being quite close to the UDA'.

The dogs, cats and rats on the streets of the North knew of Barr's paramilitary associations. Over the next few days, as the impact of Sands's death and funeral passed over the assembled heads of the *Today Tonight* current affairs team, I made up my mind that the only proper course of action was to resign, not just because I had no respect for the programme's leadership and the lack of accountability, but because the culture was so deliberately personally oppressive that it was grinding me down, as it did Forbes McFall. He too resigned and went off to a stellar career with the BBC.

Apart from its connection to my professional difficulties at RTÉ, the IRA hunger strike of 1981 had another very personal resonance for me.

During the years when I was growing up in Belfast, my mother's sister Bridget lived in Andersonstown with her husband Harry Pickering and their twelve children, who were of similar ages to my siblings. Bridget was my favourite aunt, and her daughter Pauline my closest friend among my cousins. They are two of the women I admire most in the world, for faced with any amount of hardship their innate graciousness and fortitude never failed them. Their family story says much about the ways in which context, circumstance and luck can nudge a life out of kilter, down rough unlit paths.

Harry, a fine amateur musician and gardener, found work hard to get and was unemployed for long periods. Bridget worked as a cleaner at St Joseph's teacher-training college. The Troubles brought a trough of difficulties to their door. It started when my cousin John, the eldest boy in the family, was convicted of riotous behaviour when aged only sixteen. He had been in town buying shoes and was carrying them under his arm as he headed home on foot, for an outbreak of the commonplace street violence had caused buses and taxis to stop running. Hard of hearing, he was cautiously circling around the edge of what had turned into a confrontation with the army when he was stopped and arrested by a military 'snatch squad'. He got short shrift in court, and was sentenced to six months in St Patrick's Training School, a reformatory. When he got out, his anger forged a commitment to the IRA, for whom St Patrick's was as good as any recruitment office.

John was soon interned without trial in Long Kesh, and when he was eventually released it was clear his focus remained on being a 'freedom fighter', as he told me when I met him for the first time in many years at a funeral. Relatives had tried to get him a job with decent prospects, but he was having none of it. Having seen at close quarters the stress his imprisonment had caused his mother and family, I admonished him in strong terms, but in the summer of 1976, when I heard on the news that two IRA men on the run from security forces were holding a hostage at a house near where I lived, a blanket of dread descended on me at the thought that John might be one of them. He was. He was captured and later sentenced to life imprisonment for his part earlier that day in the appalling murder of an elderly Protestant man, the owner of a local filling station, William Creighton.

My aunt Bridget's life now consisted of attending court hearings to catch a glimpse of her son, and prison visits, which she found debilitating and draining. John's politics were not hers, nor were they mine. His actions offended the deep Christian faith and values that she and I shared. But he was her son. I visited her often during those times to give her whatever support I could, and was incensed on one occasion when, in distress, she showed me a list of expensive items she could not afford but was being asked by Sinn Féin to supply for her prisoner son. The deliverer of the list got an earful from me.

Republican prisoners campaigned unsuccessfully for five years for the restoration of Special Category Status, under which they had been treated as political prisoners. In 1981 the protest escalated into the hunger strike led by Bobby Sands. When the Troubles broke out, Sands was a teenager living in the mainly Protestant Rathcoole estate, on the northern outskirts of Belfast. His family, like all the Catholic minority who lived there, were terrorised by loyalist paramilitaries and forced to leave. My husband Martin's family, living in a loyalist part of east Belfast, were similarly evicted: loyalists had invaded their home, trampling on a picture of the Sacred Heart of Jesus, wrecking the place and leaving them homeless. They were rehoused in Rathcoole, where they were pressured to give money to support loyalist causes and where Martin's youngest brother Kevin, then in his early teens, was tortured by thugs and had the letters UVF carved into his arm with a broken bottle. They were rehoused again, this time to Finaghy in south-west Belfast. Their new house was the former home of a police officer who had been driven out by the IRA. For many people there was no escape from the wretchedness that enveloped life during the Troubles, just different adaptations. Bobby Sands took one path. Martin took another.

By August of 1981, ten hunger strikers had died and the political temperature was out of control. The British government's actions and inaction had created the impetus for a manifest shift in Catholic political allegiances towards support for Sinn Féin – a shift that key players in the United Kingdom, Northern unionism and the Republic culpably failed to recognise.

On 7 September 1981, my cousin John Pickering joined the hunger strike – and his mother found her unique and courageous public voice. At a meeting of the strikers' relatives at the Lake Glen Hotel in Belfast, she stood up and announced that if her son fell into a coma, she would give permission to the prison authorities for his life to be saved by force-feeding. She went home to find her windows broken by protesters. When the hunger strike was formally ended, on 4 October, republican prisoners and Sinn Féin blamed her and Father Denis Faul, who had campaigned for an end to the strike, for breaking it.

John Pickering's girlfriend for several years was Bairbre de Brún, a teacher and later a prominent member of Sinn

Féin and advocate of the peace process. She would become Minister for Health in the first power-sharing government in Northern Ireland and later a Member of the European Parliament. At the time of the hunger strike, she was one of a number of people, including Father Faul, who helped Bridget get through the woes she now faced every day.

John refused to see Bridget for some time after the end of the hunger strike. I wrote to him, pointing out how much she loved him and that she had remained faithful to her vocation as a mother despite her opposition to the path he had chosen. He likely heard a lot of that from other sources. Eventually visits were resumed, and he even wrote a beautiful poem in her honour. Today it is reassuring to see him a middle-aged devoted family man, a staunch supporter of the Good Friday Agreement and a convert to politics as the best solution to political problems.

My old boss at Trinity, Robert Heuston, got wind of my decision to leave RTÉ, and within a short time, to his delight and mine, I was back teaching as Reid Professor once again. I was glad to return, not just to academic life but to a workplace with an embedded culture of mutual respect and graciousness among colleagues.

To my surprise, no sooner had I left RTÉ than it became clear that there were people in other areas of the broadcaster who were anxious to have me continue working there in some capacity. I was offered a range of full-time and part-time presenter roles. This was welcome financially, for Martin was a full-time student again, studying dentistry, and we were now parents to Emma, born in September 1982.

With Trinity's agreement I did occasional radio programmes and some part-time television work presenting a new monthly current affairs programme called *Europa*, which concentrated mainly on life and issues within the European Union and Europe more generally. I am glad that I did, for it immediately redeemed my unhappy experience of *Today Tonight*. My colleagues on *Europa* – including presenters Conor Brady and Michael Ryan, executive produce Noel Smyth, and my old mates Ingrid Miley and Monica Cowley – were to a man and woman wonderful fun to work with, and public-service oriented to the core. There wasn't the makings of a political agenda in any of us, and life there was simply normal. Between Noel and Monica we had a plentiful supply of rapid-fire Dublin humour. It was the glue that kept us going on fast-moving weekend shoots once a month that had to produce all the ingredients for a one-hour broadcast with a skeleton crew, and I always had to be back at work in Trinity on the Monday no matter what. Lisbon, Hamburg, Madrid, Copenhagen, Paris, Bern and many other great cities (and more obscure places) were shown through the eyes of Irish people who had made their lives there.

In 1984, after I appeared as a member of the Catholic Church's delegation to the New Ireland Forum, RTÉ's strange politics reared its head again when the National Union of Journalists broadcasting branch held a meeting at which my membership of the branch was suspended for 'double-jobbing'. Reference was made to a press interview in which I had said I enjoyed working on *Europa* so much it felt like a hobby. Of course it wasn't a hobby, nor was I saying it was. I was merely complimenting the crew I worked with for the happy working atmosphere, fascinating locations and great material.

The suspension was laughable, since one of my eminent (and unfailingly kind) colleagues on *Frontline* and *Today Tonight*,

Professor Brian Farrell, was then also a full-time member of staff at UCD. He was still double-jobbing – and he was not the only one – when the union voted to suspend me and me alone. The other double-jobbers were not Northern, female and Catholic, as Gay Byrne, God bless him, pointed out in a hilarious supportive letter he sent me after the suspension. 'Don't let the buggers get you down,' he wrote. So I tried not to, and despite the suspension I continued to happily double-job, doing occasional work for RTÉ without any threatened industrial action or even hint of it from the union. I imagine fear of litigation may have stayed its limp hand. A union official, later asked by a journalist about the fact that I alone had been suspended, acknowledged that 'there were anomalies'. I replied that the plural was incorrect. I was and indeed remain to this day the sole anomaly.

After the arrival of twins in April 1985, and a failed attempt at politics as a Fianna Fáil general election candidate in 1987, I reverted to one woman, one job – at Trinity College – grateful that Martin was by then a qualified dentist and the financial pressures were off.

Many years later, as President of Ireland, I presented awards at an event for journalists. The MC, John Bowman – one of RTÉ's journalistic greats – observed in introducing me that I was the first member of the NUJ broadcasting branch to be elected President. I corrected him. I was in fact the first *suspended* member of the NUJ broadcasting branch to be elected President. The audience had the good manners to laugh heartily. I was later approached privately by a union stalwart who was not of the old 1980s brigade. He wanted to know how I might respond to having my suspension lifted. He was very genuine, but I was not interested in revisiting that sleeping mongrel, for as I told him, despite some of the then union members' hopes to the contrary, it had not held my career back in the least. Since leaving office I have made a number of programmes with and for RTÉ, and my union suspension has never been mentioned, at least not to me or by me.

Those ghastly personal times passed, and despite them I have never lost my deep affection for our national broadcaster and its community of great people and great programmes – which is why, on its seventy-fifth birthday, I hosted a party at Áras an Uachtaráin. Joe Mulholland has meanwhile accepted mistakes were made in *Today Tonight*'s Northern coverage during my time there and in his dealings with me. We have struck up a sort of circumspect rapport. For me, the episode is long over. But the ill-treatment of the mild-mannered, temperate Forbes McFall still comes between me and my sleep.

# 7

Finding myself with a two-year-old and baby twins, I learned to meditate. It helped, too, that Martin's father, Charlie, had come to live with us in County Meath after Emma was born, and he remained with us until he died eighteen years later. He helped get us through those early child-rearing years, pushing buggies the size of small cars up and down the roads around Dunshaughlin and Ratoath, where we lived amongst the most delightful, considerate neighbours. I joined the church choir in Dunshaughlin, and we had a prayer group that met weekly in our house. Martin joined a dental practice in Bessbrook, County Armagh. Then – at the goading of Cardinal Tomás Ó Fiaich, a good friend whose intervention in Martin's career plans I did not appreciate – he set up a second practice in Crossmaglen.

I would have preferred a practice south of the border, for the North was still not an alluring place. But fate intervened when, to my surprise, I was headhunted for the job of director of the Institute of Professional Legal Studies at Queen's University, Belfast. My old professor from my Queen's student days, Des Greer, came to see me in the early summer of 1987 to ask me to apply, as an earlier trawl had not produced a successful candidate. Des had been a great help to me in the period after we lost our home and I was finding it hard to get through the college workload, with so much going on in other parts of my life. He was in fact the only member of staff I had confided in, for pastoral care was not a strong feature at Queen's in those days, despite the daily violence that skewed normal life and must have taken quite a toll on many students and staff.

I took the post and, working with a strong team, we made a good job of it. The Institute had been in need of reform, some of it contentious, but over the next ten years it became a recognised leader in the field of barrister and solicitor training in the United Kingdom and further afield. My dear old friends and colleagues Sir Anthony Campbell, Turlough O'Donnell and Sir Basil Kelly – by then all senior members of the judiciary – helped steer the changes through the Council of Legal Education, representing the professional bodies for solicitors and barristers to which the Institute was accountable. They were brilliant to work with, always affirming and encouraging, and appreciative of the Institute's growing reputation. Despite the surname Kelly, Basil was a firm Protestant unionist who had once been the North's attorney general. He had a wry sense of humour, and when I suggested that two of the Institute's rooms would be named after him and Turlough O'Donnell, he insisted that not only would his room bear his full name (in case anyone thought it might be named for the Australian outlaw Ned Kelly), but he had to have the room directly upstairs from Turlough's. Turlough agreed to the arrangement, provided Basil was told that it was the first time in their career as competitors at the Bar that Basil ever got one over on him.

By the time I returned to Queen's in 1987, I had years behind me of engagement in anti-sectarian, ecumenical and cross-community work. I had also been a member of the Catholic Church's delegation to the New Ireland Forum in 1984, an initiative of the Irish government designed to create a widely inclusive civic debate on the possible constitutional shape of a future 'new Ireland'. That background interest in peace, reconciliation and inter-denominational engagement, which continued after I returned to live in Northern Ireland, probably explains why in 1991, when leading churches on the island decided that it was time to tackle the scourge of sectarianism head-on, I was asked to co-chair a representative working party. I spent two years in that very difficult investigation, followed by even more years of trundling around Protestant and Catholic parish halls discussing the working party's report, which made uncomfortable reading for all concerned.

There was a protracted background to the setting-up of the working party, which said a lot about the superficial nature of much high-level cross-community engagement. One of the saddest aspects of life on the island of Ireland was the dominance of its people's faith lives by a medley of Christian churches, which had, despite the heroic efforts of a few individuals, abjectly failed over generations to truly love or, frankly, even vaguely like one another. By the time the Troubles erupted, the sectarian horses had bolted, and from then on the churches were on the back foot – and still not exactly galloping to catch up. Without any effective working structure of collaboration between Protestant and Catholic churches, the genteel, distant reserve that characterised their relations was no match for the brash sectarianism of Ian Paisley. Anti-ecumenism, anti-Catholic, anti-civil rights and with strong links to unlawful organisations prepared to do violence at his bidding, Paisley stoked the flames of sectarian hatred, and there was little to quell them as he went from figure of fun to rampaging sectarian monster. The feeble nature of the contacts between Catholic and Protestant churches and churchgoers at almost every level offered him a landscape ripe to be exploited and fed with fear of 'the other'. His supporters saw him as an Old Testament prophet come to avenge the betrayal of Protestantism by those who offered civil liberties to Catholics.

There were other much more likely prophets, such as the inspirational Reverend Ray Davey, who had founded the pro-reconciliation Corrymeela Community as early as 1965. But it was not until 1973 – after six years of sectarian savagery – that, at the invitation of the Catholic Church, inter-church talks between mainstream Protestant churches and the Catholic Church began. There was real opposition in Church circles to seeing the Troubles as anything other than political. Many resisted the idea that there was a strong thread of sectarianism also to be dealt with. There was also a lot of historic distrust, scorn and even enmity between the churches. Doctrines and dogma got in the way. Meanwhile, in the same year that the mainstream churches embarked however tentatively upon mutual dialogue, Paisley was proposing use of the 'mailed fist'.

In 1976, an inter-church report on violence in Ireland noted that 'Ireland needs a programme to combat sectarianism wherever it is found', but there was no one to accept responsibility for creating and delivering such a programme, or indeed for having allowed sectarianism to flourish in the first place. It was a case of the churches doing what they were best at, talking out to the world from the high moral ground, while refusing to critique themselves internally.

The inter-church talks took place every two years – hardly evidence of urgency – but in between meetings there were ongoing standing committees and commissioned reports, and the beginnings of friendships that gradually led to shared views on how church leadership needed to be exercised. I attended a number of sessions from the late 1970s onwards as a Catholic Church lay delegate, and if frustration at the glacial pace (not to mention the dull, safe agendas) could have been bottled, it would have kept a long conveyor belt going around the clock. The one-day set-piece format of the biennial meetings defeated the ends of sociability.

In fairness to the churches, ecumenism was no picnic, and its technicalities were too often seen as the work of theologians and Church historians. Practical things ecumenical and inter-denominational had absorbed me since the Second Vatican Council, so anywhere there was an opportunity for such fellowship, I was generally to be found – whether at Ray Davey's Corrymeela, the Reverend Cecil Kerr's Christian Renewal Centre in Rostrevor, David Porter's Evangelical Contribution on Northern Ireland (ECONI), or the Reverend Ruth Patterson's Restoration Ministries. These were brave and daring Protestant ecumenical outreaches in their time, and all of them met regular and vicious push-back from anti-ecumenical elements within the Protestant community. I was also involved with cross-community initiatives, like Father Myles Kavanagh's Flax Trust in Ardoyne.

Protestant fundamentalists regularly hurled abuse at ecumenists, but I also saw how even the most unreconstructed redneck Christians could be won over by the forbearance of those bent on reconciliation. One complete pain-in-the-neck serial protester was David Hewitt, a former Irish rugby international, who heaped grief on the kindly Reverend Cecil Kerr more than once. David's brother Alan, a solicitor whom I knew well, was the polar opposite – a complete gentleman – and this made David's hostility to ecumenical outreach all the more disheartening.

Then came one famous night in the YMCA in Belfast. Some of us noticed David in the audience as Cecil Kerr was

speaking at an ecumenical debate, and we positioned ourselves to protect Cecil as best we could. The anticipated
heckling never happened, but at the end of the meeting
David made a beeline for Cecil. A bunch of us got there first,
ready to fend off another verbal attack. Instead, to our amaze-
ment, David was in tears. He put his arms around Cecil
and sobbed, then he embraced me and asked for forgiveness for all the times he had behaved uncharitably towards
us. Cecil, whose imperturbable saintliness always reminded
me of Father Justin, was gracious, forgiving and welcoming. I caught sight of a beaming, happy Alan: a brother's
prayers answered, no doubt. On the bumpy journey towards
reconciliation, David became a dear friend and a welcome,
energising sign that we were all capable of unlearning the
things we had learned from childhood.

At the 1987 inter-church meeting, the Protestant Archbishop of Armagh, Robin Eames, and the Catholic Archbishop
of Armagh, Tomás Ó Fiaich, suggested in a joint statement
that it was time to examine more closely 'the lethal toxin of
sectarianism which at times seems almost to have overwhelmed us'. At long last the subject of sectarianism was put
on the inter-church agenda, and the working party was set up
in 1991. God alone knows what subtle forms of resistance its
proponents had to shift out of the way before John Lampen,
a Quaker community worker, and I were invited to co-chair
it. The terms of reference asked us to look at the role of the
churches regarding sectarianism and to recommend ways in
which they could 'promote reconciliation and positive respect
for difference'.

The working party was made up of committed and high-
profile Church members of all denominations, most but not
all from the North. Apart from John Lampen and me, the

other members were Carrie Barkley (Presbyterian and past President of the Irish Council of Churches), Reverend Sam Burch (Methodist), Joe Campbell (Scripture Union), Sister Marie Duddy RSM (Catholic college lecturer), Reverend Denis Faul (Catholic school headmaster), Reverend Michael Hurley (Jesuit priest), Dr Joseph Liechty (Mennonite), Reverend Gary Mason (Methodist), Dr Kenneth Milne (retired principal, Church of Ireland College of Education, Dublin), Martin O'Brien (Catholic, Committee on the Administration of Justice), Seamus O'Hara (Catholic, retired solicitor), Muriel Pritchard (President of the Charitable Trust for Integrated Education), Paul Rogers (Catholic, head of religion at St Malachy's High School, Antrim), Reverend David Temple (Superintendent, Irish Mission, Presbyterian Church in Ireland), and Dr David Stevens (General Secretary of the Irish Council of Churches and also Secretary to the working party). The detailed and ground-breaking report (to which journalists in the South paid lamentably little attention despite the spirited public debate it generated) probed deeply into the disease of sectarianism. It tackled causes, consequences and culpability, and set an agenda for change. Over two years of often fractious meetings, the members got to know each other well, though not without being sorely tested at times. As I wrote in the introduction:

> Being part of the group was not easy. Discussions were frank. Sometimes we were cut to the quick. We heard things, said things and learned things which offended: but we had come as believers in Christ and recognized that if we could not learn to listen in love and to trust each other then we might as well pack up and go home. The Holy Spirit we hope stayed with us and we stuck with one another.

I made the most faithful friends in that group, people who later became instrumental in the Building Bridges project during my presidency. An exception was Father Denis Faul. I already knew him from previous encounters, and he had a high public profile as an arch-critic both of the IRA and of the British government. I had been looking forward to working with him at close quarters, but with every meeting I grew more and more disappointed in him. He was cantankerous and caustic; at times sexist and offensively sectarian. He never let a meeting go without emphasising that his objection to a united Ireland derived from wishing to maintain the integrity of a Southern Irish Catholic state untainted by liberal British Protestant secularism. He went out of his way to irk any liberal Protestants around the table, reserving a touch of misogynistic ire always for the blunt but never rude Carrie Barkley and especially for me.

I was inclined to forgive him a lot, remembering how kind he had always been to my Aunt Bridget, but dear God, he tried our collective patience and my chairing skills. He frightened the bejasus out of John Lampen, who generally left him to me – which was not always ideal, since I was the proverbial red rag where Denis was concerned. Any sign that I was facilitating discussion of a Protestant/unionist perspective on more or less anything brought him out in a dose of the furies. I decided to have it out with him over a cup of tea away from the working party meetings, and discovered that since I had worked on *Today Tonight*, he assumed that I (as one of only two Northern Irish journalists on the programme) was in some way responsible for its appalling Northern coverage, and for never seeking his opinion as a commentator. At least I was able to disarm that argument, but it made little difference, for he remained prickly and confrontational to the finish.

In a strange way, however, his contrarian provocation ensured that everything that needed to be said eventually tumbled out onto the table. This was no restrained forum where important things went unsaid in that cultural logic of 'whatever you say, say nothing'. Quite the reverse. Tempers and tears were not uncommon. But in the introduction to the report I explained that, by pushing through and refusing to walk away, 'We came to respect the sheer spiritual energy required of us individually and collectively to really live the Gospel in our dealings with each other.' Most members of the group became close and trusted friends. The two years we spent together were better than any master's course in conflict resolution. The working party taught me the phenomenal value of sustained encounter with 'the other' in a managed environment where good leadership and good humour were needed to neutralise negativity and keep nudging towards consensus. I also became more confident in handling the barbed and the bristly.

John Lampen and I presented the report first to the senior religious leaders and Church delegates at the inter-church talks at Dromantine outside Newry, and later to countless Church groups as we took it 'on the road' to provoke discussion and hopefully action. The backlash from day one in Dromantine made it clear to us how unprepared people were for the compromises that eradicating sectarianism would demand. Yes, everyone wanted peace, and everyone thought sectarianism was an awful thing altogether, but they drew the line at this, our first recommendation directed at the churches:

> It is vital that we find ways out of the fear, rivalry, sense of superiority and enmity which have historically characterized relations between the Churches and most Christians in

Ireland . . . the credibility of the Gospel is at stake. What has happened in Northern Ireland society calls us to a profound change of heart (*metanoia*). It calls us to face reality and abandon our myths, to accept our part of the responsibility for what has happened and find new ways of living together.

The standing committee of the Church of Ireland took particular umbrage at the report's analysis of policing as 'members of one community largely policing the other'. It was an analysis the accuracy of which would be borne out several years later by the Patten Commission on policing, which led to the replacement of the Royal Ulster Constabulary by the Police Service of Northern Ireland. Umbrage also was taken at the report's concentration on Northern Ireland and the slight attention paid to sectarianism in the Republic, which was described as 'too comfortable'. That was a fair comment, but sectarianism in the South was another day's work: from the outset, the main focus and preoccupation of the report had been on – and had to be on – Northern Ireland, where so many were dying.

The report was described years later by historian Marianne Elliott as the most notable thing to have come out of the inter-church talks. It was, but of itself it changed little. *Metanoia* needed owners, activists who would make it happen. In church hall after church hall, John and I met good people who were prepared to try to walk in the shoes of the other. We also met good people who resolutely would not, for they saw themselves as the sole victims here and theirs was the only true version of the past.

In 1994, after the first IRA ceasefire was called, Ardoyne's Father Myles Kavanagh CP, intuiting correctly how vexed the issue of policing was in Catholic communities, brought together a group to organise a conference on policing. The concept was that individuals, organisations, politicians, senior members of the Royal Ulster Constabulary, the chair of the Police Authority, and the chair of the Independent Police Complaints Commission would gather in one room. All would have the chance to have their say and to listen. It had every prospect of being a nightmarish screaming match. Myles asked me to chair it.

Two things worked well, besides the power of Passionist prayer. The first was that, in a gesture of remarkable goodwill, all the catering was done by local Protestant women from the Shankill Road, old neighbours of mine and of the Passionist monastery. Those women were not likely to be happy with some of the things said, but they knew how important honest dialogue was while the shooting and bombing had stopped and in order to keep it stopped. The second thing was my insistence on a respectful non-interruption protocol, so that every speaker would get space to speak, and would be listened to respectfully no matter what came from their mouths.

The proceedings were conducted with remarkable calm and courtesy, even though at times some of the stories were so awful (and so personally familiar) that it was difficult to hold back the tears or the anger. The conference was hailed as a huge success. David Cook, chair of the Police Authority, remarked in public that he was moved, shocked and dismayed by the experiences of decent local people as they described their dysfunctional everyday interactions with members of the RUC.

In the aftermath of the conference, six working groups were formed to draw up an analysis of the problems and a charter for the future of community policing. I was one of three facilitators, along with TCD graduate and Ardoyne native Paul Shevlin and Professor Mike Brogden, director of the Institute of Criminology and Criminal Justice at Queen's University. The published report called for an independent commission on policing and the introduction of a new community police force capable of holding the trust of both communities. Many of the report's insights and recommendations eventually came to pass, first with the establishment in 1998 of the Patten Commission and secondly with the implementation of the commission's recommendations, leading to the establishment of a community police force known as the Police Service of Northern Ireland.

Frustrated by the limitations of the one-day format for the inter-church talks, I managed to persuade the organisers to move to a two-day residential conference to encourage greater social interchange between the delegations. The first such residential event was held in November 1995 at Emmaus, a retreat house outside Dublin. I spent the free evening with fellow delegates of all denominations watching in disbelief as Cardinal Cahal Daly, in an ill-advised appearance on the *Late Late Show*, waxed breezily defensive over the Catholic Church's child sex abuse scandal. His infamous clash live on air with Passionist priest Father Brian D'Arcy was a vivid illustration of Catholics' diminishing trust in the Church hierarchy. Our Protestant colleagues discreetly withdrew in embarrassment for us, leaving me to have a fairly animated discussion with several Catholic bishops, among them Bishop Seamus Hegarty. The first set of Catholic Church guidelines on child protection were due to be published shortly and it was evident from Cardinal Daly's words on the *Late Late Show* that the Church still planned to deal in-house with abuse allegations against priests, rather than reporting the allegations to the police. I told Bishop Hegarty that the bishops were heading for serious trouble if that was the case.

At Bishop Hegarty's request, I met with one of the legal advisers to the committee that had drafted the new child-protection guidelines. He was an old and highly regarded friend of mine, Belfast solicitor Ted Jones, an expert in criminal law. We chewed the issues over but ultimately disagreed on whether the guidelines, which were to cover the island of Ireland, should include mandatory reporting by Church authorities to the civil authorities of allegations of abuse made to the former. Mandatory reporting was not then a requirement of the law of Ireland, though it was in Northern Ireland. It was at that time a controversial subject within the social work and legal professions. Even so, I remained concerned that trust in Church management authorities was ebbing away as a result of the abuse scandals and that, regardless of what the civil law provided, the Church needed to deal with allegations at arm's length by handing them over to the appropriate civil authorities. Ted was obviously worried enough and persuaded enough to report my views back to Bishop Hegarty, and so at the Bishop's invitation I went to see him in Derry with my old friend Dominic Burke, a childcare expert whose views coincided with mine. We hoped we could persuade Bishop Hegarty to advocate, with Bishop Forristal, who was overseeing the committee's work, amending the guidelines to require mandatory reporting of allegations to the civil authorities. Intervene he did, and to good effect, for in the end the published guidelines included mandatory reporting. It was ironic that the inter-church conference that weekend probably did more good for intra-Catholic talks than for ecumenism.

\*

The success of the Institute of Professional Legal Studies was probably the reason why, in 1995, I was appointed the first female pro vice chancellor of Queen's. In this role I led the first neighbourhood outreach initiative from Queen's to its hinterland, which took in the wealthy middle-class suburb of Malone and the loyalist working-class stronghold of Sandy Row. In discussions after Orange band practice in the Sandy Row community centre, I learned how few children there ever went to grammar school, how remote their lives were from the university, how they circumnavigated the perimeter of the campus rather than walking across it for fear they would be spotted as people who did not belong there.

We started an initiative to end that estrangement and to provide support to the schools that would give local children the realistic hope of aspiring to college education. Some of the children from the local school would be present at my inauguration as President, and I was moved to see them there, for invitations were easy to issue but, for children from the heartland of loyalism, not always easy to accept. The vice chancellor, Sir Gordon Beveridge, asked me to help set up university outreach centres in Armagh and Omagh. It was a complicated enough task, but in the negotiations I got to know the members and staff of the local councils and the local politicians, among them a number of senior unionists. Some of these relationships would last well beyond that outreach project.

Father Alec Reid, a Redemptorist priest based in Clonard Monastery in west Belfast, was, in his unobtrusive way, a seminal figure in the peace process. He worked in the shadows where no one else would go, talking and listening to paramilitaries, hearing how tired of war they were becoming, and intuiting that they could be persuaded to try an alternative to violence if such could be convincingly constructed, and if champions could be found to bring the republican movement on board.

The man with the most comprehensive and compelling vision for a peaceful, reconciled Ireland was John Hume. The man at the head of the republican movement was Gerry Adams. It was Alec who conceived of the idea to create a dialogue between the two men, out of which would come the ideas and language that eventually persuaded the IRA to end the war, disband, and entrust the future exclusively to politics. In 1988 he brought the pair together, commencing the secret talks that eventually came to be known as the Hume–Adams initiative.

Clonard Monastery was situated between the Shankill and Falls Roads, a Protestant/loyalist stronghold and a Catholic/republican stronghold cheek by jowl. During the Belfast Blitz, the monastery had sheltered people from all sides, laying the foundations of a cross-community trust that Alec and his colleague Father Gerry Reynolds would develop into the Redemptorists' Peace Ministry.

Alec grew up in Nenagh, County Tipperary, and was a handy hurler in his youth. He arrived as a young priest in early 1960s Belfast just as the Catholic Church embraced the greater ecumenical openness promoted by the Second Vatican Council. He threw himself into it from the outset, and in the years that followed he developed friendships and collaborations with a wide circle of men and women from other denominations.

The onset of the Troubles placed Clonard Monastery right on the front line of sectarian violence, and Alec was in the thick of it, day in and day out, on the street trying to talk down rioters, in homes comforting the bereaved, in prisons working unsuccessfully but relentlessly to end prisoner protests and the hunger strikes. In March 1988, he administered the last rites to two soldiers murdered on the Falls Road by the IRA during a republican funeral; photographs of him kneeling over the body of one of the soldiers were seen all over the world. In his pocket that day, I later learned, was one of the first draft documents to emerge from the Hume–Adams initiative, which had only just begun. The document was covered in blood.

The dialogue continued for several years, and with Alec using all his connections to engage the British and Irish governments, the work of the three men paid off. Over the course of 1993, Hume and Adams issued a series of joint public statements setting out their view as to how the conflict could be resolved. On 15 December 1993, the British and Irish governments, led by John Major and Albert Reynolds respectively, issued the Downing Street Declaration, which incorporated many of the Hume–Adams ideas for bringing about peace. Crucially, the British government declared it had no 'selfish strategic or economic' interest in Northern Ireland and that if a majority of Northern Ireland's voters were ever in favour of a united Ireland then it would be facilitated. Furthermore, in any official talks towards a peaceful constitutional settlement, parties associated with paramilitarism could participate if they forswore violence. These were essential tools with which to persuade the IRA towards peace. Within the year, not only had the IRA declared a ceasefire, but so too had some of the loyalist paramilitaries.

The Hume–Adams roadmap to peace provoked outrage from various quarters. Unionists were exercised by the legitimation of the ambition for a united Ireland, and many nationalists were exercised by the legitimation of political parties immersed in paramilitarism. But the progress towards a consensual settlement continued, and with help from President Clinton's special envoy George Mitchell, the structure of talks and the principles that would guide them began to crystallise. The process was always fragile, and susceptible to the ups and downs of realpolitik. It collapsed in February 1996 when the IRA – which claimed to be frustrated by the British government's demand for full disarmament as a precondition for peace negotiations – broke its ceasefire and bombed Canary Wharf in London's dockland district, killing two people and wounding many more.

Father Alec had been working on the Hume–Adams initiative on his own. With his health in as parlous a state as the peace process, he needed help, and after discussions with his superior in the Redemptorist order, Father Brendan Callanan, they decided to approach Jim Fitzpatrick, the eminent chairman of the *Irish News*, and myself. Our task was to help the Hume–Adams process find favour among as many influential people as possible on the nationalist/republican side, in the hope that the IRA could be persuaded to resume its ceasefire, and create the conditions in which Sinn Féin could be admitted to peace talks.

In the aftermath of Canary Wharf, trust was in short supply and cynicism abounded. But, after a hiatus, the Hume–Adams talks resumed, and Father Alec believed that Jim and I had the wherewithal to bring others on board in support of the process. We began to meet regularly with Father Alec, John Hume and Gerry Adams, and to listen while they analysed how best to pull the republican/nationalist side together at a time when it was in danger of shattering into even smaller pieces.

Jim and I had two initial target audiences: the leadership within the nationalist and republican constituencies, and certain key members of the media. So much depended on the breadth of vision of the personalities, and their generosity of spirit. Some in the media and the SDLP were deeply sceptical of Sinn Féin's genuineness, and indeed exhibited hostility to Jim and me as well as expressing scathing umbrage at John Hume's involvement with Gerry Adams. Within certain republican quarters, distrust of the British and disdain for the moderation of the SDLP was so deep-rooted that Adams was seen as naïve and a betrayer of their tradition. Not all of what Jim and I heard was expressed in public, but Hume and Adams were well aware of it and of the dangers it placed them in personally and politically. Some of it probably surprised them, as it did Jim and me, especially in its vehemence. The Irish Independent group of newspapers in particular conducted relentless attacks on Hume, often authored by columnists with no appreciable experience of Northern Ireland but with strong views on it. They put him under immense stress.

Jim and I began to get some raw insight into what John Hume was up against. There was no greater champion of democratic politics and no more formidable opponent of paramilitarism. But as the Troubles became almost a way of life for two generations, and with no end in sight, he knew the only path to permanent peace lay in the full inclusion of all sectors of the community, including those completely estranged from democratic politics and seduced by the power of conflict. He knew they needed to be persuaded that there was a better way. He also knew that the IRA would be more likely to listen to Gerry Adams than to him. If Adams could be persuaded, then he in turn might persuade the republican movement. That was the vision Hume committed himself to in his dialogue with Adams: complete conversion to democratic politics and an end to paramilitarism. He believed that if republican violence ended, it would open up space for the political discussions that could bring about an agreed political settlement.

Hume was the only nationalist politician in Northern Ireland with the skill, personality, insight and stature required to bring a critical mass of nationalists and republicans behind his plan for the delivery of a lasting peace. He was the first to see that future healthy relationships within Northern Ireland would need firm structures based on shared governance and parity of esteem and backed by an international treaty. He was the first to see that North–South relationships needed to be recalibrated and underpinned by new life-enhancing structures. He was the first to see that the relationship between Ireland and Great Britain was also out of kilter, and required new institutions to move beyond the morbidity of the past. And he was the first to articulate the great opportunity for reconciliation offered by common citizenship of the European Union to people divided by identity and political ambitions. Not everyone understood his genius. Not everyone was capable of understanding it.

John's unyielding courage in the face of pressures, accusations, and complaints from all quarters, including reasonably close quarters, sent him soaring in my estimation. He was not just a prophet for our time, but *the* prophet. It was hard at times not to be disappointed in some of those who, in private, excoriated him. After our first set of outings, Jim and I were despondent. But then we had the great good fortune to meet people of far-sighted vision who transcended party politics and kept a focus on the prize of peace. Among them were Dr Joe Hendron and the late Eddie McGrady of the SLDP: civil, decent, big-picture men for whom peace trumped party and tribe.

I was already well acquainted with the party's deputy leader, Seamus Mallon, having spent a lot of time in his company on a trip to the United States in 1995. He could be prickly and hilarious in the same sentence, and he had the mischievous facility to raise a row where none was needed. Martin and I discovered that particular trait as we tripped around Virginia with Seamus and a number of unionist politicians in advance of President Clinton's seminal White House Conference on Trade and Investment in Northern Ireland, which had been brought about almost entirely by Hume's efforts. Visiting an impressive frontier culture museum in Staunton, Virginia, Seamus observed out loud – as the rest of the group had done more quietly – the complete absence of African Americans among the actors on the working period farms, or indeed of any mention of them. He just could not let it go, and kept needling at one of our hosts, whose redneck politics hung openly around him but who was otherwise a man of genuine hospitality that inhibited the rest of us from getting overly confrontational. At dinner with the same gentleman, Seamus's provocation followed the trajectory of his intake of whiskey, and he cross-examined our by now unashamed white supremacist host until the latter felt compelled to lift his trouser leg to reveal an ankle-strapped handgun. Terrified, we grabbed the heroic, delighted Seamus and retreated.

I have long admired Seamus's courageous political leadership, and though relations between him and John were not always straightforward, Seamus's objections were never about living in the shadow of Hume, the celebrated and successful international statesman, but simply and genuinely about

differing strategic perspectives. He was a thoughtful character, living rather isolatedly in the unionist enclave of Markethill
in County Armagh under persistent sectarian threats to himself and his family.

It was galling, at the White House Conference, to see John
Hume arrive alone, unannounced, ambling into the hotel
reception just off the plane from Ireland, exhausted and hungry, and with no reception committee for the man whose
efforts had largely brought the Conference about. Meanwhile,
at the same venue, two massive posses of officials, cameras
and guests had formed around Sir Patrick Mayhew, the then
Secretary of State for Northern Ireland, and Sinn Féin's Gerry
Adams. Martin and I took a very weary John in hand, sorted
out his room and a meal, and notified his colleagues and the
organisers of his arrival and of our view that he deserved better. There were no complaints from John himself.

The soft social mechanics of the conference worked wonders for relationships between unionists and nationalists. So
too did the few days of holiday pre-conference that delegates
from the North's different political parties spent in each
other's company, well away from the usual fray and forming
a united front to keep Seamus Mallon from getting us all assas-
sinated. There is nothing like a common danger to create a
common purpose. The value of the house of the President, of
non-threatening encounters around themes of common
interest, and of hospitality generously shared – all of these
made an impression, and would eventually inform the 'Building Bridges' project when I became President of Ireland.

To maintain the relationships and the momentum created by
the White House Conference, President Clinton visited
Northern Ireland in November 1995. His persistent interest

in Northern Ireland had helped nudge a sluggish peace process to life, and his even-handed outreach to all sides was a masterclass in the art of diplomacy. Part of Clinton's success lay in broadening the issues. He took the focus off the narrow constitutional question, where there was little prospect of consensus and every certainty of communication breakdown, and looked instead at the things everyone was concerned about, like jobs, investment and trade. I learned a lot from his ability to park the highly contested issues while building communication and consensus around issues likely to promote cross-tribal agreement.

The final event on his schedule was at Queen's, where I was the person designated to greet him before introducing him to the assembled guests. He started off by saying, 'Jim King told me you have a story about him and a hammer that I have to hear.' So while the guests and press watched and wondered, I told him the story.

Jim was a very close friend of mine, with roots a few miles from my father's home in County Roscommon. A former Vice President of Harvard, he had worked for Presidents Kennedy and Carter, and had been appointed by Clinton in 1993 as director of the US Office of Personnel Management. It was an unwieldy institution that needed a radical overhaul and modernisation. Jim was an organisational genius and a man who did not like sitting behind a desk. He also had a legendary sense of humour. He famously commandeered a wheelbarrow, placed the outdated 10,000-page personnel manual into it and wheeled it to the trash can.

He often visited us when he was in Ireland, and had arrived the previous summer to our cottage in Roscommon where Martin and my cousin Eugene McGreevy were rebuilding an old dry-stone wall, chipping and battering the stones into place – with better results on Eugene's end of the wall than Martin's, which had a distinct curvature. Jim expressed disgust at the state of the tools they were using to dress the stone and their skill levels in general, and, being related to the proprietors of King's hardware store in nearby Boyle, he headed off to get proper implements. He arrived back with an alarming-looking hammer, which he placed in Eugene's hand with instructions as to how it was to be used. Eugene brought it down on a stone with full force, whereupon the heavy metal head flew off and, if not for a mighty leap in the opposite direction, would have taken Eugene's head with it. When it was established that the only thing injured was Jim's pride, we all let him have it with full-throttle scoffing, for he had once been chair of the National Transportation Safety Board under President Carter. Clinton loved the story, but unknown to us, the BBC, which was televising the event, had no audio, and so there was much speculation in the production box about the subject of our lively conversation. I got more than a few queries about it, but maintained a discreet silence.

Nine years later, in 2004, my son Justin was interning with Jim at the Democratic convention in Boston, which selected John Kerry as the candidate to challenge George W. Bush. We were fast asleep when the phone rang, our very excited son having forgotten it was 4 a.m. in Roscommon. 'I have just met a future President of the United States,' he enthused. I asked what he thought of John Kerry, assuming that was who he meant. 'No, no, no. The future President is called Barack Obama.' The name was unfamiliar and sounded unlikely, so I jumped to the wrong conclusion: 'Would you tell Jim King to stop feeding you alcohol and get to bed.' Instead, he spent the hours before dawn listening quietly while Jim and a multitude of other senior Democrats discussed the prospects for electing America's first president of colour. When Obama got the nomination four years later, Justin took leave of absence from his job and went to campaign for him. Jim King died in 2019 while working on a stone wall at his home in Rockport, Massachusetts.

Exactly a year after President Clinton's White House Conference, his special envoy, George Mitchell, was sufficiently trusted and embedded in the Northern Ireland political scene to secure agreement to a list of six principles to which all parties would subscribe if they wished to participate in the peace talks. The Mitchell Principles cleared the way for the inclusion in the talks of those whose association with paramilitarism had denied them access to the negotiating table in previous peace efforts. At least that was the theory, and it won out in the end.

The loyalist paramilitaries and their associates, including Ian Paisley's DUP, did not sign up to the Mitchell Principles or participate in the peace talks. However, in the summer of 1997, the Orange Order cancelled a number of parades that would otherwise have become potential flashpoints for interface violence. The IRA restored their ceasefire on 20 July. The Hume–Adams plan had delivered once again and the peace process was back on track. David Trimble, my former law lecturer at Queen's and now head of the Ulster Unionist Party, took the historic decision to enter talks that included Sinn Féin.

The tide had begun to turn.

# 8

In the summer of 1997, I was working as pro vice chancellor of Queen's in Belfast and living in Rostrevor. Our children had finished their primary education at the local village primary schools and were all now at the St Louis Convent in Kilkeel, a beautiful twenty-minute drive along the northern shore of Carlingford Lough. The twins, aged twelve, were in first year, and Emma, aged fourteen, was in third year.

They loved that school; it was just the getting out of bed part that caused minor morning ructions. I had at least an hour's drive to work, and Martin was dividing his time between dental practices in Bessbrook and Crossmaglen. It does not take much imagination to picture the weekday-morning scene. Justin, ever the organiser and the mediator of fair play, policed the use of our two bathrooms to ensure everyone departed on time, clean, clothed, and in the right car or bus going in the right direction. It would have been total mayhem but for Martin's father, who kept things calm in the kitchen as cornflakes and porridge packets were drop-kicked from cupboard to cooker or table. I made a point of seeing the children off, mainly to ensure that the girls' school skirts exited the house at the regulation knee length and maintained that length at least as far as the bus stop. When they got off the bus at the school, I knew my old pal of Ardoyne days, now a teacher of Irish there, Kathleen (Boyle) Collins, might be on skirt patrol, and so there was a passing chance the girls would enter the school in the same sartorial state they had left the house and not disgrace us entirely.

The most urgent thing on my mind that summer of 1997 was that I needed to write a book based on a series of lectures I had given on reconciliation at the World Christian Meditation Seminar held that year in Dublin. My immediate predecessor to give the seminar was the Dalai Lama, and his book of lectures on the Beatitudes was outstanding. Now it was my turn, and I felt pressure to do justice to my belief that the commandment to love one another had a transcendent capacity to heal even the worst of toxic divisions between people, and that it was capable of transforming the unhealthy relationships within Northern Ireland, between North and South, and between Ireland and Great Britain. Each claimed a Christian heritage, which, though often abused in order to foster division, could yet be harnessed to foster, at the very least, a culture of basic good neighbourliness. If I had learned anything from my life and work in Ireland, North and South, it was that there existed a huge reservoir of decency, an appetite for peace and a growing willingness to compromise, all of which were ready to be shaped into a force for structured and sustainable reconciliation.

Justin, being the most computer-literate person in the family, decamped with me to Dublin for two weeks in early August, during which time the rough text made it onto the word processor – despite several dramas caused by me hitting the wrong button and deleting when I should have been saving. Father Laurence Freeman, a Benedictine monk and director of the World Community for Christian Meditation, came from his London home and stayed with us in Rostrevor towards the end of August, during which time I finished the book with him hovering at my shoulder to make sure it got over the line. We were just about to celebrate the last full stop when the news came that Princess Diana had tragically died. It hit Laurence hard, for he knew and greatly admired her.

It had been on my mind to talk to Laurence about something completely different, but I had postponed the conversation until the book was done and dusted. With Diana's death weighing on his mind, I didn't bother, and so he returned to England unaware that there was some ongoing talk that I could be a candidate in the forthcoming Irish presidential election. As far as Laurence was concerned, I would be spending the following summer helping him set up training courses for meditators at the new Christian meditation centre in the monastery of San Miniato al Monte near Florence, as we had arranged many months earlier.

The talk had been a very quiet murmur for some months since March 1997, when Mary Robinson announced her intention to leave the presidency early to take up the role of United Nations High Commissioner for Human Rights. My mind had immediately turned to John Hume as her possible replacement. He was head and shoulders above any other politician of his era, and his wife Pat was not far behind him in terms of ability and endurance.

I knew that the former taoiseach, Albert Reynolds, was a possible candidate, and his track record as a peacemaker was outstanding. But government numbers were on a knife edge, and Albert was a sitting TD. If he were to win the presidential election, the resulting by-election could impact adversely on the government's stability, and that left a question mark over the likelihood of him being chosen. Michael O'Kennedy, a former European commissioner and government minister, was also in the frame, but as a sitting TD he had the same disadvantage as Albert.

One of my closest friends, Harry Casey, was the first to moot the possibility of my candidature, initially to Martin and then to me. Harry was a teacher of religion in the Classical School, Navan, and a writer of religious texts for second-level students. Secular and ecclesiastical politics were grist to his mill. He had boundless enthusiasm and energy, and a vast capacity for organisation. Over the summer, while I was writing the book, Harry and Martin were taking soundings and preparing the groundwork in the event that John Hume would decide not to run. Father Alec Reid met John in early July and formed the view, which he relayed to us, that John would indeed not be running – a view John subsequently confirmed publicly in early September.

Martin, Harry Casey and our friend the Belfast solicitor Denis Moloney went into overdrive, contacting every friend and acquaintance across the entire island and far beyond, from churches, the professions, politics, business, sport, the media, the arts and every other conceivable sphere, urging them to spread my name as a presidential possibility. They were energised by the amount of positive feedback they received. Now it was time to sharpen the focus and see if it was feasible to consider seeking the Fianna Fáil nomination.

I had a lot of faith in the wise political and personal judgement of Mary O'Rourke, then deputy leader of Fianna Fáil and a government minister. We went to see her at her modest, welcoming home in Athlone. While her husband Enda made the tea, Martin and I broached the idea of me becoming the Fianna Fáil candidate, with the clear mission of using the emotional reach of the presidency to build bridges of healing across the many unreconciled relationships conferred on our island home by history and circumstance.

We talked through the radical pathway I believed was

navigable to a much healthier set of relationships, for I was sure that despite much tentativeness on the part of the North's fundamentalist politicians, the people of Northern Ireland were ready to compromise. But I also knew that a stable peace would depend on the quality of the three inter-locking sets of relationships John Hume had identified as critical to a permanent peace: the community relations within Northern Ireland, the relationship between Northern Ireland and its neighbour to the south, and the relationship between the latter and Great Britain. I knew how deeply many Northern unionists distrusted the Republic of Ireland, seeing every gesture of conciliation as a Trojan horse leading to their worst nightmare – a united Ireland. Somehow we had to build trust, and while the politicians worked to deliver a robust international peace treaty based around compromise and consensus, the work of reconciliation would only be beginning.

Ireland was changing rapidly, thanks to the impact of massified second- and third-level education. Its image of itself was changing. Its political and religious dynamics were changing. The conservative, Catholic anti-British weft was loosening. Twenty-five years of membership of the European Union had helped to provoke a modernising impulse and a rethinking of the old ways of doing things, as had the radical presidency of Mary Robinson. Britain too was changing. It was tired of the Northern conflict and anxious for peace. Its outdated image of the Republic was being updated. The time was absolutely right to harness the surge of intellectual energy and to deliver an innovative vision for island-wide peace through respectful partnership based on parity of esteem.

With strong family roots on both sides of the border,

having lived in both jurisdictions, and having expended a lot of energy in trying to comprehend the complexities of both, I could see this was a unique moment of opportunity for someone who could use the soft yet powerful quasi-pastoral role of the presidency to build bridges of simple non-threatening good neighbourliness across all the wounded fragments the peace process was trying to heal, and to be a steady, sure guide across the changes produced by convulsive times. If I had any doubts about Fianna Fáil's support for that vista, they were dispelled that day in Athlone with Mary O'Rourke; but there was still a lot of realpolitik to be addressed. Mary set out the obstacles to getting the nomination. First and foremost, I would need to engage with the parliamentary party members individually.

A formidable network of contacts and advocates went into action, with so many people pleading my case in writing that by the time I eventually got to make my own case in person to the party leader and newly elected taoiseach, Bertie Ahern, he complained that he could paper the walls of Government Buildings with the correspondence he had received on my behalf. He neither encouraged nor discouraged me, but told me to keep in touch with Séamus Brennan, the government chief whip, to see if I gained any traction with the members of the parliamentary party. To say I was not the bookies' favourite would be an understatement.

As a former Fianna Fáil party member, I was afforded the opportunity to address the parliamentary party meeting at which the presidential candidate was to be chosen. Two other possible candidates, Albert Reynolds and Michael O'Kennedy, also spoke. Going into the meeting, I had not the foggiest idea who was likely to vote for me, and as the TDs and senators passed Martin and me in the corridor, no

one was giving anything away. In fact, judging by the coolness, I felt my chances were slim. I had been told I would
have five minutes' speaking time, so I had written a three-
minute speech, believing no one ever got too exercised about
a bad short speech but they would surely never forgive a bad
long one. Martin and I waited outside the meeting room,
unsure about the running order or protocol. Dr Rory
O'Hanlon was chairing the meeting. General Secretary Pat
Farrell came out and asked me who was proposing my name.
The answer to that was easy: I had no idea. He went back
into the meeting and returned a few minutes later to say that
the other candidates had agreed there would be no propos-
ers or seconders; that I would go first as my name came first
alphabetically; and that I would have three minutes! Just as
well I had exactly three minutes scripted, timed and off by
heart.

I was escorted into the front of that packed, stuffy and
tense room – Martin remained outside – and given the floor
immediately. It was a sea of inscrutable faces.

I have a dream for the eighth presidency of Ireland which I
hope you will recognise as your dream too ... Ours is a
complex and a thoughtful democracy ... There are many
fault lines in our country, some new, some centuries old ...
The presidency offers a powerful symbol in which the many
unreconciled elements of our society can find a common
home ... We have come to realise that the emotional reach
of the presidency is much, much greater than its modest constitutional reach ... In a real way the President personifies
this country ... I want to be a President who brings a cool
head to protecting the constitution and a warm heart to each
person that constitution exists to defend. A President who

can show each person that he or she is utterly respected and valued . . . I am a Northerner who has lived through the worst of the Troubles, whose roots are in Roscommon, who made her first married home in Dublin and reared her children in County Meath, who taught law in Trinity College for many years, who got inside the skin of every part of Ireland as a journalist with RTÉ . . . I have come to understand how important is our debt to the future . . . One life . . . can make a difference. You know what you want for Ireland . . . I hope you will decide that you and I can embrace our future together.

There were two rounds of ballots, at the end of which I was selected. Albert was visibly upset, but very gracious in defeat. I was heart-sorry for him, for his contribution to the peace process was massive, and but for the parliamentary numbers he would likely have been selected.

The Progressive Democrats, who were Fianna Fáil's partner in government, endorsed me as their candidate a few days later. And so my campaign was launched, the slogan 'Building Bridges' appearing suddenly on posters all over the country. Noel Dempsey, the Minister for the Environment and Local Government, was appointed my campaign manager. He was tough and formidable. I would have to trust him no matter what, and I did, subject to one reservation. On day one I told him of the work undertaken with Father Alec Reid and Jim Fitzpatrick and the renewed Hume–Adams talks under the Redemptorist Peace Ministry. He thought it would make great press, but I told him it had to remain confidential. The ministry's work was central to the peace process; it was highly sensitive; and it could be terminally damaged if I was seen to be revealing it for political gain.

There were five candidates, all of whom I knew – some quite well – and all of whom I liked. I took the view that the campaign was a very important job interview, and my mission was to let the voting public get to know and evaluate me. It was not my place to denigrate the other candidates. It was in truth a field of fine, admirable people who had made significant contributions to Irish civic life in a variety of different ways.

I knew Adi Roche well enough to know what a very sincere and good person she was. Through her record as an outstanding champion of children and founder of the Chernobyl Children's Project, to which she had dedicated her life, she shone as a human being of exceptional compassion and hard work.

Dana Rosemary Scallon had been a neighbour in Rostrevor. Martin and I were friendly with her husband Damien and other members of the Scallon family over many years, and had held our wedding reception in his family's hotel in Newry, the Ardmore, the day before it was blown up. Their children and ours had been at school together in Rostrevor. I knew Dana mainly as a pop singer, remembering how her victory at the Eurovision Song Contest had enthralled us in 1970 as a very welcome distraction from the daily diet of violence. More recently, she had carved a career as a Catholic campaigner and singer working in Alabama with the Eternal Word Television Network (EWTN), a wealthy conservative Catholic broadcaster. When Martin and I, in May 1990, had organised a fund-raiser in Warrenpoint for a new Poor Clare convent to replace the condemned building on the Cliftonville Road in Belfast, Dana had agreed to perform pro bono, helping us to raise a lot of money for what we suspected even then was going to be a temporary fix for an emptying convent of elderly but much-loved nuns.

Derek Nally, the only male candidate, was a former police officer. He and I were very well acquainted going back many years. He had asked for, and I had willingly given him, considerable help when he was setting up the first Irish victim support organisation. He knew my pacifist politics and values well, and I respected him for his civic-minded conscience.

Fine Gael politician and MEP Mary Banotti was also well known to me. I admired her and her sister Nora Owen, also a politician and former government minister, for their dedication to public service and in particular to the advancement of women and the modernising of Ireland.

For the most part the candidates treated each other with courtesy and respect, but any campaign to become the country's first citizen and primary ambassador was always likely to be tough – and it was. It had been no different in past presidential elections, including the most recent one, when Mary Robinson endured sexist comments that in the end proved counterproductive and helped rather than hindered her election.

The campaign trail was a curious mixture of rallies and appearances up, down and across the country, in halls, pubs, hotels, clubs, houses, restaurants, fairs, marts, matches, local shops, shopping centres . . . A lot of chicken sandwiches and crisps were eaten on the road between venues, and yet all of us had dropped a clothes size by election day. Denis Lawlor, Fianna Fáil volunteer and driver extraordinaire, saw more of me during those days than Martin, who still had patients to look after on some of the days. There were a lot of encounters with photographers, journalists and commentators, a few of whom I knew and most of whom I did not.

Each day, each engagement and all the advertising was planned by an impressive back-room team, directed by Noel and guided by Pat Farrell, Jackie Gallagher, Des Richardson and P. J. Mara, as well as the Progressive Democrats' Garvan McGinley and Liz O'Donnell, a former student of mine. Not since working in RTÉ had my hair and make-up been so perfect, thanks to the work of Sarah Ashe and Mary Bruton, who turned up at the crack of dawn each morning to sort me out for the day. Eileen Gleeson, along with her sister Kate, took my clothes in hand, setting Irish designers Deborah Veal, Miriam Mone and Mary Gregory on me to rid me of the female-academic-on-the-loose look. The small apartment we had bought in Dublin after moving back to the North in 1987, and which was our family weekend bolthole, became Candidate Central.

The atmosphere within the team was good-humoured and collaborative. There was no time for anything but getting on with it. Also, Noel was boss. He knew that the media tended to hunt in feverish packs. There was little evidence that they had done much in the way of research about my career to date. The years of ecumenical, inter-Church, anti-violence campaigning did not figure much in the coverage. The *Sunday Independent*, which I had successfully sued for libel ten years earlier, published an article by Eoghan Harris in which he described me as a 'tribal timebomb'. Anyone reading his comments could have been forgiven for thinking we had worked together and that he knew me well. In fact, although he had previously worked at RTÉ, we'd never met. He was later man enough to admit he had been wrong about me, but during the campaign he was gratuitously vitriolic. More importantly, he was an adviser to Derek Nally.

After the leak and publication of a Department of Foreign Affairs memo purporting to describe my political beliefs, Nally saw an opportunity to attack me and insinuate that I was a closet Sinn Féin supporter. The campaign had already become rather nasty, with very personal and hurtful attacks being made on the frontrunner, Adi Roche. I had offered her my support and sympathy, and it was no surprise when the guns (a word used advisedly) were turned on me. Derek Nally issued a public statement. Although he had known me and my politics and principles for years, and had asked me to work with him because of them, he now felt that I 'was not a proper person to be President of the Irish Republic'.

The fact that the allegations were groundless and opportunistic was as nothing by comparison with the immediate danger in which they placed my family in Rostrevor. The children were there in our family home with their grandfather just a few miles from Kilkeel, a loyalist paramilitary stronghold – and the loyalists were not on ceasefire. The RUC instantly recognised the danger and put a plan in place to protect my family.

Even though by then the renewed Hume–Adams talks had succeeded in pushing the IRA to renew their ceasefire, scepticism abounded that summer about the bona fides of the IRA and about allowing Sinn Féin into multi-party peace talks. Such scepticism would have been particularly acute in Kilkeel. Up until Nally's intervention, my children went unprotected to school in Kilkeel on the school bus. Now they and all on their bus were potential sitting ducks. They were scared out of their wits.

By the time I was due to do a live studio discussion with Derek Nally later that day, I was angry at Nally and his team of advisers and also desperately worried about the consequences for my family. Nally waved a newspaper theatrically during the programme and asked if I had any association with Sinn Féin. I had none, and said so. I had never supported them and never voted for them. All my life I had been opposed to the use of violence for political ends.

There followed a media feeding frenzy, as the pack followed the scent of blood. Nally continued his attack a few days later at a debate in Trinity College hosted by the Hist. I quickly realised that I was the one on home turf. The others, God help them, were in the terrifying bearpit I had first encountered in the mid seventies, and it showed. The vocal, not to say at times raucous, support I received from Trinity's debating audience at that event helped me to face down Nally's wrong-headed personal attacks. These people and this forum had heard me speak again and again over two decades. I was no stranger there, and they knew what I stood for and what I stood against.

Nally got the message loud and clear that night that he was on a hiding to nothing. He crumbled and admitted that my word was good enough for him. As we were leaving the building, I told him that I did not like 'what this election has done to a decent man'. I could see by his reaction that he was heart-scalded and torn, but since he had now publicly accepted the allegations were untrue, I left it at that. The following day, his campaign manager unfortunately reiterated the allegations. The *Irish Times* scathingly described Nally as being 'in the grip of his advisers'. By the end of that turbulent week, Nally declared on the *Late Late Show* that it had been a mistake to let Eoghan Harris join his advisory team.

The tide had turned against Nally, but for me the misery

was to continue when additional leaked memos were published the following Sunday. One of them contained remarks attributed to the SDLP's Brid Rodgers, which included serious allegations about Jim Fitzpatrick and myself. Rodgers was among those most hostile to the Hume–Adams talks, though the memo made no direct reference to the talks or my role in them. I felt the only way I could properly respond was to disclose my work with the Redemptorist Peace Ministry, and I was not prepared to do that, because the Hume–Adams talks were both confidential and still ongoing. (Even now, over twenty years later, I do not feel at liberty to share more than the barest details of them.) They were too important to jeopardise, and much more important than me or my candidacy.

That Sunday, with the affair now entering its second week, I made up my mind that I would withdraw my candidacy the following morning rather than reveal the existence of the talks and my role in the process. I went to bed determined that first thing in the morning I would be giving Noel Dempsey the bad news. Things turned out differently.

In the morning, Martin turned the radio on – and there was the head of the Redemptorists, Father Brendan Callanan, disclosing my honest-broker role in the peace ministry. He had issued a statement the night before, explaining the ethos of the ministry and how Jim Fitzpatrick and I came to be involved.

The Redemptorist Peace Ministry team is non-political, i.e. it does not purport to support, nor does it in fact support, the position of any political party. The benchmark of the Redemptorist peace and reconciliation team is the call of the Gospel to seek out ways and means of developing and promoting a more peaceful, a more reconciled and a more just society. Mr Jim Fitzpatrick and Ms Mary McAleese were invited to join the peace ministry team precisely because they share these convictions. Their contribution to the peace ministry in association with us has been a valuable one. It is deplorable that because of this ministry they would be in any way slighted.

The noble Jim Fitzpatrick also had his say: 'This was a genuine and sincere initiative, and it is both hurtful and malicious to suggest any subversive motivation by any of the individuals involved. Professor McAleese is an honourable and trusting individual who is totally committed to peace.'

Just then the doorbell rang and the postman handed me a package. It was from a nun in England: Father Justin's sister Gemma. In the parcel was the crucifix Justin had worn from the time of his novitiate. Sister Gemma's note simply said, 'You might need this.'

Noel Dempsey was determined that I should say nothing until other credible voices joined those of Father Callanan and Jim Fitzpatrick. And they did. John Hume called the allegations 'an outrage'. Seamus Mallon rubbished the idea that I was ever a Sinn Féin supporter. Brid Rodgers, in an *Irish Times* interview, said she wished 'to refute the unworthy implications from some quarters in relation to Professor McAleese, Mr Fitzpatrick and Father Alex Reid'. Joe Hendron was characteristically blunt: 'This woman is no Provo.' I got a standing ovation at a rally in Galway. It took a Northern commentator, Tom Kelly, to search my past record and write in the *Irish News* that 'Never has Mary McAleese espoused violence. All her on-the-record comments stated very clearly her opposition to all forms of violence.' The

SDLP had a policy of not getting involved in elections in the South, but Eddie McGrady, appalled by the innuendo against me, broke with the policy and announced that he was endorsing my candidacy.

The SDLP's support was crucial, but support came also from many others who had come to know me over the years as a peacemaker. The Protestant ministers Sam Burch, Ken Newall and Tim Kinahan issued a public statement saying that in all their contacts with the Redemptorist Peace Ministry, including with me, they had never detected any political agenda. Dr David Stevens, with whom I had soldiered on the working party on sectarianism, issued a statement saying I was 'not a Sinn Féin supporter or supporter of violence'. Colonel Harvey Bicker, a UUP councillor on Down District Council, said I was the best person to lead Ireland into the next century. John Taylor, deputy leader of the Ulster Unionist Party, declared firmly that I was an able person with whom he had worked easily and I was no supporter of violence.

Ghastly and hurtful as the clamour of accusation had been, the supportive response from those who knew me over many years was healing beyond measure. It opened the door that allowed me to play my part in Ireland's future.

On the afternoon of 30 October 1997, Martin and I were in the Portmarnock Hotel watching the election count coverage with our children when, at around 4.30, Eileen Gleeson flung open the door and announced: 'We've done it!' From there it was a sprint to the tiny apartment in Ballsbridge to meet my parents and siblings, who were in various stages of shock and excitement, and then another sprint on to the Parliament Hotel to get dressed and wait for word that it was time to go across the street to Dublin Castle for the official announcement of the election result. A group of colleagues from Trinity were already at the hotel, waiting to celebrate.

The taoiseach, Bertie Ahern, and tánaiste, Mary Harney, who had been so strong, calm and supportive throughout the arduous campaign while also running the country, arrived wreathed in smiles. Together we walked the few yards to the castle. Everywhere I looked there were familiar faces: people from the North who had jumped in their cars to be present for the moment when the first Northerner became President of Ireland. I spotted Denis Moloney and his sister Maria, Harvey Bicker and his wife Elizabeth, Harry Casey and his wife Mary, and face after face of friends from Cork and Coleraine, Belfast and Ballyvaughan, Rostrevor and Roscommon, of men and women who had made my election their business. I knew even then that I would never be able to thank them adequately, though I tried when my name was announced as the winner with 58.67 per cent of the vote. There were commiserations for the other candidates: Mary Banotti, who came second; Dana Rosemary Scallon, who came third; Adi Roche, who was fourth; and Derek Nally, who came last. All of us had been bruised and battered by the experience to some extent, but all were still standing and respectful of one another at the finish.

As we left the podium, several complete strangers gathered around me with a puzzling sense of purpose. They were to be my companions for many years ahead, the security detail attached to me now I was President-elect. They were members of the Garda Special Detective Unit and they still tell the story of how, when we got back to the Portmarnock Hotel after a riotous and packed party at the Herbert Park Hotel, I thanked them and shook their hands as I got out of the car. I headed though the hotel entrance to the lift. They were still behind me, so as the lift door opened I thanked them again, said goodnight and got in. They got in too. At the bedroom door they stood on while I asked myself: just how far do they go? I thanked them once more, wondering if they would follow me in. They didn't, but next morning when the door opened onto the corridor, there they were again – as they would be every day for the next fourteen years! The children were bemused, mostly by the fact that it took me so long to figure out what was going on.

The official parchment of my election was presented to me next day at Dublin Castle. It was my first introduction to Lieutenant Colonel Des Johnson. His next job was to introduce me to the right way of reviewing a guard of honour, a regular set piece for all heads of state. The first was to occur on the day of my inauguration. What could possibly go wrong, walking up and down two very straight lines of soldiers? At McKee Barracks I was to discover that a lot of things can go wrong, and Des Johnson took pains to point out all the places where mistakes were regularly made. He showed me a video of President Robinson reviewing a guard of honour. Before she had taken two steps, he was saying that this was wrong and that was wrong. By the time she had finished, two minutes later, there was an itemised list of infractions, not one of which was obvious to me. I thought it looked perfectly fine. My attempts at light-hearted banter were met with a certain coolness.

Worse still, a mock guard was waiting in the yard for me to undergo a rehearsal. Pure dread descended on me. Lieutenant Colonel Johnson escorted me to the spot marked with an X on which I was to commence the operation, which suddenly seemed as complicated as blindfolded brain surgery. Martin and Eileen Gleeson were attempting to suppress

. My mother, left, with my father's cousins Norah McAreavey and May Fitzpatrick, shortly
after my birth. That's me in Norah's arms

2. Sitting on Bronco the donkey outside my
grandparents' cottage in Caraward, Co.
Roscommon, with my father

3. My first communion, May 1958

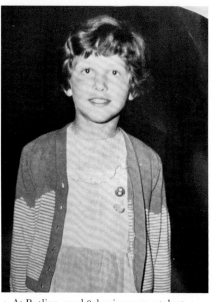

4. At Butlins, aged 8, having won a talent contest with my Irish slip jig

5. With Martin at the Aquinas Hall annual dinner dance, 1970

6. Northern Ireland's bar was all male until Patricia Kennedy (left), Eilis McDermott (right) and I qualified in 1974

7. Wedding day: 9 March 1976. Our dear friends Tony and Myles O'Reilly were murdered that morning by loyalists; the news reached us that night

8. A headshot from 1979, when I was working on *Frontline*: relatively happy times for me at RTÉ

9. Fr Alec Reid: An unassuming but seminal figure in the peace process, with whom I worked on the Hume–Adams talks

10. With schoolchildren on the campaign trail on Inis Mór, 1997

11. At the announcement of the count result, with (*from left*) Mary Banotti, Dana Rosemary Scallon and Derek Nally

2. Celebrating with my family after winning the presidency: (back row left–right) Nora, Claire, Damien; (front row left–right) John, Catherine (Kate), Dad, myself, Mum, Phelim, Clement, Patrick (Pat)

3. At the opening of the Island of Ireland Peace Park in Messines, Belgium, on Armistice Day 1998. Understanding the role of Irish people of all persuasions in the First World War was a crucial piece in the reconciliation jigsaw (Maxwell Photography)

14. Visiting Pope John Paul II at the Vatican in 1999. We got off to a bad start when His Holiness opened with a sexist joke (Maxwell Photography)

15. With Mary O'Rourke, a friend and trusted advisor whose encouragement and guidance helped me decide to stand for President (Maxwell Photography)

16. I always suspected that Ian Paisley would drop his extreme sectarianism once he saw political benefit in doing so, and so it proved. In 2010 he and his wife Eileen came to the Áras, where we had been welcoming loyalists since 1997 (Maxwell Photography)

17. The last big ambition of my presidency, to host Her Majesty Queen Elizabeth II for what would be the first-ever visit by a British monarch to independent Ireland, was finally realized in May 2011. Everything was planned in great detail, but as we walked together into the State Dinner at Dublin Castle, there was a very pleasant surprise ahead of me (Maxwell Photography)

18. With the Obamas, just three days after the Queen left Ireland. President Obama drew a huge crowd for his speech in College Green in Dublin to round off a remarkable few days (Maxwell Photography)

19. I took a dim view of the Vatican's plans for the World Meeting of Families in Dublin in August 2018, and I had it in mind when I suggested that the theme of Dublin Pride that year should be 'We Are Family'. Martin and I marched with our son Justin and his husband Fionan. (Fergal Phillips, *Irish Independent*)

their laughter at my discomfiture. Suddenly I had an idea – a good one, even if born of panic and a determination to vindicate my predecessor. I smiled sweetly at Des Johnson and suggested that before I attempted the ritual, it would be helpful if he did it first so that I could witness an expert at work. After all, the only film I had seen was, as he had pointed out himself, focused on flaws, so it would be much appreciated if there was a first perfect run-through.

He was a bit stunned. Martin and Eileen were looking as if they had actually herniated by this point, as were several senior officers, among them the Chief of Staff. This was an unexpected and unscheduled turn of events. Poor Des set off, making an obvious mistake at the outset and several more before it was over. He was apologetic to the point of apoplexy. I was delighted, knowing that no matter what I did now, short of doing the review backwards, it would be good enough. I took my place on the X and on the signal did my first ever review of a guard of honour. It was perfect, absolutely flawless. The soldiers looked like they might spontaneously combust with hysterics. Des was gracious, announcing that I was a quick pupil. I graciously replied that I had a good teacher.

The weekend after the election there was only one place we all wanted to be and that was at home in Rostrevor, knowing it would be as much a leave-taking as a welcome home. There were thousands outside the house and in the village square as we walked from our home up the street to the chapel for Sunday-morning Mass. The Longstone pipe band led the way, playing a rousing rendition of 'Star of the County Down', past the Old Corner House pub, our first home in the village, and on past the Church of Ireland church where my children had had their first experience of shared ecumenical prayer, past Justin's old school, and into the church where we were married, where our children were baptised and made their first Communion and Confirmation, and where I was my sister Claire's bridesmaid. I remembered what Father Ailbe had said to Martin and me on our wedding day in 1976 as I arrived to meet my groom at the altar: 'Eyes down for God and Ireland.'

Back at the house, plain-clothes gardaí and RUC officers mixed together in the kitchen drinking tea. A lot of new, unexpected friendships would be made over tea and scones in our new home.

I wanted the inauguration to be a celebration of the neighbourliness I knew we were capable of. Eileen Gleeson and I deliberated at length on the ceremony, the guest list, the atmosphere I wanted to create, the messages I wanted to convey, the speech I wanted to deliver at this particularly charged moment in history.

Why was it such a curious moment? I was the first President from Northern Ireland, elected in an election in which I did not have a vote, and on a promise to be a bridge-builder. It was a huge act of faith by the electorate. We were still six difficult months away from the Good Friday Agreement of 10 April 1998. In November of 1997, few would have put money on that, or on the agreement's overwhelming endorsement by twin referenda on both sides of the border. Politically things remained fraught. But the IRA were back on ceasefire. And with two new Prime Ministers, Bertie Ahern and Tony Blair, and a new Secretary of State, Mo Mowlam, plus the active involvement of President Clinton and his envoy George Mitchell, there was a convergence of pragmatic leaders who got on well together and who were willing to invest the vast time and effort needed to pull Northern Ireland's sharp political fragments together.

Remembrance Sunday, when the dead of the Great War are commemorated, fell on 9 November that year, two days before the inauguration. Historically, few Catholics took part in the annual commemorations, and the stories of the many tens of thousands of their forebears who had fought and died in British uniform had gone untold, failing as they did to serve the vanities of a divided history. I knew that if the true story of the sacrifices made by Catholic, Protestant, unionist and nationalist in that war was told, it could help to unify us. And it might provoke us to critique the foundations of things we held dear and that kept us at wary arm's length from one another.

Martin and I attended the Remembrance service in St Patrick's Cathedral in Dublin with Colonel Harvey Bicker. An Ulster Unionist councillor, a former member of the British Army and the Ulster Defence Regiment, he had written to me before I was elected, in fact before I was even selected as a candidate, telling me he had observed me over some years, believed in my commitment to building bridges, and was willing to help in any way he could.

How tentative things were back then. Protocol was not keen that I personally lay a wreath, as it had not been done before. So Harvey offered to lay a wreath on my behalf, and protocol conceded. The service was particularly poignant since it was the tenth anniversary of one of the worst atrocities of the Troubles. On Remembrance Sunday in 1987, as people gathered at the cenotaph in Enniskillen, the IRA had detonated a bomb, murdering ten people and injuring dozens. Gordon Wilson had lost his daughter that day, holding her hand as her life ebbed away. Yet no hatred or thirst for vengeance had ever compromised his Christian forgiveness and his insistence on loving those who had hurt him so unimaginably. When he was later appointed to the Irish Senate, I had written to him not just to congratulate him but to tell him how important a voice his was, precisely because he came from the unionist community north of the border. It was a voice we needed to hear, and he should never feel inhibited or intimidated but should speak his mind no matter what. He had written back saying that of all the letters he received, he had taken most courage from mine. Now I took courage from him and his legacy.

While many, understandably, may not have been impressed or persuaded, Gerry Adams chose on Remembrance Sunday 1997 to say publicly that he was 'deeply sorry' about what had happened at Enniskillen. Sorrow for atrocities was rarely heard from supporters of the IRA. Indeed, the opposite was more usually the case and that really rankled, often rubbing salt into open wounds. Still, the words had been spoken. We all knew that the establishment of a permanent peace would need a lot more sorrow for the past if we were to gather the forbearance needed for a historic political compromise.

Many hours of planning went into the inauguration ceremony. It had to be more than a formulaic set-piece event. It had to reflect the hopes of so many for a different future, one characterised by a new and sincere good-neighbourliness. That was what we wanted for our children, and so we planned to have Dublin Castle's yard ring with the shouts of eight hundred children bussed from all over the island, the children of loyalists, republicans, unionists, nationalists, Catholics, Protestants, Jews, Muslims, atheists, Irish, British, new immigrants . . . The dignitaries and politicians who attended would walk though that throng and, I hoped, be energised by their innocence and their dependence on us to do the right thing for them.

The eight hundred children from all over Ireland were mixing giddily and happily when the presidential Rolls-Royce slid into the historic cobbled Castle Yard to their smiles and cheers. Among them I saw the uniforms of St Louis Kilkeel, the school my children would now be leaving, and Kathleen Collins shepherding them. All skirts the regulation length! We were both a long way from Ardoyne. For a second I choked at the idea that my own children would soon be wearing different uniforms and missing their old lives desperately. I said a quiet prayer that they would forgive me in time for visiting all this upheaval upon them and would come to see the value of their sacrifice.

When I recall that day, it is the sea of children I remember, and two pieces of music. The first was 'Star of the County Down', played as I walked up the aisle in St Patrick's Hall to the podium where I would be inaugurated. The second was a hauntingly elegant piece, 'An Droichead' ('The Bridge'), which I had asked the legendary piper Liam O'Flynn to compose and perform for the occasion. He played it as I left the podium to greet a special group of twenty-five people, sitting up front among the official state dignitaries. They had been chosen to represent Ireland North and South in all its diversity. The packed hall and its overflow room were filled to capacity with a mix of politics and perspectives never seen before at such a ceremony. For many of the audience, especially those from the unionist community, just being there was a personal bridge crossed with generosity. It augured well for the work that lay ahead.

Chief Justice Liam Hamilton administered the presidential

oath and handed me my seal of office. He was a very fine judge and I knew him well, but in 1983, as a young, enthusiastic academic, I had critiqued one of his judgements on a criminal matter in a legal publication. Academic critiquing of appeal court decisions was central to the UK system from which I had come, but was still in its infancy in Dublin. No matter how scholarly or valid, it was interpreted as personal criticism back then, and it had not been appreciated by at least one of Justice Hamilton's great friends, especially coming from a female blow-in. They were still unaccustomed to academic lawyers rooting around in their thinking, as another Supreme Court judge, Niall McCarthy, told me a little apologetically while agreeing with what I had written: 'Ah, Mary, would you go easy on poor Liam. You know he is not in a position to argue back!' If Liam was still smarting fifteen years later, he showed no sign of it, mercifully.

It was time to make my first speech as President, to send out an invitation to all sides to get behind the work of building bridges. As the Northern Irish poet Louis MacNeice had said long before, 'a single purpose can be founded on a jumble of opposites'. I noted the coincidence that this was also Armistice Day, and spoke of 'nationalist and unionist who fought and died together in those wars, the differences which separated them at home fading into insignificance as the bond of their common humanity forged friendships as intense as love can make them'. We too had suffered from:

> the cruelty and capriciousness of violent conflict . . . [Gordon Wilson's] words of love and forgiveness shocked us as if we were hearing them for the first time, as if they had not been uttered first two thousand years ago. His work and the

work of so many peacemakers who have risen above the awesome pain of loss to find a bridge to the other side is work I want to help in every way I can . . . The distrusts go deep and the challenge is awesome. Across this island, north, south, east and west, there are people of such greatness of heart that I know with their help it can be done . . . There will be those who are wary of such invitations, afraid they are being invited to the edge of a precipice.

During the campaign, one of my closest friends, Mary McGonnell, had sent me a poem she thought would help me through. I had phoned the poet earlier that week and asked if I could use it in my speech. He was delighted, and so my address finished with a dedication to those who were nervous and fearful of the changes we all needed to make if we were to make peace. 'To them I have dedicated a poem written by English poet Christopher Logue, himself a veteran of the Second World War: *Come to the edge/ We might fall/ Come to the edge/ It's too high!/ Come to the edge! And they came/ And he pushed/ And they flew.'*

I concluded by asking for prayers for me and our country, so that we might use the next seven years well 'to create a future where, in the words of William Butler Yeats, "everything we look upon is blest".'

I brought Father Justin's cross and picture with me into Áras an Uachtaráin. I also brought a new light to replace the one that Mary Robinson had memorably lit in an upstairs window at the start of her presidency as a symbol of welcome for the Irish abroad, and which she took with her on leaving.

Some years earlier, my dear friend Davey Hammond – Belfast Protestant, contrarian extraordinaire, poet and film-maker – had given my children the gift of a Tilley lamp to be used on walks on the dark country roads of rural Roscommon. He had visited us on holiday there, and late in the evening insisted we all head out for a ramble in the faint moonlight. He sang snatches of songs and recited children's rhymes the whole way, undoubtedly causing consternation to the quiet folk who inhabited the sparsely distributed cottages. We had battery-powered torches. He was not much impressed, and a week later a parcel arrived addressed to Emma, Sara and Justin with a disc of the children's rhyming songs and a Tilley lamp with the instruction that it was to accompany them on country walks on moonless nights.

The lamp was lit with oil, but between the election and the inauguration, and without consulting Davey, I had it electrified, and it was installed as a welcome to the Irish abroad and especially to our estranged neighbours in the North, with whom, over the years ahead, we hoped to develop a happier relationship. If the world had been made up of people like Davey Hammond, there would have been no need of building bridges! He had a gift for friendship like no one I have ever known, and for songs and stories he was in a league of his own. He subsequently forgave the electrification.

In 1995, Davey had accompanied his friend Seamus Heaney to Stockholm for the award of Seamus's Nobel prize, wearing memorably big yellow boots. He wore the same boots a short time later when Sir Patrick Mayhew gave a reception in honour of Seamus at Hillsborough Castle. I was standing close by Davey when Sir Patrick made his obligatory speech and then, having quoted lines from the famous poem 'Digging', presented Seamus with an actual spade. There was audible shock, for in one interpretation it was as if he was telling Seamus to give up the pen and go back to digging potato drills. Knowing Sir Patrick, I very much doubt that thought had entered his head. Rather, some aide had deemed it a good idea and landed him in it. Davey's face turned puce and he uttered a string of invective, barely sotto voce and so violent that I thought he would bring the police down on us. Mayhew, he said, was being deliberately provocative. I offered that it was just innocent thoughtlessness. The Secretary of State hadn't a notion what 'Digging' was about. That cut no ice with Davey. Now it was a toss-up which of us, me or Mayhew, Davey would spiflicate with the spade first. It was the best sideshow at any formal reception I have ever been at, bar none.

Our first meal in the Áras was an official inauguration lunch with an array of guests, among them former President Paddy Hillery, whose seat collapsed as he sat down. Quick as a flash he looked at me and said, 'I can't believe this old chair is still here!' At least he knew his way around the place, which was more than we did. When the guests had gone, we headed upstairs to the set of austere rooms that were to be our home for the next seven years. There was no time to unpack, only to change into a new set of clothes for the evening party back at Dublin Castle. My outfit, designed by Mary Gregory, was a full-length silver silk dress cut on the bias with a matching coat. It was beautiful, but not suited to travelling in the broad, deep seat of the elderly Rolls-Royce, which had no seat belt. I rolled, slipped and slithered all the way into town, so that by the time we pulled up at the castle door, the outfit was wrapped around me like an Egyptian mummy's bandages. We were greeted by the taoiseach and his then partner Celia Larkin. I grabbed Celia and made for the ladies' room, where she held the coat while I ran around until the dress had unravelled back to its intended shape, by which time we were both in stitches.

Back at the Áras for our first night, we gathered in the gloomy sitting room, exhausted but not yet ready to go to bed, with so much to talk about. Justin was sent to make tea, and luckily was just prevented from putting an elegant Georgian silver teapot to brew on the stove. He quickly sussed out where the biscuits were kept and we went to bed happy! My father-in-law Charlie, who had lived with us since Emma was born and would be living with us in the Áras, did what he did every night before going to bed. He went around all the rooms pulling out plugs and turning off lights, including the electrified Tilley lamp. Justin, always one step ahead of the posse, spotted the darkness on his night rounds, and the 'eternal' light of welcome was restored.

On the second night, a couple of our close friends, Michael and Deirdre Delaney, joined us for our first private family dinner. There were big fancy plates under smaller fancy plates, each of them with a harp image in the trim. Deirdre had the bright idea that before we could eat, each of us had to line up the harps on our two plates. We were slightly terrified of the staff, which was ridiculous, for every one of them was slightly terrified of us: we were all unknown quantities to each other. But the harp-alignment exercise provoked the first of many laughs we all shared together.

Our living quarters were above and adjacent to the offices of the secretariat, and sat in the middle of what was pretty much an open thoroughfare. There was little privacy. I was not sure how we would acclimatise to being on permanent parade. By happenstance, the discovery of asbestos meant that we had to move out to allow for renovations. I was able to sequester rooms in a far corner of the house known as the West Wing, and it became our private family home, well away from the official life of the Áras. Thankfully it had its own back door, where abandoned bikes, hurls, helmets and school bags looked a lot less alarming than they did when strewn at the front door of the President's official residence.

# 9

Immediately we set to work honouring the promise to build bridges. There was an urgency to it. The conflict in Northern Ireland was ongoing, but a lot of effort was being expended in trying to bring it to an end. Over the thirty years of the Troubles there had been a number of failed inter-governmental attempts at constructing a peace agreement. Each had contributed to a body of experience and insight that became useful tools in the hands of a new generation of peacemakers. Some worked on the visible front line of politics; others worked in back channels.

My job, once elected, was to use the office of the President to explore the areas of long-standing distrust and estrangement that could, I was sure, be bridged by a sustained effort at friendship-building. From 11 November 1997 it was time to put into effect all we had learned over years of living and working on both sides of the border. The Áras was to be a welcoming place, especially to those who had never considered visiting it. The first thing to do was to open the house to the general public for the first time: we established public visits to the state rooms every Saturday, and eventually created a visitors' centre that told the history of the house and the presidency. The Saturday visits included a wander around my office, which made Friday evenings a rush of tidying – not something that comes naturally to me, for I love to see a desk covered in open books, papers, in-trays, out-trays, pictures, Post-its, pens, paper clips and all the paraphernalia that screams there is work to be done.

Martin and I, with the help of Harvey Bicker and Denis Moloney, devised an intensive seven-year plan to reach out to the unionist community, including the hard-to-reach loyalist constituencies. It was to be a patient and sustained effort to draw them into a new era of good neighbourliness. We also made plans to bring together people of all faiths, politics and perspectives, putting particular emphasis on those who lived and worked away from the limelight in each of the strands that made up civic life. Some years down the road, when we organised a dinner for members of the judiciary North and South, a friend who is now a Northern high court judge was bemused to discover that the lady who cleaned his chambers had been to the Áras long before him.

A principle with which we began, and which we maintained faithfully throughout, was that none of these encounters would be staged for photo opportunities or publicity, and that everything done would be to build genuine lasting friendships. With the many Northern unionist friends and contacts we already had between us, the work started immediately, building up phone and email lists of people and groups we wanted to engage with. We developed a network of people and organisations in the Republic willing to help us grow a wide and strong web of cross-border hospitality, centred on the home and the role of the President but radiating out to and including every single county. The response was phenomenal. We received great support from the taoiseach and government, whom we kept fully informed of what we were planning to do, so there were no surprises.

A group of stalwarts rapidly gelled into a formidable team of volunteers, with Martin, Denis and Harvey at the centre doing the heavy lifting, along with Áine de Baroid of the Department of Foreign Affairs. Martin soon gave up his dental practice to work on Building Bridges full-time and pro bono, as he had promised Bertie Ahern months before he would do if I was elected.

The scene was set for my first visit north, three weeks after the inauguration. It was my first trip on the government jet. In my innocence I had assumed we would jump in the car and head up the road to Newry, but a security briefing made it clear that was highly unlikely for the time being, mainly because members of the Royal Ulster Constabulary were regularly targeted by republican paramilitaries, so it was not advisable to have them hanging about the border waiting to escort me onwards. It was ironic that in order to get me to venues in the North, it was safer for me to travel through loyalist areas, where the RUC wouldn't be bothered, rather than through republican areas. So I got used to travelling in unmarked cars at unremarkable speeds and carefully obeying every red light through loyalist strongholds. Some of the accompanying staff may have been on the far side of fidgety, but having been raised in such a place myself, I was relaxed enough to be able to knit, to the manifest bemusement of the police officers. The perils of knitting in an official presidential car, sometimes travelling at speed on meandering country roads in order to get to an event on time, occasionally prompted Martin to prophesy that I would be the first President in the all-time history of presidents, any presidents, anywhere, to stab myself to death in the middle of a purl row.

I talked often with Mo Mowlam, the Secretary of State for Northern Ireland. She was thrilled that I would be visiting the North, but none too happy about the protocol rules that specified she should accompany me throughout my trips. 'Look, love, let's start as we mean to continue. You come and go as you please and I will not be tripping over you except in your house in Dublin on my weekends off.' And that was how it worked out.

Martin and I arrived at Belfast airport to be greeted by Colonel Charles Hogg, the Lord Lieutenant for Belfast and brother of my old friend Billy Hogg from Warrenpoint. He greeted me in Irish, learned specially for the occasion. I just about held back the tears, for knowing his background I also knew that in this gesture he was helping build bridges from the other side of all those divides. It was one of those singular moments when the deep yearning for peace and willingness to compromise to achieve it reveals itself in a simple act of generosity.

We took the not-so-straight road to Newry, where the Newry and Mourne council laid on a special reception attended by unionists and nationalists and republicans. Almost all of them were well known to me, since they represented the area I had lived in for the previous ten years; and many of them had teeth or dentures well known to Martin. Danny Kennedy, an Ulster Unionist councillor who could sometimes be a bit sour, was anything but that day, remarking naturally and accurately that 'she knows we don't give her our allegiance, but that does not mean we cannot be gracious'. And he was, and they all were, especially those from Rostrevor and Warrenpoint, old neighbours trying to come to terms with this radical turn of events.

Later that day I returned to Ardoyne. Ann McVicar of the Shankill Women's Centre was waiting to greet me at the Flax Centre, a cross-community initiative of the Passionists with which I had long been involved. Here was a troubled and troubling place that could be transformed by peace – but it was far from finished with suffering, as events would show.

That very night, a young Catholic father was murdered nearby by loyalist gunmen.

Things became easier as time went on and word went out about our seriousness of purpose and the authenticity of our agenda, which was to create a culture of good neighbourliness. Within a short time, a visit to the North by the Irish President was no longer an exceptional or remarkable event.

Less than a month after my inauguration, I took Communion in the Protestant Christ Church Cathedral in Dublin. If I had committed all seven deadly sins in public I could hardly have caused a bigger furore in fundamentalist clerical circles, which had little insight into just how fundamentalist and clericalised they were.

By way of background I should explain that I had neither the intention nor the right to be a Catholic President for Catholic Ireland, which was what those circles expected and desired. Since our island had suffered greatly from the vanities of religious exclusivity, I intended to show respect at the highest level of the state to all faiths, all denominations, and those who embraced none of the above.

Growing up in Northern Ireland among self-styled Christians, both Protestant and Catholic, had introduced me to what I described in my book *Love in Chaos* as the 'ya-boo school of theology; the my-God-is-bigger-than-your-God school of theological bullies'. Participation in decades of inter-church ecumenical talks had introduced me to the dual reality whereby both sides saw themselves and themselves alone as victims and martyrs of the other, and as having God exclusively on their side. And sectarianism still ruled hearts and minds – and streets – in Northern Ireland. My experience of the working party on sectarianism had shown me that it would be no easy task to find a formula for interrupting and reversing a culture of deep-rooted sectarianism, transmitted and reinforced through home, parents, family, clan, community, church, school, peer group, workplace, playground, media, pastors, politics, politicians, doctrines, dogmas, sports, clubs, identities, flags, emblems, music, marches, histories told and untold, true and untrue. But the political terrain was shifting. Ordinary people, tired to death of grief and its human cost, were quietly affirming a new willingness to compromise.

One of the first things I did on entering office was to write to all the churches and faith systems, essentially inviting myself to join them in worship if they would or could have me. I was invited to St Andrew's Catholic Church on Westland Row for a Mass on 30 November, celebrated by then Archbishop Desmond Connell, to mark the start of my term of office. He referred warmly to my inauguration speech and announced: 'She will be a builder of bridges in a spirit of reconciliation and love.'

Yes, well, that was the general idea, but a week later it was the archbishop himself who took out his ecclesial Sherman tank and drove it over that spirit of reconciliation. That was the week I responded to the invitation from Christ Church Cathedral. King James had worshipped there before the Battle of the Boyne, and King William had done the same after winning the battle. Where better to share my first worship as President with the Protestant community?

The cathedral had really taken the Building Bridges theme to heart, for the Warrington Male Voice Choir was there. This was a poignant reminder of two little boys, Johnathan Ball, aged three, and Tim Parry, aged twelve, who had been murdered in Warrington, in the north of England, by the IRA in 1993.

Walton Empey, the Archbishop of Dublin and the wisest and humblest senior churchman I have ever known, devoted his welcome to the importance of building bridges. The homilist that day was the special envoy of the Archbishop of Canterbury, Terry Waite, who had been held hostage in Beirut by Islamist paramilitaries. He knew a thing or three about the need for reconciliation across sectarian divides, and he spoke with an agonising quiet passion. Martin and I, along with our accompanying children, took Communion. The Catholic Lord Mayor of Dublin, John Stafford, did the same.

It is hard now to credit that it was the first time a Catholic Irish President had taken Communion in a Protestant church. It never occurred to me not to. Nor did it occur to me to tell anyone of my intention to do so. I never planned to create controversy. I simply intended a gesture of respect for the offered Eucharistic hospitality. The cathedral was not notified in advance, protocol was not notified in advance. I had not discussed it with anyone, not even Martin and the children. There was no need. I had been taking Communion in Protestant churches for years, and it was entirely a matter for them to do as they chose. They too chose to take Communion, showing the respect for Anglican Eucharistic tradition they had been raised to have.

However, the taking of Communion in Christ Church drove certain Catholics and even the odd Protestant cleric to historic levels of apoplexy, which were revealing of the rigidities that inhibited the free flow of the great commandment to love one another. The spokesperson for the Catholic Bishops Conference issued a statement saying my action 'took everyone by surprise' and that they 'hoped the issue would not arise again'. Father Denis Faul pronounced that I had breached the Catholic Church's code of canon law. There were many other more soothing, most supportive voices. But Denis Faul's angry factionalism had once again done us all a favour, as it had done during the discussions of the working party on sectarianism. He had lifted the lid on the thinking that lurked under the surface of an all too easily assumed ecumenical mask. The truth genie was out of the bottle and would have to be dealt with.

A week and a half after my visit to Christ Church, Archbishop Connell lit the touchpaper when he pronounced that for a Catholic, 'partaking of the Eucharist in a Protestant church is a sham'. The intended insult to the Protestant churches was unmistakable. It was almost three weeks before Archbishop Connell got around to offering an apology, by which time a tribe of well-known Catholics, led by the US Ambassador (and my new next-door neighbour in the Phoenix Park) Jean Kennedy Smith, had taken Communion in Protestant churches.

Shortly before his elevation to cardinal in 2001, Archbishop Connell reignited the controversy in a published interview, when he criticised the Church of Ireland for offering its Eucharist to Catholics and remarked that Archbishop Walton Empey 'did not have much theological competence' and would not be regarded as one of his church's 'high fliers'. When I read it I didn't know whether to laugh or cry, so I phoned Archbishop Empey to offer my support. Even he, with his great soft heart, admitted to being hurt by Connell's words.

I told him a story that was not about Connell, but that, for me, said all that needed to be said about that condescending metaphysician and inept pastor. The story came from my father. Years earlier, he had been attending Mass in County Donegal. On exiting the chapel he had noticed some elderly women gathered around what looked like a recently dug grave, close to the church door. A curious and sociable cratur – or as my mother might have said, 'nosy as get out' – he ambled over to see what the attraction was. The headstone belonged to a former parish priest, and its lengthy inscription told of a man who had many degrees and had been a noted university scholar. As a biography, it could have been written of Desmond Connell. My father commented to the women that they were fortunate to have had such an erudite parish priest. The oldest lady fixed him with a distinctly severe stare and replied, 'Actually, sir, a far stupider one would have done us!' There then ensured a catalogue of complaints about long, turgid Sunday homilies that induced comatose stupefaction from one end of the church to the other. That too could have been written of Connell, for I had had the recent benefit of hearing orations delivered by both archbishops, and to say Walton Empey won hands down would be an understatement. Walton was discreet enough not to comment and we left it at that.

For all that Archbishop Connell and his supporters raged that he was the victim of a biased press (which had, in fact, accurately reported his remarks on both occasions), he was in the end the victim of his own narrow clerical formation and rather dull personality. These had armed and primed him with an autonomic prickly defensiveness of the Catholic Church, which he always saw as in need of his heroic protection. It sometimes got in the way of first championing Christ. Before long, he would be publicly exposed as the author of a carefully constructed web of deceit and cover-up regarding clerical child sex abuse. The loss of standing would haunt him to the grave.

\*

On 10 April 1998, after years of failed attempts at a negotiated settlement in Northern Ireland, politicians agreed a
historic settlement that became known as the Good Friday
Agreement. It was achieved with the relentless ingenious
help of President Clinton's special envoy, George Mitchell,
and the Westminster and Dublin governments, especially
Prime Minister Tony Blair and An Taoiseach Bertie Ahern.

Another fortuitous element was the presence of Mo Mowlam as Secretary of State. Her colossal personality disarmed
Northern Ireland's carefully spring-loaded sexist and sectarian vanities with humour and gentle mockery; and when all
else failed, she would throw off her wig and her shoes and
put her feet up on the discussion table. Something about the
fact that she was living with terminal cancer throughout her
tenure of office gave her unique permission to pierce the pre-
tensions of Northern Ireland's armoured bunkers. She and I
had become friends when she was the Labour spokesperson
on Northern Ireland from the latter end of 1994. Her
appointment as Secretary of State had filled me with anticipation, for I could see we were in something of a 'kairos'
moment, a moment filled with special opportunity thanks to
the meld of these intriguing personalities and the state of
things more generally.

I had developed a friendship with Cherie Blair while we
were working together on a joint project in London, and I
was impressed by the sincerity, empathy and brainpower she
and her husband both brought to bear on the 'Irish question'. They understood it in a way it had not been understood
for generations in Britain. In Dublin, Bertie Ahern and his
government were quick to capitalise on this convergence of
promising omens, knowing that things never stay the same.

The agreement involved serious levels of compromise

from all sides: unionists led by my former lecturer and university colleague David Trimble, nationalists led by John Hume, and republicans led by Gerry Adams. Loyalists and the DUP, led by Ian Paisley, stayed outside the process for several more years. Thanks to those willing to compromise for the sake of a just peace, Northern Ireland would have a customised system of power-sharing government between nationalists/republicans and unionists/loyalists. Governance would be underpinned by parity of esteem. The Republic's constitution would be amended to remove its territorial claim to Northern Ireland, which would remain part of the United Kingdom for as long as that was the will of its people; their desires would be tested by referendum if and when the Secretary of State was of the opinion that 'a majority of those voting would express a wish that Northern Ireland should cease to be a part of the United Kingdom and form part of a united Ireland'.

In May, twin referenda on both sides of the border revealed overwhelming support for the agreement. It was a day of great celebration and optimism, for now we knew that most people, regardless of faith or politics, shared the same desire for peace, the same willingness to compromise to achieve it, the same acceptance of the equality of the 'other'.

Not for nothing was it called a peace *process*, for ahead lay many more years of negotiation, breakdowns, fresh starts, ruptures and untold frustrations. Yet somehow the solidarity of that May referendum day held strong, no matter what harrowing grief it faced in the years ahead. And there were days of unmitigated grief yet to come.

During the campaign I had promised that, if elected, I would commemorate the Twelfth of July each year. The anniversary of William III's victory at the Boyne remained politically potent, and sometimes destabilising. In the summer of 1996, a dispute over the Orange parade at Drumcree in Portadown, which traditionally took place on the Sunday before the Twelfth, had provoked a wave of violence across the North and some of the ugliest sectarian scenes of the Troubles.

The then Secretary of State, Sir Patrick Mayhew, had announced the establishment of a commission to advise on future arrangements for parades and marches, which was to report before the end of the year. The three men courageous enough to take on that thankless task were Dr Peter North, a lawyer and vice chancellor of Oxford University; Dr John Dunlop, a former Presbyterian moderator; and Father Oliver Crilly, a Catholic priest and social justice activist. Over a period of three months, they received written and oral submissions from a wide range of interested parties, among them the Catholic Church. I was a member of the Catholic delegation along with Cardinal Cahal Daly, his co-adjutor Archbishop Sean Brady, Monsignor Denis Faul, and Martin O'Brien, a lawyer. A huge amount of work and discussion went into preparing a clear document for presentation in an oral session to the commission. Our firm view was that the entire issue of granting or denying permissions for parades had to be taken out of the hands of the police, since they were also the body charged with enforcement. We argued for the creation of an independent parades body and were gratified when the commission took that view in its final report. The Independent Parades Commission was born, but its future would be far from tranquil.

Against that backdrop, and the whole history of sectarian division symbolised by the Battle of the Boyne, the Twelfth of July events at the Áras would be the first official commemoration of that day anywhere on the island North or

South. In early 1998 we brought members of the Orange Order to the Áras and explained our plans for a shared commemoration between the descendants of the Williamites and the Jacobites. It would embrace the winners and losers of the Battle of the Boyne. The Orange Order supported the concept, but I could tell they were doubtful it would ever happen. There was ongoing violence, despite the peace process, and they were worried that at the first sign of trouble the event would be cancelled.

I made a promise then that it would go ahead no matter what – a promise that was tested to its limit when, on the night before the first Áras Twelfth, loyalists murdered the brothers Richard, Mark and Jason Quinn, aged ten, nine and eight respectively, living in the mainly Protestant town of Ballymoney with their Catholic mother and her Protestant partner. A torrent of condemnation followed from all sides, though Ian Paisley couldn't resist the urge to minimise the event, observing that worse atrocities had been committed by the IRA. David Trimble had been very much involved in the Drumcree stand-off, which was still ongoing even after his statesmanship had helped get the Good Friday Agreement over the line. Now he exhibited both deep empathy and courageous leadership, saying to the Orangemen protesting at Drumcree that 'The only way the Portadown brethren can clearly distance themselves from these murders and show to the world that they repudiate them is now to leave the hill at Drumcree parish church.' In other words, he who had been among the most prominent leaders of that harrowing protest believed its day was over and a new day had to begin.

Having liaised with those comforting the Quinn family, I decided that the event would go ahead in memory of the boys and in pursuit of a new way of Catholic neighbour engaging with Protestant neighbour, so that no child would suffer again as they had done. The atmosphere at the Áras on 12 July 1998 was tortured, but the fact that it had taken place at all and in such circumstances sent the message that we were embarked upon a solemn and acutely necessary undertaking. A softness and even greatness of heart revealed itself in the emotion engendered when I named the Quinn children, Richard, Mark and Jason, from the stage around which the guests were gathered. Whimpers became sobs and then uncontrollable tears. The children of Williamite and Jacobite cried sorely, together.

From the beginning, we described our annual Twelfth of July event as a commemoration of the events of 1690 at the Battle of the Boyne, which had given us the narrative of the winning Williamites and losing Jacobites. Their descendants had long struggled with the divisive legacy of that battle. I hoped that by commemorating the event in the company of both sets of descendants, through their music, dance, poetry and stories, we might set a new agenda conducive to mutual respect. Musicians played music from both traditions, explaining how very often the tunes were the same but played in a different style or sung with different words. Irish and Scottish dancers danced together. Irish and British army bands played together. Williamite and Jacobite poems were read. Lambeg drums thrummed around the Áras grounds and joined with bodhrans. Flutes tootled Orange tunes and segued into Irish traditional tunes. The mood lightened year on year as people grew more comfortable with and accepting of the concept. Williamite and Jacobite could meet, commemorate, sing, dance and laugh together without sectarianism raising its ugly head.

Over the fourteen years of my presidency, the significance

of our annual Twelfth event revealed itself – especially in the North. In 2000, some local councillors from Paisley's party came to the event unobtrusively and brought good wishes from 'the Big Man'. I reciprocated, telling them to tell him I hoped he did not mind that I had asked the Poor Clares in Ennis to pray for him. The following year, back came the councillors with the message that he was delighted with the prayers and to keep them going. The subject of prayer would be a recurring theme in conversations we later had with the Reverend Dr Paisley and especially with his sincere and pleasant wife Eileen, who never met us without giving us the gift of little prayer books she had compiled herself.

In August 1998, Martin and I and our children were on holiday in my father's old cottage in north County Roscommon. The place was so tiny that we spent most days outdoors rambling the countryside. On the afternoon of Saturday 15 August, we were walking on an oak-lined road said to have been walked by Cromwell's troops when I was given the horrific news that a dissident republican paramilitary group had bombed the town of Omagh. Twenty-nine people were dead, among them adults and children, Catholics and Protestants, Irish and English and Spanish, locals and tourists, children on a cross-border trip from Donegal, and a young mother pregnant with twins. Over two hundred people suffered terrible injuries. It was the worst loss of life in any of the miserable episodes of violence deliberately inflicted on the innocent during the Troubles.

I knew immediately that I had to go to Omagh, to hug and hold, to cry and comfort, to ask those who knew the perpetrators to give them up and to insist we preserve the solidarity of the Good Friday Agreement in the face of this atrocity. There was consternation in the Department of Foreign Affairs and An Garda Síochána: it was dangerous, the time was not right, it could be interpreted incorrectly . . . I knew Omagh well. I had set up an outreach centre in the town for Queen's University just a couple of years earlier and had got to know many of its civic leaders. One of them was John McKinney, Chief Executive of Omagh District Council. I phoned him and told him I wanted to go to Omagh immediately but was being told I could not. What did he think? He could barely speak, but he managed to whisper: 'In the name of God. We need you.'

Next morning, I went. The Ulster Unionist vice chairman of Omagh District Council was Allan Rainey, whom I had met on university business. He was leading the council's response to the bombing. It was a horrendous task, but he was dealing with it with the deepest wells of compassion. There were those with notable expertise on Northern security and politics who predicted Allan would have difficulty with my arrival. They could not have been more out of touch, more wrong. As I approached him among the traumatised, the bereaved, the numb, the catatonic, that man of compendious decency opened his arms, wrapped them around me and began to cry. We sobbed together and held one another tight like the bereft children of the one God that we were.

Something similar occurred a few days later in Buncrana, at the funeral of three little boys who had been on a day trip to Omagh with some Spanish exchange students when they were murdered. One of them, Sean McLoughlin, had visited Áras an Uachtaráin a short time earlier on another school trip. He and his class had left a poem for me about building bridges. It was called 'The Bridge' and it was addressed to those who opposed the peace.

Orange and green – it doesn't
matter
United now
Don't shatter our dream
Scatter the seeds of peace over
our land
So we can travel
Hand in hand across the
bridge of Hope.

I sat close to David Trimble during the funeral Mass. We hugged each other, heartbroken, at its start. He was then in the throes of pulling together the necessary political good-will to commence power-sharing governance for Northern Ireland. The pressures on him were colossal. Only later did we realise just how colossal, when the Orange Order moved to censure him and Ulster Unionist Party chairman Denis Rogan, both members of the Order, for breaching one of its rules in attending the Catholic funerals of the Omagh victims: 'You should not countenance by your presence or otherwise any act or ceremony of Popish worship.' Jesus wept! Denis Rogan hit that old protruding past-its-sell-by-date nail firmly on its head with his simple response: 'In a time of great suffering for the entire community, as chairman of the Ulster Unionist Party and in a personal capacity I believed then, and still do now, that it was the right and Christian thing to do.' David Trimble evidently was of the same mind.

Living in a Protestant community in the North, I had learned how deeply Protestants revered the sacrifice of those who fought in the Great War, especially the 36th Ulster Division, whose service at the Battle of the Somme was the stuff of proud remembrance. Yet that was not the full story of Ireland's considerable contribution to the Great War. A quarter of a million Irish men, from all over the island and both sides of the religious divide, had volunteered and served in British uniform, and almost fifty thousand had died. The majority of the dead were Catholics, among whom were many Irish nationalists. In Northern Ireland it was the sacrifices of the Protestant Ulstermen who had served in the 36th Ulster Division that were commemorated, while in the South the dominant heroic narrative was of those who fought for Irish freedom from British control in the Easter Rising, the War of Independence and the Civil War. The sacrifice of the Irishmen who died at the Somme or Gallipoli was deliberately overlooked. Yet here was a narrative that, if told accurately, could potentially unite rather than divide.

In 1985, at the Abbey Theatre, Martin and I had attended the second night of Frank McGuinness's powerful drama about the 36th Ulster Division, *Behold the Sons of Ulster Marching Towards the Somme.* There were a lot of American tourists in the audience who seemed to miss some of its bleak humour, so that we occasionally found ourselves laughing alone; but for us and many others, that remarkable play was a light-bulb experience. A small band of stalwarts led by Fine Gael politician Paddy Harte and Glenn Barr, the former loyalist paramilitary I had illegally interviewed for *Today Tonight*, set about retrieving the memories of all who had served.

Shoeboxes came out of the attic. The forgotten were remembered with both surprise and pride. Many republicans discovered a neglected relative who had served in British uniform. Scholars such as David Fitzpatrick, Jane Leonard and my old office-mate John Horne contributed to a richer and more complex historiography. New memorials were planned across the country. Old memorials were restored.

Symbolic of the healthier relationships was the opening, on Armistice Day 1998, of the Island of Ireland Peace Park at Messines in Belgium, in honour of the thousands of Irishmen of all politics and persuasions who fought and died near there in the same uniform and for the same cause. I opened the new monument in the presence of men and women from all traditions in Ireland, North and South. Some of them were the bitterest of political opponents but were suddenly relieved to have discovered a place where they could meet and embrace and remember without rancour. In my speech I said, 'For much of the past eighty years, the very idea of such a ceremony would probably have been unthinkable. Those whom we commemorate here were doubly tragic. They fell victim to a war against oppression in Europe. Their memory too fell victim to a war for independence at home in Ireland.' Messines was to change what I called 'the landscape of our memory'. Near the entrance a plaque was mounted. It read: *As Protestants and Catholics, we apologise for the terrible deeds we have done to each other and ask forgiveness.*

I had travelled to the formal opening of the Peace Park with Her Majesty Queen Elizabeth II and the Belgian monarchs King Albert and Queen Paola. The four of us went together in a state car sitting two opposite two with Queen Elizabeth and I sitting side by side. The conversation was lively, veering from comment on the ghastliness of the experiences of those who had walked the same road to their deaths a hundred years earlier, to the significance of the poppy (which was unfamiliar to Queen Paola), to the relationship between the Scottish game of shinty and the Irish game of hurling, which King Albert's brother and predecessor King Baudouin had attempted to play on a visit to Áras an Uachtaráin years before my time there. Queen Elizabeth was very knowledgeable about both games. The Belgians asked about the progress being made in the peace process, and that led to mention of the fact that the Reverend Dr Ian Paisley along with his followers were still volubly opposing the Good Friday Agreement.

Queen Paola asked, 'Who is this man Paisley? I have never heard of him?'

Queen Elizabeth replied, 'Lucky you.'

It would be eight more years before Paisley eventually engaged with the peace process, becoming First Minister in a government with Sinn Féin. Such a partnership would have been unthinkable to most people at the time I was elected, but it had always struck me as the most likely way to break through the sectarian barricades. I hadn't yet met Paisley, but I had lived under the shadow of his bullying and among his bully boys. It was evident, at least to me, that his innate narcissism made it likely his extreme views would soften if he thought he could become Northern Ireland's Prime Minister, even if the only way of achieving that was in a power-sharing government with his old enemy. And so, eventually, it proved.

## 10

In October 1998, ten months after taking Communion in
Christ Church, I paid a visit to Boston. While there, I made
a brief courtesy call on Cardinal Bernard Law to thank him
for the financial support he had given to the voluntary agen-
cies dealing with Irish emigrants to that city. Law was a
legendary fund-raiser. Since Boston was a very Irish city and
destination of choice for many emigrants, and since Law had
some Irish ancestry, he had been notably generous particularly in support of organisations dedicated to helping the
most vulnerable.

It should have been an unremarkable visit, and for the
first part it was. Accompanied at the episcopal palace by
Minister of State Liz O'Donnell, ambassador Seán Ó hUigínn
and consul general Orla O'Hanrahan, among others, I
thanked Cardinal Law warmly for all he had done. We had a
cup of tea and were about to leave for the next engagement,
which was to be at the Kennedy Library, when Cardinal Law
asked me and our delegation to step into an adjacent room. I
imagined he wanted to show us some piece of art or ecclesial
artefact, but almost immediately his demeanour changed
and I found myself in the company of Harvard family law
professor Mary Ann Glendon, whom I knew from past academic contacts.

As Holy See delegate to the UN Conference on Women
in Beijing in 1995, Glendon had implausibly portrayed the
Catholic Church as a leading advocate globally for the full

equality of women, and had shocked the conference by insisting that the use of condoms to prevent HIV/AIDS was unacceptable. More recently, in the face of devastating allegations of abuse against Father Marcial Maciel, the founder of the Legionaries of Christ, she had said she could not 'reconcile those old stories with the man's radiant holiness' and insisted that he was to her certain knowledge a saint. She certainly knew Maciel and the Legionaries well. The latter employed Glendon's daughter in Rome; and Father Tom Williams, the best-known public face of the Legionaries, was that daughter's long-term lover and had a son with her. Williams was a moral theologian and the author of books like *Knowing Right from Wrong: A Christian Guide to Conscience*. You simply could not invent this stuff. He would later leave the priesthood and is now Rome bureau chief for the right-wing propaganda site Breitbart News. Glendon, still a professor at Harvard Law School, is now also the head of the US State Department's Commission on Unalienable Rights. Maciel remained in active ministry until 2006.

On that day in 1998, Cardinal Law explained to me that Professor Glendon was there so that I (and, presumably, those accompanying me, of whom the cardinal took almost no notice) could listen while she explained just how brilliantly the Church treated women. I told him as politely as possible that I had no intention of doing so. I had done what I came to do, which was to thank him, and now it was time to leave. Suddenly he became loud and angry, denouncing me for failing to be what my church demanded, a Catholic President for a Catholic people. I explained that I found the very idea offensive. I was a Catholic, yes, but a President for all the people of Ireland regardless of their beliefs. He chastised Minister O'Donnell for sending her children to Protestant schools. A humdinger of a row ensued, and Cardinal Law was left in no doubt that I found his views sectarian, sexist and offensive. The ambassador memorably later described it as a 'double brandy day', for diplomatic nerves were shredded as Law's neck got redder and redder and his language more and more strident. He evidently was not accustomed to anyone arguing back. Professor Glendon never uttered the makings of a syllable.

I wondered afterwards if someone among the Irish hierarchy might have had a hand in briefing or provoking Cardinal Law to behave as he did. If so, the matter could not be allowed to rest. I asked my trusted friend Monsignor Tom Fehilly, a former classmate of Archbishop Connell, to recount to him the events in Boston and tell him of my concern. Tom soon rang to say the archbishop had been visibly outraged by Law's intervention, which he saw as unhelpful and an insult to the Irish people. It was a year on from the Christ Church Communion affair, and we had met on a couple of formal occasions, so relationships were cordial if a tad untrusting on my part. At the archbishop's request, we met in Tom's church in Dun Laoghaire, and Connell's distressed insistence that he had had nothing to do with the matter was convincing and more than a little humbling. He told me the name of the priest who had briefed Cardinal Law, and fortunately I have never met the man since.

That day I left Dun Laoghaire sure in my mind that the Law affair was firmly closed. I reckoned without the extent of Connell's annoyance – which, if anything, was deeper than mine – and thanks to him the entire Irish hierarchy soon knew the story. Cardinal Daly came to see me to let me know they were so furious that they had rescinded an existing invitation to Cardinal Law to come to Ireland. That definitely closed the matter. In 2002, a month after being appointed cardinal, Desmond Connell came to the Áras. It was his birthday and Martin's, and they shared a birthday cake. We seemed to have established an *entente cordiale*. Until, that is, a year later, when Marie Collins revealed Connell's calculated duplicity in dealing with clerical sex abusers, their victims and the Catholic faithful.

In 1996, in response to the emerging clerical child sex abuse scandal, Cardinal Daly had announced, amid great self-admiring slapping of episcopal backs, the introduction of the Church's first ever national child protection guidelines. They included, as I have noted, mandatory reporting, thanks to the frantic efforts of Dominic Burke, Bishop Hegarty and myself. Yet here was a woman, abused as a child by a priest, telling the public that Connell had failed to report her accusations, as the guidelines insisted he must, and that he had explained by way of excuse that the guidelines were optional, that in fact no bishop was bound by them. In canon law he was perfectly correct, though that rather important limitation of the guidelines had never been drawn to public attention, and there was no way a member of any diocese could find out if his or her bishop intended to abide by the guidelines or not. Things grew steadily worse for Connell when it became known that he had also dissembled over and over again when he denied ever paying compensation to victims out of diocesan funds. He claimed that his denials were legitimate 'mental reservations', which allowed him, by careful use of language, to claim the truth of things he knew to be untrue. The rest of us mortals call that lying.

Cardinal Law, in Boston, had done exactly the same thing when confronted with evidence that he had committed a similar vast cover-up of clerical abuse. Mary Ann Glendon expressed outrage when the *Boston Globe* won a Pulitzer prize for revealing the damage Law had inflicted on victims, on the Church and on truth.

There was a sequel to the Cardinal Law affair when, after leaving the presidency, I went to work at Boston College for a semester as Burns Scholar. Law was long gone by then and the diocese had sold his extravagant residence to the college, which was right next door. I soon discovered that the story of my biting encounter with Law was well known in Boston. The President of Boston College, Father Bill Leahy SJ, was one of those who in 2002 had told Law in rather unclerical language to resign and go to that place reserved in Catholic teaching for very bad people who fail the test for salvation. Bill took real pleasure in ensuring my first lecture was held in the very room where Law and I had traded opposing views. 'I'm sure you remember this place,' he said as he introduced me to a cheering anti-Law audience.

I know now, but did not know then, that although I had been a voluntary adviser to the Episcopal Conference, and in particular to both Cardinal Ó Fiaich and Cardinal Daly, on many occasions and on a multiplicity of issues, the Holy See kept a file on me that noted none of my help but meticulously recorded all instances of my perceived disloyalty. A curial friend tells me it is quite a large file and goes back a long way.

I had been one of the first Irish Catholic journalists to call out the Church on the abuse scandal in the 1990s, going so far in a Catholic newspaper as to describe Cardinal Daly's handwashing reaction to the Brendan Smyth affair as reminiscent of Pontius Pilate. In the Church's in-house magazine, *Intercom*, I had highlighted the absence of any Church forum to which a victim of episcopal malfeasance could appeal for redress. It caused uproar among the bishops and played a part in ending the then editor's career.

The person who fomented most of the uproar was Ireland's leading canon lawyer, Monsignor Gerard Sheehy, whom I had met while doing pro bono Church work at a time when I was heavily pregnant. He was a vain and pompous man, and in 1994 he took me to task for an article I had written about a hypothetical situation in which a child, standing at the altar waiting to be confirmed by the local bishop, was publicly humiliated when he refused to accept the perfectly legitimate Gaelic Confirmation name she had chosen. In the article I had asked what redress was open to such a child or her parents. When the article was picked up by the *Irish Times*, Sheehy publicly upbraided me for inventing a story that he claimed simply could never have happened. I wrote to him privately to tell him the story was real, but that to protect the child concerned I had presented it as hypothetical.

In fact it had happened in my parish in Rostrevor, in my presence, on the day of my own elder daughter's Confirmation a couple of years earlier, and it had happened to her friend. The offending bishop was the Bishop of Dromore, Francis Brooks, and I had tried unsuccessfully to get him to apologise to the child and her parents, at their request. He had ruined Confirmation for the entire parish, but particularly for the children gathered around the altar. Each of them had their chosen names written on a card to be handed to the bishop. The names had been written in beautiful script by the nuns who taught in their school, and not once had anyone advised against any particular name. Each of them had been carefully chosen from the litany of saints.

The following year I had no one for Confirmation, but I turned up for the Mass determined there would be no repeat episcopal performance. The entire village was there with the same thought in mind: I had never seen the chapel so packed. I was looking around for a place to sit or stand when the popular and normally easy-going parish priest, Monsignor Arthur Bradley, made his way down to me. 'We need you on the altar,' he whispered. And so I found myself sitting beside the altar servers, looking out at the palpably tense congregation and knowing I would have to face down the bishop should he be minded to create another commotion. In fact he behaved impeccably. When it was all over, the curate and parish priest wanted to know what exactly I would have done if the previous year's mess had been repeated. The truth was that I had no plan, and it was good that we never had to find out.

There would be shocking sequels for both Brooks and Sheehy. In 2009, the Murphy Report on clerical abuse in the Archdiocese of Dublin uncovered the fact that, as a leading canon lawyer, Sheehy's advice to bishops dealing with alleged clerical paedophiles was that they should ignore both canon law and civil law. In other words, cover it up and disregard the victims. Sheehy was also highly influential in how similar scandals were dealt with in other countries, for he was one of a small coterie of top canon lawyers on whom the Holy See depended for the advice it disseminated to bishops worldwide. Sheehy, who died in 2003, was in all likelihood deeply implicated in the widespread episcopal cover-up that infected jurisdiction after jurisdiction and protected paedophile priests while creating more and more child victims. Bishop Brooks, for his own part, covered up a long history of sexual and physical abuse by Father Malachy Finegan, President of St Colman's College in Newry.

My dealings with the Church hierarchy in Ireland had also

given me some unusual insights into the at times unfathomable mindset of senior clerics. In November 1996, Archbishop Sean Brady took over from Cardinal Cahal Daly as Primate of All Ireland. It was expected that Cardinal Daly would move more or less immediately from Ara Coeli, the primate's home in Armagh, to Belfast, where a house had been prepared for him in which to live out a comfortable retirement. But Daly hung on in Ara Coeli, while Sean made do with an apartment in Armagh and no settled moving-in date. Father Denis Faul and Father Raymond Murray – put up to it, I think, by the archbishop – asked me to intervene, for by now it was a matter of much muttering that the primate had to present himself at the door of Ara Coeli and wait on the step while his post was gathered and handed out to him.

I phoned the cardinal and delicately asked why he was still in the house. He blamed his large collection of books, which was taking forever to trawl through and organise. Luckily, he was planning to give most of them to Queen's University. I offered to get immediate practical help from the university to identify the books he wanted to keep and a van to shift them to the Belfast house. He was snookered and he knew it. He admitted sadly and in emotional terms that he hated to leave. He was afraid the heart would go out of him in Belfast. Knowing his obsession with writing, I asked him to consider the peace he would have there to write the books he had never had time for.

Within a week his library had been sorted out, and shortly after that he was in his Belfast home and the new primate took up residence in Ara Coeli. I was left with an unnerving insight into the loneliness that can strike a man when vacating such a position: although Cardinal Daly had a very attentive family, and although he kept very active in Church affairs, it must have looked to him as though there was no longer any place for him to fit in comfortably. He and I kept in touch and remained the best of friends through many ups and down until his death in 2009.

After the Christ Church kerfuffle of 1997 and my run-in with Cardinal Law in 1998, I hoped that a quiet discretion would descend on relations between the President and the Catholic hierarchy as we approached the two thousandth anniversary of Christendom. Unfortunately, however, within weeks of the encounter with Law in Boston, I was scheduled to meet Pope John Paul II, a man whose courage had helped to change European history but who was less committed to bringing change to the Church.

Back in the mid 1980s, I had publicly criticised John Paul II's views on women. In the 1990s, I had criticised the Church's treatment of women as an underclass. I had to assume that the Pope would likely be briefed on those matters, as well as on the Christ Church affair and possibly on the business with Cardinal Law. Because my meeting with the Pope was in service of international diplomacy, it was important to both principals to ensure that no matter what was said in private, the public face of the encounter should look perfectly normal and agreeable. It did look normal. In reality, it was anything but.

We arrived in convoy at the Vatican through l'Arco delle Campane and into the Cortile San Damaso, where we were greeted by the Prefect of the Pontifical Household, Bishop James Harvey, a very pleasant American. The delegation formed up with me in the lead, accompanied by Bishop Harvey, the Swiss Guards and the gentlemen of the papal household. The last-named are men dressed in tails who are descendants of popes and cardinals through whose efforts their families acquired titles and vast wealth, though the latter was probably waning for many of them. We had been briefed that we would be brought to the papal chambers, and after a moment or two the Pope would arrive. Just short of the turn into the chambers, a papal gentleman came towards us and took Harvey aside. The entourage stopped. Harvey then rather anxiously informed me that, contrary to the normal protocol, the Pope was in fact ready and waiting, and had rehearsed something special. He could not be sure exactly what, but he warned me half humorously to be prepared for anything. I could see he was not entirely happy.

We entered the papal chambers and I immediately greeted the Pope, asking after his health. He smiled, but when he spoke, it became clear he was addressing Martin: 'Would you not prefer to be the President of Ireland rather than married to the President?' He laughed heartily and extended his hand in Martin's direction. Martin held back, and I took the Pope's outstretched hand myself. He realised straight away that I had not appreciated his joke, and explained, embarrassed, that he had rehearsed it for me, as he had been told I had a great sense of humour. Apologetically, he said his English was poor and that the words had not come out as he intended.

The episode lasted just seconds, amid much smiling and apparent good humour. Inside I was anything but amused, and when the Holy Father and I went into a private session with his interpreter, I told him so, explaining that I regarded the joke as sexist and improper. He was visibly mortified and apologised profusely. I accepted his apology. Then, to my surprise, he began a discussion about the role of women in the Church, including women priests. That was a subject I had not planned to raise with him, not just because his apostolic letter of May 1994, *Ordinatio Sacerdotalis*, had closed the debate and rendered discussion pointless, but also, and more to the point, because my visit to the Holy See was as President of a secular state and there were other matters for discussion, including human rights, ecumenism, and the growing concerns about clerical sex abuse.

The Pope was insistent on pursuing the debate on the status of women in the Church, however, reassuring me that the debate was not closed and could continue. He appeared very anxious to please in that regard, but since our time was limited and the fluency of discussion was not helped by the use of an interpreter, this detour truncated discussion of other subjects, some of which he was clearly not keen to pursue. I raised the question of whether the Holy See might be minded to ratify the Convention on the Elimination of All Forms of Discrimination against Women, particularly since he had done a great service to humanity by ratifying the Convention on the Rights of the Child in 1990. I told him the Holy See was seen to be reticent about ratifying other important human rights treaties and that, given the issues of human rights, justice and parity of esteem that arose with regard to peace in Northern Ireland, it would be very useful if the main church in Ireland, and the only one with permanent representative status at the United Nations, led by example.

He turned the discussion to Northern Ireland and spoke with evident fondness of his 1979 visit to Ireland, when one and a quarter million people, fully one third of the population of the country, had turned up in the Phoenix Park for his Mass. He was delighted with the progress being made on the peace process, especially the signing of the Good Friday Agreement and its overwhelming endorsement by the people on both sides of the border some months earlier. We mulled over the dreadful circumstances that had prevented him from visiting Northern Ireland in 1979, in particular the IRA's sectarian murders at Mullaghmore of Lord Mountbatten and his friends, and of eighteen British soldiers at Warrenpoint. That seemed to still rankle with him, and he spoke of it as unfinished business. I told him that even so, in his speech at Drogheda, he had memorably challenged the men and women of violence, and that I felt that had contributed to the change of heart that brought about the paramilitary ceasefires and the embrace of democratic politics. I raised the slow pace of ecumenical progress with him and said that, given the role of sectarianism in the ongoing conflict in Northern Ireland, it was essential that the major Christian churches were seen to be focused more urgently on advancing Christian unity. We ended the discussion on friendly terms. He then met the rest of the delegation, whom he blessed, giving them small gifts of medals and rosary beads.

I was due to meet Cardinal Sodano, the Cardinal Secretary of State, immediately afterwards, along with minister Michael Woods, ambassador Eamon Ó Tuaithail and Secretary General to the President Brian McCarthy. The cardinal was delayed, which gave us a chance, courtesy of his secretary, to take in the magnificent view of St Peter's Square from his well-appointed balcony. Sodano arrived eventually, explaining that the Pope had called him in after my meeting with him to brief him on the backfired joke and to ask him to reassure me that the Pope hoped that by opening the freewheeling discussion on women in the Church he had persuaded me of his good intentions. I had the distinct impression that there was a concern on the part of the Pope, and now Sodano, that I might divulge the episode to the waiting press. I had no intention of doing so. I told Sodano that I had accepted His Holiness's gracious apology and we had parted on good terms. As far as I was concerned the matter was closed before I left the Pope's study, and would not be revisited until long after I had retired from public office.

As it turned out, my second visit to Pope John Paul II in November 2003 was to be much more worrisome – and this time the offender was Sodano. The formal drill was the same. We were met by Monsignor Harvey and escorted by the papal gentlemen to the papal library, where the Pope and I talked in private. He was by then a lot more frail, and his speech was slow and laboured. He cut a tragic, suffering figure, for he was manifestly in poor health yet pushing on nonetheless. By now the scandal of Catholic clerical sexual abuse and institutional abuse of children, the scale of which was just emerging on my first visit, was well and truly in the public domain – not that you would have known it from the tongue-in-cheek speaking notes suggested for my meeting by Ireland's ambassador to the Holy See, the wry Bernard Davenport. I was, per these notes, to congratulate the Pope on the silver anniversary of his pontificate, tell him An Post had issued a set of commemorative stamps in his honour, confirm that the Papal Cross was still standing in the Phoenix Park, and say that it was a delight (which it was) to be here for the three hundred and seventy-fifth anniversary of the Pontifical Irish College in Rome. That, Bernard hoped, would get us safely through the encounter with the Pope without giving him (Bernard) high blood pressure. The Pope's ill-health made any deeper discussion impossible in any case, and the tête-à-tête lasted just a few minutes. The delegation was enthralled to meet him, for it was hard to resist the conclusion that his days were numbered, and we were privileged to have even a small part of them.

As had happened in 1999, there was to be a private meeting with Cardinal Sodano, the Secretary of State, after meeting the Pope. The protocol for the meeting specified that Martin and I would be accompanied only by Ambassador Davenport. The three-page briefing prepared by the Department of Foreign Affairs said that the subjects for discussion would be the European Union's intergovermental conference on a draft constitutional treaty, the situation in Iraq, China (where I had recently met President Hu and Premier Wen), and Northern Ireland's peace process. In the event, Ambassador Davenport did not attend. Instead the Secretary General to the Government, Dermot McCarthy, sat in on the meeting.

Sodano was accompanied by his secretary, Monsignor Joe Murphy, a young Irish priest from the diocese of Cloyne, who sat behind him and unobtrusively provided translation services. As soon as introductory pleasantries had been observed, Sodano opened the discussion, saying: 'You have been briefed by the archbishop.' It was a statement, not a question, and I had no idea what he was referring to. The evening before, Archbishop Sean Brady had dropped off the 2004 Armagh diocesan calendar to the Irish College cottage where Martin and I were staying (and that would, a decade later, become my home in Rome for two years). He too was staying at the college, and we chatted for a while about the anniversary and our memories of his time as college rector, when we first got to know him. There was nothing in that conversation that could remotely have been construed as a briefing on any subject.

I looked at Dermot McCarthy and asked if he had been briefed by an archbishop on a subject to be discussed with Sodano. He shrugged to indicate that he was as puzzled as I was. So I asked: 'Briefed about what?' The cardinal introduced a topic we were singularly unprepared for. The Holy See, he said, wanted to negotiate a concordat with Ireland. He explained that the Catholic Church in Ireland provided many services, such as education and healthcare, and as a result there were substantial assets and archives that the Holy See was within its rights to protect.

Four months earlier, the RTÉ current affairs programme *Prime Time* had broadcast a special investigative report entitled *Cardinal Secrets*, which had revealed a shocking and hitherto hidden world of victims of clerical abuse in the Archdiocese of Dublin. The abuse had been covered up by both Church and state authorities. Since the RTÉ report had caused public outrage, I reckoned that there was consternation in the Holy See. I asked Sodano if he was referring to getting legal protection from the Irish state for diocesan records and archives. He seemed pleased that I had hit the nail on the head. Yes, he said, that was precisely what he intended. I asked if he had ever heard the expression 'being on the back foot', and Monsignor Murphy was obliging enough to explain its meaning. I told him that the subject he'd raised was outside my jurisdiction to discuss, but that since he had raised it I was willing to give him some free advice, which was not to pursue the matter. The Church in Ireland was on the back foot as a result of the abuse scandals now in the public domain. It was set to get worse. If he pursued the idea of hiding relevant records from perfectly justifiable public scrutiny, he would leave the Church flat on its back with a self-administered knock-out punch.

Sodano was most unhappy with this answer and attempted to argue his point more emphatically. I would not engage, repeating that the subject matter was not appropriate for

discussion between the President of Ireland and the Holy
See. If he wished to raise it with the government, despite my
warnings, so be it; but it would not be done with or through
me. A frostiness enveloped the meeting. Sodano was unaccustomed, it seemed, to being contradicted quite so bluntly.

The affair left me dreading the evening, for Sodano and I
were to be guests of honour at a dinner at the Pontifical Irish
College hosted by its rector and one of my dearest friends,
Monsignor Liam Bergin, and I was sure the cardinal and I had
already run out of conversation. My two meetings at the Vatican had not been in the least inspirational or even pleasant.
Instead I had seen at first hand a hard, political, power-
mongering side of the Church's top management structure that
was difficult, maybe even impossible, to reconcile with the
Christ-inspired Church of the people of God. Also hard to
stomach was the cloying sycophancy of the junior clerics who
worked there when they were in the presence of archbishops
and cardinals. The prevailing atmosphere was of a camp
medieval court, full of obsequiousness, intrigue, and men like
Sodano who exercised enormous power and not always with
the noblest of intentions. If it was designed to impress, it did
not. It was depressing. Luckily, at the college's dinner table I
was relieved to see that, thanks to Liam's intuitive diplomacy,
Sodano and I were not seated side by side. Sodano was probably thinking exactly the same thing.

## 11

A year before the millennium, with all its countdowns and projects, I had the idea of celebrating my mother's clan by making a quilt that would tell the story of her parents and their eleven children and sixty grandchildren. The quilt was a particular homage to our grandmother Cassie (Rogan) McManus, for her hands were never idle. She was always sewing, knitting, mending or baking, and I, who lived closest to her, had the good fortune to be taught by her night after night so that even today I have to be sewing or knitting if I am a passenger in a car or watching television or listening to the radio.

I put the idea first to my mother, who thought the notion that everyone in the family would collaborate in making the quilt was completely bonkers unless the enterprise was to be chaired by Kofi Annan. Luckily, the next person I tried out the idea on was my cousin Ethna (McAllister) Brogan, a professional artist who made exquisite commissioned quilted panels of mind-boggling intricacy. She had a more optimistic view of the family capacity for collaboration and loved the idea. Between us and her arty sisters, Kate, Claire, Roisin and Oonagh, we came up with a plan for a quilt of ninety-nine colour-coordinated squares. Soon everyone had a pack with materials, a set of instructions and deadlines. Regular quilt parties were held to check on progress and encourage a bit of competition, which was not in the least difficult. The completed squares came back from America, Australia, South

Africa, England and closer to home. I had an awful job to find two-inch-long knitting needles for mine.

Ethna sewed the ninety-nine squares together, and under her expert hand the magnificent quilt emerged telling our family story, or part of it at least. Our cousin Kathleen McAllister Bush made a book that narrated each square, I composed a suitably maudlin poem, and we held a grand unveiling in Áras an Uachtaráin, after which the quilt went on tour around each of the families. Later, it was exhibited in various museums and became the subject of talks given by Ethna when she was President of the UK Guild of Embroiderers. Now she minds it permanently, and it occasionally emerges to cover coffins.

On the day of the quilt unveiling, my mother's cousin Father Clement McManus brought a photo taken in 1912 of our grandparents John McManus and Cassie Rogan as schoolchildren in Muninabane school in the Dromara Hills. John was then aged fourteen. Cassie was nine. All the children are staring intently into the camera, with one exception: John is looking at Cassie, as he would with admiration and love until he died in 1973. She died in 1981. On 27 February 2000, most of their clan gathered around the millennium quilt, some meeting one another for the first time.

My square is number 47. It depicts a pearl cross, to symbolise the importance of Holy Cross Church, Ardoyne, and my faith/hope in a loving God, the pearl of great price that has kept me going through life's tribulations and tests. The pearls are taken from Emma's First Communion dress. I was still sewing each one of them on by hand well into the night before she wore it. Beside the cross is the blue flag of the Irish presidency, on which is mounted a harp, and below it the tricolour of Ireland, with its white band symbolising the reconciliation (yet to be fully effected) between the orange and green traditions on the island. In awkward embroidered lettering my grandmother would have sent me back to redo, I wrote the names of my husband and children. Then there are two balls of wool in the Down colours, red and black, run through with my two-inch knitting needles. They denote the utilitarian, domestic but also artistic skills handed on to us by our mother and grandmother and the overlooked work of women in making homes, and peace, one stitch at a time.

The eight squares that follow belong to my three sisters and five brothers. My siblings have featured only in passing so far in this memoir, but they are remarkable people who have lived fascinating and diverse lives, and I'm glad of the chance to tell something of their stories.

Anyone who ever received a letter or card from my sister Nora will immediately recognise her quilt square. Her missives often had no signature, just a cartoon of a cheeky laughing pigtailed girl based on Cáit, a character from the old Irish-language textbook *Buntús Cainte*, which we used at school and at home. Nora commandeered the image and has used it as her signature since she was eleven.

I have mentioned that in 1972, when loyalist attacks in Ardoyne forced us to decamp temporarily to Dublin, Nora, aged sixteen, remained on in Belfast overseen by the O'Malleys, for whom she was working in the Lyric Theatre. We all eventually ventured back to Ardoyne, but loyalist violence encroached more and more on our lives. In late 1972, my mother and Nora went to Dublin on the train for a weekend of respite from the awful tension that prevailed in our area. They arrived in Dublin around lunchtime on 1 December, left their bags in the little hotel they were to stay in on Parnell Street, and hit the shops.

After a day shopping, they parked their purchases in the hotel: material for new dresses, wool for school cardigans, and an Arklow pottery teapot. Nora remembers walking out of the hotel onto the street – a city centre with no barricades, no soldiers, no bag searches! – and breathing the air of normality and freedom with a great sense of joy and anticipation. They were planning a ramble to Cafolla's, the family's favourite café for fish and chips. That was when, in quick succession, two car bombs exploded close by, injuring dozens and killing two young men, both fathers and employees of the state transport company CIÉ.

Nora and Mammy arrived home on Sunday more fraught than when they left. Things had not been without drama at home in their absence. On the Saturday lunchtime my father and I were discussing the spate of robberies from Catholic-owned pubs in the Falls Road area. He was concerned that the Long Bar could be next, even though he paid protection money to the local IRA. He phoned the pub and told the barman to take all the cash in the tills and the safe and use it to pay any due bills to local suppliers of goods to the pub. Later, when he went back to work, he was none too pleased when a couple of young armed gangsters arrived before closing time and demanded whatever cash he had. He handed over his familiar leather bank bag, but smiled to himself at the thought that they would be mighty disappointed at its lack of contents. Still, he was angry enough to complain to those to whom he paid protection money.

Next day, he collected Mammy and Nora from the train and navigated the menacing loyalist barricade that had been erected at the high double gate to the side of our house, which gave directly on to a quiet street in a mainly loyalist area. No pleasantries were exchanged as he negotiated with them to move a piano so that he could get the car past. We were listening to the story of the dreadful events in Dublin when I saw a group of tough-looking characters come through our front gate, a small pedestrian gate that opened on to the busy main road. I shouted to my father to hide, thinking they were loyalists coming to kill him, but he glanced out the window and recognised them as the gentlemen to whom he gave the weekly payment designed to protect his premises from being robbed or worse by the same men to whom he gave the payment. They were carrying his leather bag. Unfortunately for us, all four republican thugs standing on our doorstep were in the direct line of vision of the loyalist thugs at the barricade.

The sensible thing would have been to get rid of the republican thugs immediately; but no, I had to berate them and interrogate them and invite them into the front room to do so. Nora still thinks it was the stupidest possible thing to do, and she is right. The gentlemen handed over the bag, mumbled their apologies and said the robbers would be dealt with. That prompted the interrogation from me as to how that might be conducted, as we wanted nothing to do with paramilitary policing or extrajudicial punishment. I threw in a diatribe on punishment beatings, the sectarian nature of their campaign and the sheer idiocy of thinking anyone – much less unionists – could be bombed or intimidated into a united Ireland. I told them they were a disgrace to the lofty ideals of the Easter Proclamation, at which point Nora and my father indicated that the visitors had been in the house longer than was safe and that I should shut up and let them leave. It was only when they had gone and a kind of nervous relief descended that my father opened the bag and, to his horror, found it contained a lot more than just his few paltry pounds. He spent the rest of the evening distributing the money to those businesses that had also been robbed in the same spate and were its likely owners.

In May 1974, the Ulster Workers' Council strike sent life into a new gear of wretchedness. Disruptions to electricity supply meant no light in our house, and no hot food. I was studying by candlelight for my Bar finals. Nora was working in Dublin at the time. Mammy took the train to visit her. They went to Guineys, where they bought cheap towels; then to Clery's to buy fabrics for new dresses; then to Arnotts for wool; and lastly to my mother's favourite, the haberdashery and crockery departments in Roches Stores on Henry Street. The Arklow teapot had not survived and a new one, decorated in green, was purchased.

They headed off before shop closing time and mercifully missed what ensued. A car bomb exploded on the street outside Guineys, where they had been a short time before. Two other car bombs also exploded in Dublin's city centre. A little while later, another loyalist bomb went off in Monaghan. The eventual death toll from the bombs was thirty-three. The UDA spokesman Sammy Smyth commented, 'I am very happy about the bombings in Dublin. There is a war with the Free State and now we are laughing at them.' Smyth reportedly received a punishment beating from his colleagues for the indiscretion. To this day, allegations persist that British intelligence colluded with loyalists in the bombings. While the UVF publicly claimed responsibility for the 1974 bombings many years later, it has not done so, except privately, for the 1972 bombing.

Nora worked in Dublin for a number of years as a house

mother at the Mary Immaculate School for the Deaf run by
the Daughters of the Cross at Stillorgan, where our brother
John was a student; later she went to the United States, working as a nursing attendant in New York. Ill-health brought
her home and dogs her to this day, but our children have
great memories of mad Hallowe'en parties at her little railway cottage in Rostrevor, with its painted landing pad for
witches' broomsticks and marvellous dressing-up clothes,
for she could handle a sewing machine well until her illness
robbed her of the full use of her hands. Despite her own
poor health, she has always managed to keep a weather eye
out for our father's twice-widowed and childless sister Mary,
who lives alone in a remote Midlands area. Mary prefers her
own company and is notoriously independent, making it
less than easy for people to help her – though they still do,
putting up with her feistiness and amused by the gems of
mordant wit that often break through.

John is next, the first boy in the family. I remember lying in
bed in Mountainview Gardens, aged about five. John was in
a cot at the foot of the bed, a beautiful blonde cherub of
eighteen months. I was throwing a teddy bear to him and he
was throwing it back in fits of giggles. Mammy came in. He
had his back to her. She called him. He paid no heed. She
called again and again. He kept on playing our game. I can
hear her saying, 'Paddy, Paddy, come quick. Dear God, I
think John is deaf.'

He was. Profoundly deaf. The frustration of inhabiting that
big clan of chatterboxes with quick speech can only be imagined for a child who could not participate in all those easy
conversations, who was always out of the loop and behind the
curve, no matter how hard we tried to include him.

At three years of age, he went to a nursery school for the deaf in Jordanstown. He hated that school, and getting him onto the school bus on the Shankill Road each morning was an agony of hysterics and kicking.

My parents were persuaded that the best option for his primary schooling was in Dublin, since Northern Ireland had no school for Catholic deaf children. At six he was dispatched, amid much weeping and gnashing of teeth, to the Daughters of the Cross's School in Stillorgan. The school used an oral method; that is to say they tried to teach the deaf to lip-read and speak as if they had hearing. Sign language was not only not taught, it was forbidden. I could scream just thinking of the abject stupidity of it all. Some of the children came from all-deaf homes where the only mode of communication was sign language. Years later, the Ryan Commission on Child Abuse would be told that these children were smacked for using sign language. The children, being more creative than their teachers and in need of the widest possible range of communication skills, soon devised their own rudimentary sign language, which we still use with my brother.

John was lonely and unhappy. Among the staff were some who were kind and caring, and others who were not. When John came home at the end of each term, he was the odd child out when he ventured out to play with the children of the neighbourhood. We visited him in Dublin once a month and he lived in permanent anticipation of seeing our car pull up outside the institutional front door. He loved to go to the seafront in Bray and into a café for a plate of chips, a dish never encountered at school. Each chip was lovingly soused in tomato ketchup and savoured. But the return journey to the school was always the start of the familiar crisis, as he became more and more loudly distraught. Twice he put his foot through the passenger-side window in his distress.

When it came time to change to second-level school my parents decided not to send him to the Catholic school at Cabra in Dublin, where the rest of his Stillorgan peers were going, but to bring him home to the secular school at Jordanstown, where he had attended nursery school years before. Their decision was influenced by two unpleasant episodes in his final year at Stillorgan. He developed appendicitis, which was dismissed as flu by the school authorities, and so he developed peritonitis, which was neglected until he was at death's door. By the time my parents were informed that he was in St Michael's hospital in Dun Laoghaire and seriously ill, he had been anointed with the last rites. His life was saved there by a very determined medical team, who were just plain horrified at the state in which he was admitted to the hospital and the length of time his condition had been neglected. The vulnerability of a sick deaf child at a boarding school preyed upon my parents' minds, and swayed them in favour of the day school at home.

The small problem of religion was resolved when John made his Confirmation in Dublin later that year, in a church not far from his school. The children at the school came from all over Ireland, so their parents got suited and booted and made the trip to Dublin. The rain was torrential that day. At the door of the church, the parents were stopped and told that the archbishop, John Charles McQuaid, had decreed that no family were to be admitted to the ceremony. No explanation was offered. The parents stood, belittled and bedraggled, among them a number of deaf parents struggling to understand, until my father, seeing that the custodians of the holy door had disappeared inside and that the door was unlocked, led a charge on tiptoes that brought them inside, up the stairs and into a gallery from which they watched as their children were confirmed by a manifestly cranky Archbishop McQuaid, ever after known in our house as 'that galoot'.

So John came back home to Belfast and to the start of the Troubles. His schooldays in Jordanstown were worse than anything he had experienced in Dublin, for, as we later learned, the much-honoured Reverend Dr George Grindle, who ran the Kinghan Mission for the Deaf and who was a regular at Jordanstown School, sexually abused him, threatened him with hell and got away with it. By the time John was emotionally and psychologically able to complain to the police, he was in his fifties, and with George Grindle ill and elderly, the police felt unable to make progress with John's complaint.

John left school with poor literacy in written English but excellent communication skills in sign language. In fact, it is only in and through sign language that his erudition shines. He left Northern Ireland when still in his teens, partly as a result of the loyalist attack I wrote about earlier, and partly because of two subsequent attacks on him by British soldiers.

As he was coming home from work as an apprentice hairdresser in the city centre one Saturday, an army patrol at the entrance to our street called on him to stop. He did not hear them and continued on homewards. He was grabbed by the patrol and beaten in the stomach with the butt of a rifle. I came upon the scene a few minutes after the arrival of my mother, who left the soldiers in no doubt about her opinion of their parentage. They were taken aback to discover they had just assaulted a deaf teenager. I phoned the barracks and asked to speak to the commanding officer, who was on the scene in short order. He was sincerely apologetic and disclosed that there were nights he could not sleep with worry because of the low IQ and jitteriness of many of the men under his command.

He arranged for John to have an ID pass, which he could show to the army in future. We were reassured and did not pursue the matter any further. An army photographer came to the house and took John's photograph. Sure enough, a day or two later a special identity card arrived for him. The following Saturday, at exactly the same time and place on his way home, he spotted the army patrol and reached inside his jacket for his pass. After they had battered him senseless with their rifles, the soldiers explained to their harassed commanding officer, who was now our new best friend, that they thought he was going for a weapon, and we were lucky they had not shot him.

John was on the boat to London a week later, to deaf friends and an altogether better life. He trained as a hairdresser, and later ran his own business, until a stroke in his early thirties robbed him of the capacity to work. The stroke happened in Berlin, as he left a German television studio after doing a programme on international sign language. He was in the U-Bahn station en route to his friend's apartment when he collapsed. Four nuns who were nearby quickly got him to the nearest neurological hospital, which turned out to be among the best in Europe. I spent a lot of the next six weeks there, as he hovered between life and death. Only one arm worked. He had no speech.

The doctors and nurses were outstanding. Not once did they talk across him or leave him out of a conversation. The Berlin deaf community started to work a visiting rota. They communicated with John in sign language, then with the doctors in German, and then with me in English. I was mes-merised by their linguistic competence and stunned by their spontaneous kindness. I made a mental note to see what we could do at Queen's University to facilitate third-level educa-tion for the deaf. Project Succeed, funded by British Telecom, was born in that hospital. At a ground-breaking conference at Queen's on third-level education for the profoundly deaf, the keynote speaker, Michael Schwartz, a legal scholar in New York, profoundly deaf from birth, delivered the best lecture I have ever heard on any subject anywhere. The following year, the first profoundly-deaf-from-birth student to enter third-level education in Ireland started at a sceptical Queen's University. She left with first-class honours in English and as Student of the Year, having single-handedly helped enhance the way in which lecturers communicated with students.

Getting John back to Belfast was a complete horror story. My sister Claire and I arrived with our wheelchaired brother at the airport only to be told by the woman at check-in that he could not travel. The hospitals in Berlin and Belfast, the insur-ance company and British Airways had produced a mountain of paperwork, but someone somewhere had not joined the dots. We phoned John's doctor at the hospital we had just left and were told to bring him back immediately. Meanwhile I had relayed the sad story to the head of the airline's legal ser-vice, who was an acquaintance of a friend of a friend. I have no idea what transpired between him and the Berlin airport ground staff, but when we turned up the next day, two weary sisters and one wheelchaired brother, there she was again at the desk: the Valkyrie ground agent from hell of the day before. She was halfway through the 'I told you yesterday . . .' speech when a man appeared from a desk behind her. He had been waiting for us. He hit a button on her computer and three miles of paper stuttered out. 'Mrs McAleese,' he said, all smiles in mellifluent English, 'you are going home today and so are your brother and sister. We have rostered an Irish member of staff in the VIP hospitality suite and she will arrive any minute to look after you. My colleague here wishes now to apologise for her mistake yesterday. We are so very sorry.' The Valkyrie looked murderous, but she muttered something in German that we graciously took to be an apology. There were hand-shakes all round, and then the fantastic Siobhan arrived and we knew all was going to be well.

At Belfast airport, an ambulance was waiting on the tar-mac. A room was ready and waiting at the Royal Victoria Hospital and a foot-thick file of notes had arrived already from Berlin. John was elated to be on home territory, and all went swimmingly until the first junior doctor tipped into the room bearing the file on which it was clearly stated that the patient was deaf but could speak. He instantly addressed his questions to Claire and me. Big mistake. From the bed came our brother's voice, weak but audible. 'Excuse me. I am here. You need to talk to me!' John was definitely back!

But he would never regain full health. A quadruple bypass has allowed him to play extra time but with reduced quality of life. He lives close to my mother in Rostrevor and they look after one another. He is stoical but often frustrated by how hard his life can be. He particularly hates having to live on sickness benefits, sucked into an inflexible bureaucratic system populated too often by people who don't make the effort to communicate with him adult to adult. The new deaf campus at Cabra in Dublin has opened up great new oppor-tunities for social gatherings and entertainment, which he relishes.

*

Damien gets square number 50, with its windmill and sea-scape to depict the lovely town of Skerries, where he and his wife Karen made their home. Three birds represent his three children, and a fourth came along shortly after the quilt was made.

Damien was born with a tiny black spot on his cheek. My ever-vigilant mother asked Dr O'Rawe about it, but he seemed to think initially she was worrying about nothing. By the time he was two, she had observed that the spot seemed to be changing and mentioned it to the district health visitor, who was alarmed enough to ask Dr O'Rawe to have it checked out. It emerged that Damien had a tumour. He would spend a number of the next fifteen summers in hospital getting plastic surgery and skin grafts to rebuild the half of his face that had to be removed, finally deciding at eighteen he had had enough and was happy to live with the scars.

He was the most uncomplaining child in the history of the hospital. I can still see him in his hospital bed, aged not yet three, struggling to smile as my father called to visit him twice a day. More than once my father cried leaving him behind, having heard him say resignedly over and over again, 'Daddy come, Daddy go.'

Damien became a sports teacher and a fine musician. After a spell working in a comprehensive school in England, he came home to his wife's town of Skerries and worked for years at Oberstown, a school for boys in trouble with the law. He coached hockey locally and loved it, but years of treatment had taken a toll on his bones, and after suffering multiple leg and ankle fractures he ended up in constant pain and unable to continue coaching. He eventually had the leg fused rather than amputated, trained as a sailing coach, went back and did a master's degree, and then started work with the elderly, where he found his true vocation. Karen works in a local school and is a terrific craftswoman. She comes from a family of Skerries sailors, but Damien could find no natural sailors among their first two children and had almost given up trying when he stuck their third child in a boat one day and instantly realised that she alone had the sailing gene. They are almost empty-nesters now, for their youngest is now studying human rights law in Galway and so is only at home in holiday times. The rest have moved on. One is a doctor in Dublin. The sailor is a teacher of Irish, now travelling the world on a two-year odyssey. And the eldest, a post-doctoral scientist, lives and works in Oxford. How quickly that all happened.

Our sister Kate was the kind of adorable, sunny child people routinely stopped to stare at in her pram. I should know, as I was usually the one pushing the pram. Our neighbours the Shaws adored her from the moment she arrived and spoilt her rotten. Jack Shaw owned a furniture manufacturing business, and among the things he made on a quiet day at work was a Kate-sized fully upholstered plush armchair for her use only. If it had been a throne, she could not have lorded it over the rest of us any more.

At age seven, she was Anna Shaw's bridesmaid, kitted out in the most magnificent white dress, which the Shaws had with great delicacy and kindness chosen so that it could double as her First Communion dress. They were Plymouth Brethren, and as excited about her big day in the Holy Cross Church as she was about her big day at Anna's wedding.

As I have related, the Shaws' son John became a loyalist paramilitary, and would serve five life sentences for sectarian murders. The Shaws' marriage disintegrated and our friendship drifted, until one night in Rostrevor, when we were going over old times pondering what they had been through. Kate decided to phone Jack Shaw, and found his number in the telephone directory – itself a miracle. He was unable to speak, for the tears started and just would not stop. Some years later, I managed to find out where his wife was living and wrote to her too. What awful things sectarian violence does to good people.

Kate, like me, went from the Convent of Mercy to St Dominic's. After she was attacked by a gang of Protestant girls, she was sent on doctor's advice to a boarding school in Kilkeel. Like Damien and Patrick, who were by then at boarding school in Newry for their own safety, she was a term boarder. On Sundays our family now comprised one car with half the remaining kids going to pick her up in Kilkeel, and another picking up the boys in Newry, meeting up halfway between the two in the magical village of Rostrevor for tea. That is how we came to discover the Fairy Glen, the oak forest, the salmon leap, the valley of St Bronagh, the Mournes and Carlingford Lough, and all the serene beauty of that exceptional village that would later become our home.

Kate trained as a dental assistant and worked in New York for some years. Then she moved to London and retrained as a hospital nurse, later working in the start-up of the first NHS IVF clinic. That work eventually brought her to the Royal Victoria Hospital in Belfast and home to live in Rostrevor with her arty and musical children. She is a grandmother to two little Corkmen, Fionn and Oisín, who we all hope will line out in Croke Park one day against my half-Kerry grandsons.

*

Square number 52 has a treble clef and four musical notes to announce that this is Patrick Gerard Martin's square. Otherwise known as 'our Pat', he is the natural wit of the family. The sharp end of his banter is usually reserved for his brothers-in-law, whom he thinks are useless tools, overhyped and spoilt by their mother-in-law. His wife Maura comes in for a fair amount of stick too, but she is a Newry Cox, with ten siblings, so she has plenty of backing and gives as good as she gets.

Pat is the family entrepreneur and runs a very successful wholesale grocery business. His two gorgeous daughters have run rings around him for years, but when both ended up at university in Liverpool, it was clear he was terrified they would stay. One did, but the other returned and her father is thrilled to have her living back home and driving him mad again.

For sheer goodness you would be hard put to find a finer and funnier human being, helpful to the nth degree to everyone. He and some friends have kept an amateur folk band going off and on for the past forty years. When Martin and my father ran a pub for a few months in Miami in 1981, the band came and stayed with us, playing night after night unpaid in the Lucky Leprechaun. It was Martin's first summer as a dental student and he had three months free. I was in the throes of leaving *Today Tonight* and starting again at Trinity, but I joined him and, lacking a work visa, had a very long holiday in the sun. It was the summer of the first big move into the Florida holiday market from Ireland and the UK, and the pub catered for the many Irish tourists billeted along that stretch of beach. Fitted out with huge pictures of old Belfast and old Dublin, it was the scene of many a singsong. My father had a ball for the first few weeks, helping to get it going, and it was there that he befriended a stranger who rambled in and who turned out to be Brigadier General Basilio Lami Dozo, a member of Argentina's ruling junta at the time and head of the Argentine air force during the Malvinas war.

When Pat and his friends arrived straight from Rostrevor, they were still gauche teenagers, schoolgoers, completely flummoxed by Miami. Pat started each morning by spraying them all with holy water to stave off murderous assaults by the drug addicts and crime gangs that populated North Miami Beach. They were such obvious innocents that they came to the attention of the police in the weirdest way. A young off-duty police officer, who occasionally popped in to hear them sing, attached himself to them as their personal security officer and spent every free hour minding and shepherding them.

Pat was born with what my mother always called a lucky caul, a kind of veil around his skull, which she kept in a jar for years. If he was robbed and turned upside down he would land on his feet with his pockets full of gold. He survived that summer interlude of fun, and once in a while he and the band members from those heady days get together for a charity event and re-create their harmonies and memories.

Pat and my brother-in-law Brendan are the go-to people for my mother and John when they need anything done around the house or garden. They bicker incessantly as they work, claim credit for whatever the other does well, and shove the blame on each other for shoddy outcomes. In my mother's eyes there is no one on planet earth like her son-in-law Brendan Connolly, and both Martin and Pat agree that this state of affairs is totally unsatisfactory and unjust. They are out for Brendan.

Next up is Claire on square number 53. The mystery here is how she found time to sew it, for she only lights in the house to sleep as far as I can tell. Claire and I are like twins – just born thirteen years apart. Of the nine of us, we are the most alike in terms of looks and personality, so everything I say about her will be of course highly complimentary and may thus be seen as untrustworthy – which is a pity, since it is all true.

Today she has the same organised can-do personality she has had since childhood, when from the age of six she was the gofer for the soldiers on patrol around Ardoyne who wanted to buy things from the local shops that they were not allowed to frequent. When one regiment was leaving, they asked her to ask our dad to get them Irish flags and copies of the 1916 Proclamation. It was a strange request, but they knew from the many conversations with us in our well-sheltered garden over my mother's apple pies that we visited Dublin regularly. My father duly obliged. A couple of years later – when we were living in Andersonstown, where feeding apple pie to soldiers was perceived by certain locals as a war crime – I was stopped by an army patrol on the Falls Road as I drove home from university one dark night. It was the same regiment we had known in Ardoyne, now returned for another tour of duty. I duly handed over my driving licence, which still had the old address. The soldier looked at it and shouted to his mate. They both shone torches on it. My heart sank. I could see trouble ahead and no way out. 'How's your Claire doing, then?' one of the soldiers said. 'Tell her we still remember her.' The traffic piled up behind us as I brought them up to date on Claire's life and ours.

Claire has dealt courageously and without so much as a muted grumble for years with chronic pain and multiple back surgeries. Sitting and lying down are a crucifixion for her, but running and walking are no problem, so she keeps on the move. She has been a midwife in Daisy Hill Hospital for over thirty years and is married to Saint Brendan, the mother-in-law's favourite. Brendan, a local teacher, was one of my circle of friends. When Claire first put her eye on him in her early teens, he was inclined to swat her away like an irritating fly, since he was so much older. But when she arrived home from nursing training in Belfast with a hand-some young doctor one weekend, Brendan Connolly suddenly realised he had liked being irritated and was bereft that she had given up on him.

I was her bridesmaid when she married Brendan. On the morning of her wedding, she and I carefully transported the wedding cake to the hotel where her reception was to be held. Just outside Rostrevor, we were stopped by an army patrol. I was driving and was asked for my licence. The law says I can be asked to furnish evidence of identity, but a sol-dier has no authority to ask for a person's driving licence. At that time soldiers routinely ignored the law, and when they asked for ID most people gave them the licence anyway. But by this time it was a point of principle with me, and though the licence was sitting in view on the dash, I told the soldier I would give him my work ID instead, since he had no authority to ask for the licence. He insisted he had, and I insisted he had not.

Claire was a little stressed, as we had to get to the hotel, deliver the cake, get back home, get her hair and make-up done, get my hair and make-up done, get into our frocks and get to the church in the following three hours. Losing time at an army checkpoint had not been factored into our tight schedule. We were stopped on a narrow road and the traffic was beginning to build up behind us. I was asked to get out of the car and open the boot for a search. The not-so-nice soldier had that power, so I did as I was told.

The day before, I had cleared out my office in the Law School in Trinity College to bring my books home for the summer. The boot was crammed with criminal law texts, a barrister's wig and gown. Now the soldier looked a bit frazzled. 'You a lawyer?' he asked.

''Fraid so,' I said. I asked to speak to his commanding officer.

He muttered into a walkie-talkie and a nice commanding officer appeared in front of the now half-mile-long queue. I explained the problem. He made no argument, simply said I was correct and apologised. He instructed the soldier to ask for ID and strode off. I got back into the driver's seat and the chastened soldier duly asked through gritted teeth for some ID. I gave him my driving licence. Claire was by now the colour of the icing on her cake and barely able to speak.

Cake delivered, we returned by the road we had come and the patrol was still there, but there had been a shift of personnel and the not-so-nice soldier was now stopping traffic on our side. I wound down the window to be greeted by the familiar refrain: 'Driving licence, please!' Claire went into a faint. I took the licence from the dash and put it into the glove compartment. 'Remember me?' I enquired. 'Let's just skip the bit where I tell you that you are wrong and go straight to the bit where your commanding officer does that AGAIN and then I make a formal complaint.' We were waved on without ID or further comment, though Claire did mutter some expletives unbecoming of a bride. They were directed not at the army but at me, my choice of career, the misfortune of having me for a sister and bridesmaid and chauffeur.

Everything went smoothly after that – at least until seven of her eight siblings took to the stage at her wedding reception to give their rendition of the Eagles song 'Lying Eyes'. It was our only communal party piece, but it was not exactly suited to the occasion. My mother brought out from her arsenal of looks the almighty glare, and that ensured there was no encore; that and our profoundly deaf brother acknowledging for the first time that there were occasions on which he was almost glad to be unable to hear.

Claire and Brendan have two kids, blessed with mathematical brains that must come from the Connolly side, and to our great delight both now work in Dublin. I love to see them teaming up with our kids, just like in the old days in Rostrevor.

Claire's summer holidays for many years were spent in Belarus, working in homes for people with physical and intellectual disability. Her garage, our garage, my mum's garage and Pat's garage were all depots for the mountains of clothes, medicines, sports equipment, medical equipment, toiletries and toys she gathered by fair means and foul to load into the lorries that annually ferried a team from Daisy Hill Hospital to Belarus. After their stuff was held up and siphoned off by crooked officials at a border checkpoint one year, Claire learned the lesson and thereafter travelled with a sheaf of formal-looking documents stamped with the words 'Official Government' and dated and signed by the fictitious General Governor of Northern Ireland. The border guards were completely impressed, and the hardy Northerners were waved through thereafter like VIPs.

Her fellow volunteers on the trips tell horror stories of having everything but the clothes they stood in robbed from them by Claire on the last day, to be given to the patients.

One poor unfortunate arrived home sockless and minus his underpants. People in South Down run when they see her approach, for they know she is collecting for some great cause and there will be no escape until they and their money are parted. In the days before her back gave up, she organised morning dance lessons in the Belarus institutions, where people were routinely turned out into fields like cattle and left there all day in pyjamas that never saw a washing machine for weeks on end.

Brendan humours her. He has the dinner ready when she gets home. The garden he lavishes attention on is like the Chelsea Flower Show. He can put up shelves, take down shelves, put up pictures, take the squeak out of rusty hinges, lay tiles, paint his daughter's apartment, jump to his mother-in-law's calls, win half-marathons, read the lesson at Mass and help run the local GAA. Who is the lucky one in our house?

Claire and I used to turn up in the same outfits, bought separately and in ignorance of each other's choice. Once Brendan even came up behind me and gave me a vigorous hug, only to discover he had got the wrong sister. He was years getting over the mortification. Our Pat made sure of that. Nowadays that scenario is unlikely, for apart from the thirteen-year age difference, which now regrettably shows more and more, Claire can eat anything and still wear the same size clothes she wore as a teenager.

At an event in the state guest house at Farmleigh, a former Labour Party leader made great play of introducing me to Bobby Kennedy's daughter Kathleen Kennedy Townsend. He was mystified to see us hug warmly, old friends from the days when Claire had worked for her during her gap year.

*

After Claire came Phelim – square number 54 on the quilt, with the motif of his Air Corps wings from the days when he was a military pilot, a tooth to mark his change of career to dentistry after an accident ended his flying days, and a curl belonging to his red-haired girlfriend Helen, now his wife. They met on a plane going to London. She and her aunt were sitting beside him, and in order to engage her in conversation, since he liked the look of her, he told her it was his first flight and he was so nervous he would be grateful for the distraction of someone to talk to. Helen obliged, and they are long since married with two daughters.

Phelim was a cute kid and had the good fortune to be the baby of the family for three whole years before, to his great dismay, he was usurped by the arrival of Clement, the last of us. During those three years he was unmercifully spoilt. My parents had by then completely abandoned all efforts at disciplining the younger Leneghans and left that to the older ones. Phelim was my shadow. Wherever I went, he went too.

The mayhem we lived through affected him deeply, and turned him into a quiet, brooding child by the time my parents moved to Rostrevor and tried to establish some kind of a normal life. The living accommodation was cramped, the pub's long, noisy hours encroached into family life, money was very tight and settling in took time. One evening a customer remarked to my parents that they must be so proud of Phelim's performance in the school musical. What performance? What musical? He had not bothered to tell any of us. More than that, we had never known he could sing. Luckily there was one more performance. We decamped in large numbers to watch the Star of the Sea boys' primary school version of Franz Lehar's *Merry Widow*. There was no doubting who the star was. An eight-year-old Phelim brought the house down with his pitch-perfect rendition of the waltz 'I Love You So' and three encores.

It was hard on him and Clement when I moved to Dublin in 1975, but they came and visited often. During those early years I was taking flying lessons at Weston aerodrome, and Phelim often came with me to watch as I practised take-offs and landings under the careful supervision of the great Darby Kennedy, with his handlebar moustache and terse turn of phrase: 'That was not so much a landing as a near-controlled crash. You were crashing, but luckily I was in control.' I imagine that is where Phelim got the idea to become a pilot, though he complained so bitterly through his first few months of army training, with early mornings on parade, that I reminded him his mother had nine children and his grandmother eleven and plenty to complain about that knocked his little quibbles out of the ballpark. On the day he got his wings we were all assembled outside after the ceremony to watch while four of the newly qualified pilots performed loop-the-loops in tiny jets four feet apart. Our mother was not a happy spectator. The daring performance filled her with dread. She turned and asked where Phelim had gone. No one told her until he was back on the ground.

Some years later, by which time he was a flight instructor, I was on a silent retreat with the Jesuits at Manresa, near the seafront at Clontarf. From my window mid morning I saw a helicopter flying over Bull Island. I stopped what I was doing and said a prayer for Phelim and all pilots. That evening I walked to the garage shop next door and bought the paper. Phelim's face was on the front page. His plane had suffered engine failure and had crashed into the sea a few miles up the coast. He and the student pilot were alive and unscathed. It was a horrendous event in which he had shown great skill and courage, heading out to sea to avoid coming down over houses and schools, then helping the student to escape and swimming to shore in godawful weather.

At a routine medical his hearing was found to have deteriorated, so he was grounded. He was devastated, and though offered the job of working as a ground instructor, he could not face being around planes but not flying them. He was twenty-nine and had a degree from Queen's in aeronautical engineering. I told him to think about other career options, pointing out that Martin had changed from accountancy to dentistry at thirty. Maybe I was too specific. He is now a dentist. Probably the biggest disappointment in his life (and ours), however, was his decision to withdraw from the Down football panel because travelling north three times a week for training was just not feasible with his Air Corps workload. That year Down won the All-Ireland!

Square number 55 on the Millennium Quilt marks the end of the Leneghan litter. My mother had to sit Nora and me down when she was six months pregnant and tell us that another baby was imminent, for we had failed to notice the evidence.

In my school year of over seventy A-level students, no one else's family was increasing, multiplying and filling the earth as mine was, and among my classmates there was a bit of interest in the forthcoming birth. My mother had by then run out of girls' names, and had offered that if the child was a girl then my class in school could choose her name. She had already decided a boy child would be named Clement

Justin after not one but two priests, our Redemptorist cousin Father Clement McManus and the local Passionist Father Justin Coyne.

The day after Clement's birth, when I had delivered the news of his sex to universal disappointment, I felt I had to make up somehow for this egregious error. We were plodding our way through the New Testament and I had noted the recurrence of the word 'circumcision'. I who had four brothers, all circumcised, and a baby one about to be, asked Mother Laurentia what the word meant. The other sixty-nine young ladies sat back waiting for the fun to begin. Laurentia blanched, drew back the sleeve folds of her long pre-Vatican II habit, and indicated with actions to that effect that circumcision was a reference to a small circle inscribed on the lower arm. I am not sure how we did not all spontaneously rupture an internal organ.

My schoolmate Delia Skan and I went to the Belfast Central Library that afternoon, obtained a medical dictionary and copied out the straightforward if anatomically graphic entry for the word. In a state of feigned perplexity, I read it out in class next morning while my classmates tried to avoid collective organ failure. I enquired of our benighted teacher why there was such a large discrepancy between her description and that of the dictionary. Unfazed, at least to the naked eye, Laurentia dismissed the matter, saying doctors had peculiar names for things.

Amazingly, no one died laughing, but someone couldn't leave well enough alone, for that afternoon I was called to the headmistress's office and asked to give an account of myself. Sister Virgilius was a young head teacher from an Ardoyne family who were friends of my mother's family. She was sarky and conservative but not without humanity or humour, as I discovered that day. Halfway through my detailed narrative, which involved the truth, the whole truth and nothing but the truth, she swung around in her swivel chair so that she had her back to me. I kept on talking to the chair back. When the story ended, she turned through another ninety degrees. I was astounded to see that she had her regulation large starched white cotton handkerchief stuffed in her mouth and tears were running down her cheeks. With some difficulty she managed to let me know that if I ever, ever, ever disclosed to another soul that she had laughed at Laurentia, she would do something dire but unspecified that I would not like. That warning provoked another outbreak of hysterics, and I was shooed out of her office as she stuffed the handkerchief back in her mouth.

There was a sequel, though not a dire one. By far the best headmistress I ever had was Mother Urban, who had wisely left St Dominic's in her fifties to go off on the missions in Angola. On a trip home she did a retreat in a monastery close to where I lived with Martin and our children, and arrived unexpectedly at our door. After the traditional cup of tea and catch-up, she revealed the true purpose of her visit. She wanted to hear from the horse's mouth the story of Laurentia and circumcision. She had heard it second- and third-hand but did not want to pass up the chance to get the fullest possible account. I shooed the children out of the room and told the story. Urbie returned to her retreat house in rare form.

While my parents had not run out of male names, apparently the entire tribe had run out of available godparents, for my brother John and I were dispatched to the chapel with the newborn to have Clement christened the following Sunday. There was no party, no cake, no fuss. My mother was too ill to get out of bed and so had not been 'churched', as was required then. This practice required women to obtain a cleansing blessing of sorts after giving birth before they could attend church again. The baby was dressed in his well-worn family christening gown and a matching white bonnet and matinee coat I had knitted, and was wrapped in a white blanket my mother had crocheted. I carried him on foot to the chapel and back. The ceremony was timed for the late afternoon, when the long file of penitents attending Confession would have tailed off. We missed by a couple of weeks the introduction of the new baptismal rite following on from the Second Vatican Council, and so the last child of the family was probably the last child in Ardoyne to be baptised according to the old rite, with its exorcisms of the devil and placing of spittle on the infant's ears and nose.

If being named for two priests was intended to nudge the child towards an ecclesiastical career, it failed spectacularly, for Clement Justin left the Catholic Church in early adulthood and embraced Buddhism. What we did not know for many years, until he was almost fifty, was that our favourite baby brother, the apple of everyone's eye, had been appallingly abused for years, physically and psychologically, by Father Malachy Finegan, his school headmaster and, as it turned out, a vicious serial physical and sexual predator. Finegan may also have been a police informer. He particularly preyed on first-year boarders who cried at night because they were lonely for their mothers. He died of natural causes before he could be prosecuted for his many crimes. The local bishop, John Mc-Areavey, a canon lawyer, former colleague of Finegan's and friend to my family and especially my brothers, four of whom attended the school, acknowledged that he was aware of the accusations against Finegan and their veracity when he presided at Finegan's funeral. He later resigned, saying it had been an error of judgement to have done so. As my mother remarked, Finegan was lucky to have died a natural death considering the many young men who suffered years of mental torment as a result of his abuse, none realising until too late that they were legion. On the day my brother's story broke, he spent hours on the phone taking calls of support from his former schoolmates. Many of those conversations started with 'me too'.

Like his eldest sibling, Clement graduated in law from Queen's. He then trained as a producer with the BBC, set up a film institute in Northern Ireland, went to work for Endomol in London on the first of the reality TV shows, and taught at the National Film and Television School at Beaconsfield Studios outside London, where he met his wife Hester, then also a television producer. Having specialised in film health and safety, he set up his own consultancy business, with which he has travelled the globe, working with Disney on the *Star Wars* franchise and a litany of other big productions. He and Hester, now a primary school teacher, live in her picturesque home village just on the edge of the South Downs, with their twin teenage daughters.

My maternal-side clan is huge and has its own strange but effective communications system that makes Facebook look like two tin cans and a piece of string. We hear about each other and care about one another, though we've taken so many different paths. Granny was a stay-at-home mother. Granda drove a bread-delivery van. None of their children graduated from university, but many of their grandchildren did. They became teachers, lawyers, doctors, nurses, civil servants, secretaries, social workers, dentists, hairdressers, entrepreneurs, film producers, chefs, builders, bankers and more. None of the sixty entered religious life or became a priest. We meet up at occasional family events – a ninetieth birthday, a wedding of the next generation, a funeral. We are scattered but not severed. The bonds of family are pliant and durable. But the Troubles undoubtedly scarred us, and our grandparents' decision to live in Ardoyne set us directly in the path of a brutal history.

# 12

Martin and I, having grown up in loyalist areas and suffered considerably from sectarianism, believed that unionists of all hues, including loyalists and loyalist paramilitaries, had to be talked to, listened to, argued with, and persuaded that the country south of the border was not the badlands, but a good neighbour. There was no gateway to the hard-to-reach loyalist communities without going through the gatekeepers, which is to say the paramilitaries; but they had no unified structure or leadership, and often feuded with one another. The largest of the paramilitary groupings were the Ulster Defence Association (UDA) and the associated Ulster Freedom Fighters (UFF); there was also the Ulster Volunteer Force (UVF) and its associated Red Hand Commandos (RHC), and the Loyalist Volunteer Force (LVF), a UVF breakaway group based in mid Ulster. Some were on ceasefire and others were not, and that presented immediate difficulties.

We decided to concentrate initially on engaging with the mainstream unionist community, eventually breaking through into the loyalist communities in late 2002. A key facilitator of all of this work was Denis Moloney, who drew on his extensive network of unionist friends and acquaintances and whose work as a criminal lawyer meant he knew many of the main loyalist players personally.

In our engagements with unionists and loyalists, it was important to us that the experience of Southern hospitality would be of the highest order. It would be a sign of respect.

Many among those being invited from the North would be people who would be shocked to be asked, people who expected to be always overlooked, who never thought they or their concerns mattered to anyone south of the border. Loyalists who had been accustomed to entering in the dark through back doors – especially in the days when Paisley used them privately but denied them publicly – were quick to tell us how much they appreciated being welcomed at the front door of the Áras. Inside they met nationalists and republicans from all over Ireland.

During the dreadful weeks in 2001–2 when the children of Holy Cross Girls' Primary School in Ardoyne were harassed on their way to school by loyalist neighbours, we invited the girls and their parents for a day of respite. Father Aidan Troy CP, who helped them cope every day of their ordeal, reminded them that their tormentors were victims of their upbringing and formation. Later, many of the men and women who had harassed the Holy Cross girls came to the Áras too, and we sat around lunch tables where they mixed with people from all walks of life in the South and talked frankly about the sheer stupidity of it all and how quickly things run out of control when neighbours live in ignorance of each other.

Informal introductions of strangers over breakfast or lunch at the Áras were sometimes followed by a day in each other's company. We organised visits by cross-border groups to McKee Barracks, the National Museums, the National Stud, the Japanese Gardens, Shelbourne Park greyhound stadium, Croke Park, the Curragh racecourse, the government guest house at Farmleigh, the US ambassador's residence, the RDS, the Dáil and the Seanad, the Bank of Ireland's House of Lords, An Bord Bia and European Union institutions in Brussels.

Invitations usually went out in the form of a personal phone call from Martin. Having come once, people were asked to come again and to bring their friends, particularly those friends who might hitherto have had great difficulty with the prospect of visiting the Republic. The friendship network grew, and in the North we made contacts across every sector and stratum. Some people were plainly nervous – sometimes as much about visiting a grand house as about its occupant. On one occasion, my future sister-in-law brought her staunch unionist parents to a family pre-Christmas gathering at the Áras. While her mother happily came inside, her father stayed outside in the car for a while before rather sheepishly coming in; eventually he joined our annual rendition of 'The Twelve Days of Christmas'.

My brother's mixed marriage took place in the Methodist church in our overwhelmingly Catholic home village of Rostrevor, where community relations were relaxed and friendly, and not, as might have been expected, in the bride's overwhelmingly Protestant home town of Ballyclare. Rostrevor's small Methodist community worked round the clock to prepare the pretty little church and were thrilled, for it was their first wedding in quite a while.

In September 2002, Martin had his first meeting with Andy Tyrie, former supreme commander of the UDA, the loyalist paramilitary organisation that had masterminded the 1974 Ulster Workers' Strike, thus ending the hope that the Sunningdale Agreement could bring about a shared government and a reconciled community. Tyrie had backed Bill Craig's 1972 call to 'liquidate the enemy', and my family had been among those at the receiving end of the reign of terror conducted under his leadership. It was members of the UDA who had attacked our Ardoyne home, first with bricks and subsequently with machine guns.

By the time Martin visited Tyrie's east Belfast home, the latter had forsworn paramilitarism and embraced politics. His idea for an independent Northern Ireland had not gained much traction, but it was evidence of fresh thinking. He was interested in the Building Bridges project, and he carried a lot of weight within the loyalist community. He immediately set about working closely with Martin, organising groups from loyalist working-class estates to visit the Áras. There was no agenda at these gatherings beyond just chatting and listening to each other's stories.

On 6 December 2002, Denis Moloney rang Martin from Belfast. He was in the company of Jackie McDonald, the UDA's brigadier for south Belfast. Denis put Jackie on the phone. Jackie agreed to organise a group from his area and bring them to the Áras a few weeks later. Then he changed his mind, saying the time was not right.

It certainly was, in many respects, a very fraught time. The Northern Ireland Executive had recently been suspended (and would remain so until 2007). The DUP remained hostile to the Good Friday Agreement. The British and Irish governments were using every possible form of pressure to move the paralysed peace process forward, but things were so bad that Tony Blair had felt compelled to postpone elections in Northern Ireland to the end of May 2003. The UDA was not on ceasefire, and as a consequence it was politically ostracised. The UVF, by contrast, had been on ceasefire for three years and had developed a political presence through the work of David Ervine and Billy Hutchinson in the Progressive Unionist Party (PUP). They were supporters of the Good Friday Agreement and were well integrated into the political discourse of the peace process. We believed that someone had to talk to the UDA to try and persuade them that the time for politics had come, the time for paramilitarism was over, and the future lay in getting behind the Good Friday Agreement. As the work began to gain traction, Martin kept key senior politicians, civil servants and police on both sides of the border fully briefed. He thus became an important conduit between people who had never met one another.

On 3 February 2003, not long after that initial conversation with Jackie McDonald, Martin had no fewer than six engagements in loyalist areas of Belfast. Tensions were running high, for within the UDA internecine fighting had broken out, with deadly consequences. Before Christmas, Martin had organised for the children from Mersey Street Primary School, located in a loyalist stronghold in east Belfast, to visit the Áras and perform their nativity play. Prior consultation with parents had been very positive, but nonetheless it was a giant leap for the school authorities to give their blessing. The children took easily and happily to the Áras, dressed up as it was magnificently for Christmas. Now, Martin's first call was to Mersey Street Primary School to explore the possibility of a visit from me, which later happened.

His second call that day was to the East Belfast Mission, a community regeneration initiative of the local Methodist church in the area where Martin had grown up. It had once been a vibrant working-class district, but the shipyard and old smokestack industries on which it relied for the employment of thousands of mainly Protestant workers had either closed or shrunk drastically. Now it was experiencing a level of disaffection that often played out in sectarianism, and the interface with the local Catholic community was frequently violent. The regeneration project for the area was known as Skainos; it needed help and champions. Martin had introduced its originators to the businessman Michael Smurfit, as a result of which the Smurfit Foundation gave €50,000. Today, the Skainos Centre is a hive of community-building activity on a level that would have been hard to foresee on that February day. Among its most extraordinary developments is the Turas Irish-language project, designed, according to its outstanding leader Linda Irvine, to 'connect people from Protestant communities to their own history with the Irish language'. Two hundred loyalists take weekly classes there.

On that day in February 2003, the leaders of the East Belfast Mission, Reverend Gary Mason and Glen Jordan, agreed to invite me to come and see the mission's work, which I duly did some time later, getting a very warm welcome and a good turnout from that audience of loyalists, including senior paramilitary leaders. There were no protests, and no massive police presence was necessary. I came and went, greeted and treated respectfully.

Martin's third engagement that day was a discussion over lunch with six community workers in loyalist areas, including Andy Tyrie and Sammy Douglas, who later became a DUP member of the Northern Ireland Assembly. They complained about the difficulty of getting funding to create serious interface initiatives that would reduce sectarianism. Martin told them that if they could come up with a credible cross-interface project, he would do his best to help them source funding. Over years of contact, Sammy Douglas became a solid friend. We discovered he had a collection of fridge magnets, and for the fun of it I brought him back one of Pope John Paul II and one of the Vatican from our 2003 visit to Rome. He rang us one Christmas to say he was just coming out of midnight Mass in Martin's old Catholic parish church, St Matthew's, which had been the scene of countless loyalist sectarian attacks.

Engagement four was at the manse of the Hollywood Second Presbyterian Church, where Martin met with the Reverend Norman Harrison and members of the select vestry. He invited them to visit the Áras, and two weeks later they came to lunch. From there, he went across to north Belfast and to the home of staunch Orangewoman Georgie Fannon, executive member of the Shankill Women's Association and a prominent protester at the Drumcree stand-off. Georgie had been part of a group that had come to the Áras, and we were both very taken with her personality and enthusiasm. She had also brought me a Veda malt loaf. If you have never lived in Belfast, you cannot know the ineffable joy the sight of that bread brought after years of living without it in Dublin. Roughly sliced and slathered in butter (not any substitute stuff), it is indescribably scrumptious and one of Northern Ireland's best-kept secrets. Also amazing toasted – and buttered as above. Georgie lived where I used to live, and she was interested to see what kind of place I now called home – hence her first visit of what would be several to the Áras. She attended my second inauguration in Dublin Castle in 2004, and said before she died that it was the best day of her life.

Martin's sixth engagement that day was at Taughmonagh Social Club, the headquarters of the south Belfast brigade of the UDA. The ostensible purpose of the visit was to meet representatives of Dunmurry Young Men's Football Club and invite them to bring a group to the Áras. The place was forbidding, with graphic UDA murals and slogans not designed to make an Irish Catholic nationalist at ease. Martin was, to his surprise, greeted there by Jackie McDonald. It was their first meeting of many. They chatted for an hour about the kind of legacy they wanted to leave their children and how they could work together to deliver it. They agreed to keep in touch via Denis. As Martin drove out of the car park, the police officer who accompanied him said: 'The last time I was in that car park a sniper was shooting at me from the roof of the club, and the last time I met Jackie McDonald was in a raid on his home.'

The UDA's violent internal feud had resulted in the deaths of two of Jackie's colleagues a few days previously. Leadership of the organisation was bitterly contested between competing factions concerned about the politics of a ceasefire and about control of their involvement in drugs and criminal activity. Martin was impressed that Jackie was willing to meet him in those frenzied circumstances, when Jackie himself was very much a potential target; and Jackie was impressed that Martin would talk to him in the absence of a ceasefire. Both were walking on thin ice, but to a vital purpose. Before he left, Martin was sure that Jackie was convinced that paramilitarism was a zero-sum game and that the future lay in consensus-based politics.

He was right. On 22 February 2003, the UDA and UFF announced a one-year ceasefire. It gave our outreach a timely impetus.

On 8 April, Martin was back in Belfast. Jackie McDonald had a problem. He was due to visit Texas with a group from Glasgow Rangers supporters' club, but given his past, he could not get a visa. Martin pointed out to him that travel on an Irish passport would not require a visa, and Jackie agreed to apply for one. Martin got him the forms. Jackie posted them to the Áras so that Martin could make sure they were filled in properly, and they were duly posted from a prime Dublin address Jackie was yet to visit.

Second item on the agenda was funding for Dunmurry Young Men's Football Club's development plan, which included an all-weather pitch with floodlights. Keeping young men away from sectarian trouble was an imperative to which politicians and the better-known philanthropical funders paid disappointingly little attention. Martin agreed that if they came up with a viable costed plan, he would try to put them in touch with corporate or individual funders to whom they could apply for help. The Manchester-based Mayo businessman Joe Kennedy immediately stepped up with generous support which made a huge difference.

The second meeting that day was a lunch with two members of the DUP: Willie Hay, a member of the suspended Northern Ireland Assembly, and Joe Millar, the former mayor of Derry. They let it be known that, despite the hostile public position of the party's leaders, the DUP were willing to move towards political accommodation with Sinn Féin when the time was right.

On 28 April, the Dunmurry Football Club group arrived at the Áras with Jackie McDonald. As we sat down in the state reception room for lunch, Jackie stood up and presented me with a Rangers scarf, an Ulster flag, a bouquet of flowers and a bottle of champagne. It was evident that everyone from the club had invested in a new shirt and tie for the occasion. If ever an event witnessed powerfully to the deep human desire for reconciliation and capacity for simple acceptance of difference, that lunch was it. Martin took the group on a tour of Farmleigh, and over afternoon tea the club's costed plan was handed over for onward evaluation by a potential funder. Martin, for his part, had the unique privilege of handing Jackie his newly minted Irish passport.

On 21 May, at the Stormont Hotel, Martin met the entire inner council of the UDA and the Ulster Political Research Group (UPRG), the UDA's advisory body on politics. These were the hardest of hard men, and despite being on ceasefire they were believed to have continuing involvement in sectarian violence as well as ancillary criminal activities such as extortion. The atmosphere was tense, and apart from Jackie, not one of the loyalists present, including the brigadiers, made eye contact with Martin. Denis Moloney, acting as MC, asked Martin to speak. In a diary entry he composed later, Martin wrote: 'I reckoned I had about 10 minutes to connect or end up with a disastrous meeting.' He began by speaking about his own background as a Catholic living in a loyalist part of Belfast, and about the family's experience of having to flee their home. He spoke as well of my own family's similar experiences. Then, as he noted in his diary,

> I talked about the future of this island and how we all had a responsibility to make it a better place for the next generation. I said that it would be impossible for me to create that better place on my own for my children, and neither could they on their own for their children. But that maybe together we could shape it for all our children. They agreed with that. I also said that now that Mary and I were living in Dublin, she as President, there was nothing that said we had to get involved in anything to do with the future of Northern Ireland. However, we both felt a great loyalty to the place of our birth and would be prepared to do anything that we could to promote permanent peace and reconciliation.

Martin's words seemed to soften the mood, and in the dicussions that followed, a plan was agreed for future meetings. The first of these was just five days later at the K Club in County Kildare, where Martin played golf with a group of ten that included senior loyalists, Jackie among them, and business people from the South. It was a hospitality day, but unknown to Jackie, the business group had evaluated the Dunmurry Football Club's plan, and they presented a cheque for the full amount of the refurbishment. Jackie was in tears. He had hoped for some help, but the generosity completely overwhelmed him. He spoke about how much it meant to the club and how much it would mean to the future of the youngsters who used it. They had never experienced anything like the kindness of that gesture.

A month later, in the Bank of Ireland's offices in the former Irish House of Lords in College Green in Dublin, the bank's governor, Laurence Crowley, hosted a meeting of senior business people, civil servants and media analysts from the South, and representatives of the UDA/UPRG. It was the first ever serious engagement between a who's who of the Dublin establishment and the leadership of extreme paramilitary loyalism, and it was not without drama. Getting the loyalists to Dublin proved more complicated than originally expected. Martin had arranged for a bus to pick them up, but they were worried that a bomb could take out the entire UDA leadership, so a convoy of people carriers was organised instead. All were thoroughly examined before leaving to ensure there were no bombs or listening devices. Despite the checks, the loyalists were so fearful of surveillance that they travelled in complete silence. One of them remarked at the impressive front door of the Bank of Ireland, 'The last time I was in a bank, I was there to rob it and was wearing a bala-clava.' He did not elaborate further.

The UPRG wished to develop as a political party, and we wanted to help them. As we had seen with Sinn Féin, and to a degree with the Progressive Unionist Party, it was easier to keep paramilitaries away from violence if they felt they had a voice in constitutional politics. Noel Whelan, a busy barris-ter and political analyst, volunteered to advise the UPRG on how to conduct local election campaigns. I was very con-scious that Noel, unlike others, was self-employed, and the amount of unpaid time and effort he devoted to the work was considerable, but he was passionate and determined and above all impressively effective. The loyalists had never met anyone quite like him, with his grasp of politics, his enor-mous personality and energy, and his generous nature. As far as he was concerned, this was for our island's future, and he was delighted to be involved. His efforts undoubtedly helped loyalism absorb and embrace the language that brought them along the road to permanent ceasefire and democratic politics.

A number of key Southern civil servants were now involved in the project, including Tim O'Connor, the joint Secretary of the North–South Ministerial Council; Maura Grant of the Department of Education; and Tim Dalton, Secretary General of the Department of Justice. To keep high-level offi-cials on both sides of the border fully in the information loop, there was a lunch meeting at the Áras in November 2003. We were sensitive to the possibility that our outreach could be seen as unwelcome interference. We offered to step back and hand over all our contacts to the civil servants if they felt that anything we were doing was unhelpful. The reaction was unanimous. On no account was the work to stop. It had proved its worth and its importance. It had to continue. With that reassurance, Martin brought a delegation of Southern politicians – among them minister Noel Dempsey, Fine Gael leader Enda Kenny, and Liz McManus TD – to meet the UDA in Belfast and tour loyalist areas.

By that point, the impending expiry of the UDA's twelve-month ceasefire was exercising minds greatly. The leadership was worried that the Ulster Political Research Group, which now represented them in public, was under intense media scrutiny as a result of the criminal activities of the UDA. Martin had noticed in some of their meetings that, confronted by people with university degrees and professional qualifications, they became prickly and defensive, and sometimes missed important opportunities for useful dialogue by breaking off talks too soon.

The UDA/UPRG conducted a review of the one-year ceasefire in the lead-up to 21 February 2004, when it was due to expire. Tommy Kirkham, a senior member of the UPRG and a member of Newtownabbey Borough Council, relayed its content and their future plans to Martin. I remember a white-faced Martin reeling with disbelief as he explained what the UDA now planned: the ceasefire would be extended by a mere three months. This news would be communicated to the Secretary of State, Paul Murphy, at a meeting to be held at Hillsborough Castle.

A very frank discussion ensued between Martin, Tommy Kirkham and Jackie McDonald that left the loyalists in no doubt of Martin's view that their plan was in every regard unacceptable. A three-month ceasefire would confirm the view of the Northern Ireland Office that the current ceasefire was no more than a short-term tactic designed to extract as many concessions as possible. The British and Irish governments would quite simply not respond to such blatant toying with peace. The loyalists, having brought themselves in from the political and establishment cold, would instantly return to being marginalised and isolated at the political level. Another consequence would be that Martin and I would have to withdraw from our engagement with them, for it would look – and feel – like we were being cynically used. Work on all the various projects that we were developing together would cease.

Martin's manner is normally emollient, patient and diplomatic, but time was of the essence. He became emphatic. This was the moment for the UDA leadership to enhance its credibility by persuading its followers to an indefinite ceasefire and the embrace of political dialogue towards a shared Northern Ireland. If they took that path, governments could engage with them, police could work with them in dealing with their disastrous criminal element, and Martin and I would have a strong hand when trying to persuade others in civic society to connect with them.

This was Tommy and Jackie's first real encounter with a tough-minded Martin McAleese. He offered to advise on a draft statement from the loyalist paramilitaries if it announced an indefinite extension of the ceasefire, and promised to help secure an assurance that loyalists would not be frozen out of future political talks.

On 14 February, Martin met privately with Jeffrey Donaldson of the DUP for the first time, in the home of Denis Moloney's sister Dr Maria Moloney, another quietly effective labourer in the field where bridges were being built. They discussed the ceasefire issue. Martin made Jeffrey aware that an important discussion between himself, Tommy Kirkham and Jackie McDonald on the possibility of an indefinite ceasefire was scheduled for later that day. Jeffrey was anxious to be as helpful as possible. He told Martin to tell the loyalists that if their ceasefire was extended indefinitely and if serious efforts were made to stop drug-dealing and criminality, then the DUP at the highest level would engage with them.

Martin relayed the message to the loyalist leaders. A draft statement announcing an indefinite ceasefire was debated word by word, line by line. Tommy and Jackie were convinced that such a ceasefire was the right way forward, but now they had the uncomfortable task of trying to persuade their colleagues. Their decision to do so was an important breakthrough, and it was their courage and conviction that won the day. On 24 February, a statement was issued by the UFF and the UDA, together with a short statement by the UPRG, announcing an indefinite extension of the cessation of military activity. It also said that loyalists, while remaining 'deeply suspicious of the intentions and objectives of the republican movement', wished to 'develop relationships with the broader nationalist community based on mutual respect and equity'. Within a short time, the UPRG was at Hillsborough Castle meeting Secretary of State Paul Murphy, who impressed them with his sincerity.

The trust between Martin and Jackie McDonald was to prove important early in 2005, when I was preparing to attend an event commemorating the liberation of the death camp at Auschwitz. In a live interview before leaving for Poland, I pointed out that anti-Semitism was often passed from otherwise good Christian parents to children. Such parents, I said, 'gave their children an irrational hatred of

Jews, in the same way that people in Northern Ireland transmitted to their children an irrational hatred, for example, of
Catholics . . . in the same way that people give their children
an outrageous and irrational hatred of those who are of a different colour . . .' I had failed to note that the transmission of
sectarian attitudes worked both ways in Northern Ireland,
and the outrage from unionists was understandable. I apologised immediately and profusely, and was grateful to those,
including Jackie, who publicly said that the mistake was unin-
tentional and was contradicted by everything I stood for.

I had to rebuild trust with the unionist community, and so
Martin and I redoubled our efforts 'to fill the centuries'
arrears', as the poet John Hewitt put it. Denis and Harvey set
about helping me to mend fences. To the great credit of the
unionist and especially the loyalist communities, the invitations to meet them on their home turf in Northern Ireland
continued apace, and there was no let-up in the visitors to
the Áras.

By September 2005, I was visiting a Protestant primary
school in the tough and exclusively loyalist Taughmonagh
estate. Jackie McDonald was worried that I would be offended
by the sight of the Union flags with which the estate was
festooned, and wondered if they would have to come down.
I told him to leave them where they were. They were part of
the identity and culture of the people I was visiting and I
wanted to respect that. Parents were given the option of
keeping their children at home if they were opposed to the
visitor. Only one child out of 177 stayed away. The day was
full of fun. The spotlight on the school was rewarded when
contracts for a much-needed and long-awaited new building
were signed some time later.

At the start of January 2006, An Taoiseach Bertie Ahern

and his family came to the Áras for dinner. Martin used the opportunity to brief him on recent conversations with members of the UPRG. They wanted help, by way of grant aid from both governments, to set up a staffed office, which would assist in bringing them in the direction of an even playing field with other political parties. Martin told Bertie there was a case to be made for such help, but it was undoubtedly risky and would have to be fully open and transparent. Bertie agreed to take the matter back for discussion with Michael Collins of the Department of the Taoiseach, who had a special role regarding Northern Ireland and was one of the most insightful and helpful civil servants we encountered.

Six weeks later, what would become the Conflict Transformation Initiative (CTI) had begun to take shape. It was to be a three- to five-year project aimed at assisting a loyalist transition from violence to more productive political, economic and social channels. The political element was to be funded by the British government and the social element was to be funded by the Irish government. At the request of the British ambassador, Stewart Eldon, a meeting was held at the Áras to discuss the proposed initiative. The British were on board with the concept, but were anxious to choreograph the roll-out so that British government money would be the first to come into play.

Two months later, the Secretary of State for Northern Ireland, Peter Hain, came to lunch at the Áras. Martin briefed him on the evolution of the UPRG and the UDA, its leaders, and the tensions within its inner council over the future of paramilitarism. He said they yearned for acknowledgment from the British government of their place, their voice and their entitlement to respect. For years they had viewed themselves as effectively the paramilitary wing of the DUP, but they had no place at any table. Some of them had a paranoid belief that they were being intentionally cold-shouldered by the British establishment, and at the same time embraced by the Irish establishment, as part of a deliberate plot between Westminster and Dublin to drive them towards a united Ireland. Hain was worried that the British government could not be seen to fund any political party of any hue, and that included the UPRG. A more nuanced and complex vehicle for the transformation of loyalism would have to be constructed.

Not everyone within loyalism welcomed even the most helpful interventions from south of the border. Towards the end of the summer of 2006, Áine de Baroid of the Department of Foreign Affairs, who worked intensively with Martin in his engagements with loyalism, was subject to threats from elements within the UDA in south-east Antrim. Martin met Dermot Ahern, Minister for Foreign Affairs, and Dermot Gallagher, Secretary General of the Department of Foreign Affairs, to discuss the situation, and all agreed that Áine's safety demanded that she cease travelling to Northern Ireland for the time being, while continuing to build relationships and hold meetings from Iveagh House in Dublin.

Martin also took the opportunity to raise his concerns about ongoing efforts to undermine Áine's work that came from more official sources both North and South. Within the Northern Ireland civil service there was top-level resistance to the Conflict Transformation Initiative. The resistance arose from concerns about the lack of loyalist weapons decommissioning and the high level of sheer criminality that continued to flourish in the paramilitary groups. Deadlines for British government decisions announcing funding came and went, and the loyalists became increasingly frustrated.

Martin and Áine held meeting after meeting to encourage them to keep believing in dialogue.

In October 2006, the St Andrew's Agreement created the possibility of a resumption of the Northern Ireland Executive, to be led by this time the DUP and Sinn Féin. But Sinn Féin's reluctance to back the reformed policing system in Northern Ireland held back progress. In December, I mentioned on the *Marian Finucane Show* that a number of my own relatives had joined the Police Service of Northern Ireland (PSNI). Peter Hain rang me shortly after to say how important an intervention that had been. In his view, it had tilted the scales in favour of Sinn Féin passing a motion supporting the new policing arrangements in Northern Ireland, which they did in January 2007. This move opened the gateway to the creation of the most curious government Northern Ireland ever had, with loyalist demagogue Dr Ian Paisley as First Minister and former IRA chief of staff Martin McGuinness as deputy First Minister, co-equal leaders of a power-sharing executive.

Finally, in the spring of 2007, Peter Hain announced the British government's decision to fund the Conflict Transformation Initiative for three years. The initiative was to be managed and the money administered by Farset International, a much-respected community development company. Farset hosted a UPRG workshop chaired by Sir George Quigley and attended by the PSNI chief constable and deputy chief constable, senior civil servants, and a litany of UDA personnel. The presence of Sir George, a veteran civil servant and businessman, was very telling. Few had as compendious a knowledge of Northern Ireland's complexities, and his chairmanship was a sign of how important the initiative was and how seriously it needed to be taken. Loyalist spokesmen committed unequivocally to ending paramilitarism and embracing much-needed social regeneration.

Martin was delighted that things had got this far, and was especially pleased when the role of the Irish government and of the Áras was mentioned as seminal in bringing the loyalist paramilitaries to this point in the transition process and in getting the British government to engage with them. But already there were straws in the wind indicating that all would not go smoothly. Loyalist decommissioning was frustratingly slow to materialise. Some within loyalism wanted to have their cake and eat it.

A few weeks later, members of the IRA's army council and the UDA's inner council met for the first time in public, in an initiative designed to promote reconciliation and decommissioning. IRA army council member Sean (Spike) Murray shook hands with UDA inner council member Jackie McDonald. Also present were members of the Orange Order, and senior officials from the Northern Ireland Office and the Republic's Department of Foreign Affairs. Sean Murray, who proved to be hugely important in developing the relationship between loyalism and republicanism, promised to work with loyalists to develop a 'common strategy' to deal with interface issues and to 'tackle social deprivation, poor educational achievement and a host of other issues which have blighted working class communities'. The meeting was by any standard historic. It was clear the UDA/ UPRG were serious about decommissioning and were preparing the ground within their own constituencies to bring it about. They were also giving a clear indication that the war with the IRA was over.

One SDLP assembly member, John Dallat, had been vociferous in denouncing government funding of the Conflict

Transformation Initiative. Martin initially hoped that the SDLP's Margaret Ritchie, who was to be the new Department of Social Development Minister, would be more helpful and pragmatic, but in fact the opposite proved to be the case. The skilful, experienced negotiators from the outstanding first generation of SDLP leadership were no longer in the front line of political life, and the consequences of this were becoming increasingly apparent.

Hoping to head off disaster, Martin went to meet the minister-designate in her offices in Downpatrick. Margaret Ritchie explained that she came from a rural background and had had little interaction with loyalism. She said she wanted to keep the money over which she had control for people who deserved it, and that did not include loyalist paramilitaries. Martin explained that as an east Belfast Catholic he had a lot of direct adverse experience of loyalist paramilitarism, as had his Ardoyne wife and her family. That was precisely why we dedicated so much time and effort to working with loyalists. He told Ritchie of the courageous and credible leaders he had encountered within loyalist paramilitarism who were trying to move to the politics of peace, but whose communities were mired in poverty and educational underachievement, which created an incubator for criminality and paramilitarism. The UPRG and UDA believed that tackling those levels of disadvantage was an essential pathway to ending paramilitarism and the culture of violence, and a fresh emphasis on a mutually respectful shared society would help tackle the inbuilt sectarianism within loyalism. The purpose of the CTI was to support this work. It was clear as they parted that Ritchie was not persuaded. Arriving back to the Áras, Martin was despondent.

Within a short time of becoming minister, Ritchie announced her intention to withdraw CTI funding within sixty days unless the UDA engaged meaningfully with the Independent International Commission on Decommissioning (IICD). Martin, normally calm and sanguine, confessed to me that he was never more ashamed to be a nationalist, for Ritchie's decision in his view was wrong-headed and potentially damaging to the ongoing loyalist engagement with the peace process.

At the same time, we were aware that Ritchie's reluctance to trust loyalism was far from a minority position or an unreasonable one, given their failure over many years to decommission and to deal effectively with criminality. There were episodes of shocking violence against the police in loyalist estates in the summer of 2007. But Ritchie was giving little or no credit to the distance already travelled by more progressive elements within loyalism, and the timetable she imposed was an impossible one.

While there was still time, Martin offered to help gather as much support as possible. Meanwhile he impressed on Jackie the realities that decommissioning and criminality had to be dealt with head-on; that loyalists should make no media comment; that street violence must end; and that they should quietly continue their work towards making a substantial statement on Armistice Day regarding steps they planned to take to commit fully to peace and parity of esteem. Intensive rounds of private discussions were arranged with Peter Robinson and Jeffrey Donaldson of the DUP, and Martin McGuinness's adviser Aidan McAteer, in the hope that they could soften Ritchie's red line.

At the request of Niall Burgess of the Department of Foreign Affairs, Martin went to see Ritchie in her office at Stormont in the hope of persuading her to soften her position. He emphasised that the CTI was the UDA's roadmap to the future. But the lady was not for turning.

On 16 October 2007, Ritchie withdrew the CTI funding. Within minutes of her announcement, we became aware that she had acted without referring the matter to the next Assembly Executive Committee meeting, scheduled for the 18th – a day we had been dreading. The news that she had acted unilaterally raised the prospect that her action could be tested in court, and that that might create a period of some respite. Afraid of chaos within the already fragile UDA leadership, Martin liaised intensely with Jackie McDonald on the drafting of a meaningful package for release on Armistice Day that could chart a possible way forward. There is no doubt that Jackie McDonald ploughed a lonely furrow during those days. His fellow loyalist leaders were ready to throw in the towel, but he was determined to forge on, and to go it alone if necessary. He was rightly worried about reprisals from within loyalism, and also the continuing threat from republican paramilitary dissidents.

Martin kept closely in touch with small loyalist community-based projects, which were now fearful that everything was going to collapse down around them. Spirits needed to be kept as buoyant as possible. In late October, he and Áine de Baroid met the UDA leaders at Farset. Some were in favour of proceeding with the Armistice Day statement – details of which, to their annoyance, had been put in the public domain after a meeting they had had with Ritchie in September. Others felt that to go ahead with that plan would seem to their supporters like capitulating to Ritchie. There could be a violent reaction.

Áine presented a paper setting out what the Armistice Day statement might usefully contain, and guidelines for handling media questions about its context and content. Martin explained that the fledgling executive had little option but to back Ritchie publicly. He was hopeful that the courts would take a strong line on her failure to follow the Ministerial Code, but that would take time. The courts did eventually find Ritchie in breach of the code, but for the moment the only way forward for the UDA was to do the right thing and make the statement they had promised to make.

Martin met the loyalist leaders on 7 November at Farset with a list of suggestions as to how the draft statement could be usefully honed and enhanced. He caught wind of a view held by one key figure that new, unhelpful conditions might be attached to the final draft. He told the loyalists in no uncertain terms that such a move would be disastrous.

Áine was hovering over the text of the statement like a mother hen. She met two of the loyalist leaders on 9 November and relayed to them that the statement had to be unconditional. Two days later, it was:

> The UDA believes the war is over and we are now in a new democratic dispensation that will lead to permanent political stability . . . the organisation intends to continue through a process of transformation that will ultimately achieve a Northern Ireland based on equality, justice . . . where no sections of our people are left behind regardless of religion, politics or identity . . . The ballot box and the political institutions must be the greatest weapons . . . It is our intention . . . to . . . direct all our energies into developing our communities . . . All active service units of the Ulster Freedom Fighters will as from 12 p.m. tonight stand down with all military intelligence destroyed and as a consequence of this all weaponry will be put beyond use . . . To be involved in crime and criminality is to undermine the cause.

There was jubilation around our breakfast table that morning, though tempered with the understanding that this was a beginning, not an end. The statement made it clear that for loyalists the future would be within the United Kingdom, and they were scathing about what they saw as Irish nationalism's determination to exclude them from the new shared future. The ending of the alienation of loyalism would be the work of decades.

When Áine de Baroid was redeployed to the Department of Finance, the response from loyalists was sadness and disappointment. Áine was a powerhouse, with a level of commitment to bridge-building that must at times have baffled some of her colleagues. She had an encyclopedic knowledge of loyalism and a patient manner devoid of ego or edge, which allowed trust and friendships to develop with ease. Now she was gone, and at a crucial juncture, but she could take pride in successfully helping to bring the UDA in from the cold.

Over the years working on issues concerning Northern Ireland, Martin had come across a number of people whose skill, insight and reliability had been very helpful to the Building Bridges project. He asked them to form the nucleus of a civic society group, which would regularly engage in encounters with the loyalist leadership. Stephen Kingon, Brian Rowntree, Briege Gadd, Pat Colgan and, later, Christy Mannion became the core group members. The initiative started in June 2008, and continued at an intensive level until I left office in 2011. It was highly complex and ambitious work – probably too ambitious given the range of issues and interactions it required between loyalists and a broad assortment of senior politicians, local councillors, senior civil servants, religious leaders, nationalist and republican leaders, the GAA, ex-prisoners, community activists, grant-awarding bodies, philanthropists, European institutions, European and US ambassadors, and university vice-chancellors. There were relentless meetings and discussions, position papers, projects, proposed initiatives, applications for funding, arguments, fallings-out, re-engagements, and on and on . . .

The group met with the UDA leadership, with the exception of the breakaway south-east Antrim element. The meetings took place at the offices of Invest Northern Ireland – the point being (as it was back in 1995 at the White House Conference) that the focus here was not on constitutional issues but on practical everyday things that could lift a community out of the torpor of the Troubles. The group helped the UDA identify the issues it saw as essential to the well-being of loyalist communities, and to work up and cost specific proposals.

That the group was making real progress became clear when on 16 June 2009 the UDA performed its first act of decommissioning and promised more would follow later in the year. The formal announcement was made eleven days later. The purpose of the interval was to allow time to alert Hillary Clinton and Congressman Richie Neal, among other well-disposed American political figures, so that they could respond positively to the decommissioning and encourage its completion. Loyalists had felt excluded from Capitol Hill, where Irish republicans and nationalists seemed so comfortable. Martin organised for them to meet a visiting delegation from the US Congress in Dublin two days after their official notice of the preliminary act of decommissioning was announced. Richie Neal, Chair of the Friends of Ireland in Congress, reassured them that they would be listened to.

At a lunch at the Áras in July, Martin briefed Sinn Féin on the plan for accessing help for disadvantaged communities. Getting them on board with a shared plan with the UDA was an ambitious aim, and in subsequent meetings it became evident that the difficulties were substantial. Republican communities were already in the throes of applying for funding for similar projects, which this initiative could stymie or slow down. It was increasingly clear, too, that the money for the initiative was going to be very hard to pin down from either the Northern Ireland Executive or the British government.

On 6 January 2010, the UDA confirmed in a press release that it had permanently decommissioned all its remaining weapons. A week later, the full inner council of the UDA came to Áras an Uachtaráin for a dinner to mark the decommissioning. Martin entertained them. On my desk a few yards away I looked at the photos of Tony and Myles O'Reilly that greeted me each morning, and quietly said a prayer of thanks that there would be no more such deaths.

In June 2013, courtesy of a decision by both Louth and Meath county councils, a beautiful bridge over the Boyne Valley was renamed in my honour, in recognition of the Building Bridges project. Among the guests were ex-paramilitaries and politicians from North and South of all persuasions, as well as members of the Orange Order and the Royal Black Preceptory. From where we stood we could see the new interpretative and visitor centre at the Boyne battle site, now a tourist attraction for the descendants of both Williamites and Jacobites to enjoy in peace.

There were strong signs of the likelihood of that peace and good neighbourliness sustaining. In the Republic at government level there had long been a growing consciousness that within a short few years the era of sensitive anniversaries would be upon us, with the centenaries of the last visit by a British monarch, the Somme, the Rising, the War of

Independence, the Civil War, 1920 Bloody Sunday and Partition. Planning started early, with the aim of encouraging a reconciliatory generosity of spirit rather than the stoking of old embers of resentment. It found its initial expression in 2006 with the holding of the first ever official commemoration on the ninetieth anniversary of the Battle of the Somme. Layer upon layer of divisive old presumptions and prejudices was being stripped away and new ground was being seeded with a harvest to share. Official commemoration of the Easter Rising, which had been abandoned during the Troubles, was reinstated, and enjoyed sensitively and respectfully by a much broader church from North and South than in earlier times.

In 2007, Martin and I made a trip to the Somme museum in Belfast and were welcomed there by the Reverend Dr Ian Paisley and his wife Eileen. It was our first meeting. They were warm and friendly, and between us there was plenty of familiar Belfast banter. By then he was, as I had predicted, First Minister of Northern Ireland, having eventually brought the DUP in from the political cold of its opposition to the Good Friday Agreement.

Ian Paisley's personal physician was Dr Ian Adamson, an unusual and hugely likeable man who over the years became a great friend and supporter. At his invitation, on Columbanus Day in November 2010, I paid a visit to the Ullans Centre in Belfast, which celebrates the Ulster Scots tradition and language. The event was in honour of the sixth-century monk St Columbanus, who during the Dark Ages had sailed from Bangor to the European mainland and re-established the intellectual tradition of European Christianity though his many monastic foundations.

I was to speak after Dr Paisley, and since the Pope (any

pope) was not beloved by Paisley, and since Columbanus had had a lot to say on the subject (albeit a sixth-century pope), I judged it politic to stick to safer territory. I needn't have bothered. Paisley's speech was larded with papal references wittily and respectfully delivered. I was even more pleasantly surprised when former UDA commander Sammy Douglas quoted extensively from St Augustine. It was surreal. I hadn't had such rich theological conversations in the Vatican! I had to pinch myself to be sure I was not at home in bed, asleep and dreaming.

## 13

An ambition of the Building Bridges project from the outset was to arrive at a time when it was possible to invite Her Majesty the Queen for the first ever state visit by a British monarch to the Republic of Ireland. The last time a monarch had set foot in Dublin was 1911. My second and final term was to end in 2011. There were a lot of fences to mend and pieces of the peace process jigsaw to be put in place before such a visit could happen.

The Irish community in Britain was large and of long standing. Although many had prospered and made a huge contribution to British society, there was a legacy of historic discrimination, to which the IRA campaign had added a level of renewed fear and exclusion. Many Irish had felt the imprint of the Prevention of Terrorism Act, some with good reason, many unjustifiably. I was a co-founder of the Irish Commission for Prisoners Overseas and worked closely with the priests and nuns who were helping families cope with the fallout. I was particularly involved with the campaigns to establish the innocence of the Maguire family, the Guildford Four and the Birmingham Six, all wrongly convicted of terrorist bombings, so I knew the extent to which the British justice system had become compromised by the pressure to convict someone, anyone, for the diabolical crimes of the IRA. There were, too, the poor innocent victims of those crimes and the people who lived in fear of more bombings. So there were contemporary raw wounds as well as the still livid scars of a troubled history between the coloniser and the colonised to be taken into consideration as we laid our plans. Yet both Ireland and the United Kingdom were partners in the European Union and relationships had been warming visibly. A visit from the Queen could cement the progress made and send a powerful message that mutual respect and good neighbourliness would be at the heart of future relations.

From discussions over the years about the possibility of a royal visit, I was aware that there was a fair degree of resistance to it within political, civil service and security circles on both sides. The caution was understandable, for if anything went wrong, the progress that had been made in Northern Ireland and in our steadily improving relationships with Britain could be jeopardised. There was also a section of the population none too enamoured of the idea of inviting the Queen under any circumstances, given the baleful history of British rule in Ireland. Yet this was our neighbouring jurisdiction, with whom we had, and would continue to have, multiple layers of connectedness.

I had no doubt we were capable of hosting a visit that could bring about a historic and authentic healing. Having discussed the subject a number of times with the Queen, both in London and in Northern Ireland, I knew how much the ghosts of the past weighed on her, how sad she was to have been unable to visit the Republic during her long reign, and how much she desired an opportunity to contribute to a new concord and harmony in relationships between Ireland and the United Kingdom.

The political conditions set by Bertie Ahern for such a visit had been met in the North, but Bertie had left office in 2008 and I was now a lone voice pushing for the visit. I had already batted away nervous suggestions that the Queen could come for a half-day visit to test the public appetite. That would not constitute a state visit, and if we were going to do it at all, in my view, we needed to do it absolutely right, with great generosity and magnanimity. I had not the least doubt that we could. But the politics of the day were in turmoil, as the government dealt with the economic crash.

Bertie's replacement as taoiseach was Brian Cowen, whose period in office was fraught. He had too much on his plate to contemplate a royal visit. Then, in February 2011, the pressure on Brian forced his resignation and a general election, which brought Fine Gael to power. I saw my chance. The new taoiseach would be Enda Kenny, with whom Martin was particularly close. I asked Brian Cowen if he would do me one favour before he and his government left office: would he announce that an invitation was to be issued to Her Majesty the Queen? This was an unlikely idea, tossed like a grenade into what was for him an awful time in his life, but he very graciously did not dismiss it. He thought about it, and then with sound political judgement said he would issue the invitation provided that the incoming taoiseach agreed. Enda did not hesitate. The invitation was sent.

The British ambassador to Ireland at the time was Julian King, who was surely tested in the following weeks and came through brilliantly. It is a measure of how much the Queen wanted to come that, from her diary, which is set years in advance, four days in May were immediately made available. She would arrive on the 17th and depart on the 20th, making hers by far the longest state visit by any head of state in my time as President.

We had just weeks to prepare. Bureaucrats and securocrats on both sides of the Irish Sea went into planning and

protocol overdrive. They were superb in terms of organisation and execution, but as discussions got down to the
nitty-gritty of where exactly the Queen would go and where
she could not be expected to go, I realised (at about the same
time as the Queen did) that we needed a simple back-channel
through which we might have a passing chance of getting
things we both wanted onto the visit agenda.

On 16 March, as we were planning for the following day's
St Patrick's Day reception at the Áras, a perplexed Secretary
General Adrian O'Neill came into my office to say that Julian
King had asked to bring a colleague to the reception, and
that the colleague wanted a few minutes in private with me.
Adrian was inclined to decline the request until I asked the
name of the colleague. It was Edward Young. I pointed out
that he was Deputy Private Secretary to the Queen.

Mr Young was engaging, relaxed and funny. He and I had
rather longer than ten minutes in a closed session to which
no one else was admitted. We were agreed on the importance of building on the success of our joint visit to the Island
of Ireland Peace Park at Messines, so clearly a visit to the
Great War memorial at Islandbridge was essential. I told him
I had three other things I would love to see on the Queen's
agenda, which would make the difference between a good
visit and a great visit. The first suggestion was the laying of a
wreath at the Garden of Remembrance in Parnell Square in
Dublin, which commemorates all those who fought for Irish
freedom over the centuries. To do that early in her visit
would silence the begrudgers and soften a lot of hardened
hearts. It would, without words or elaboration, put the healing of history's wounds right at the very top of her agenda.

The second suggestion was a visit to Croke Park, the home
of the Gaelic Athletic Association – Ireland's most important,

far-reaching and influential sporting and cultural institution
bar none. I told Edward Young that one of the stands in the
ultra-modern 82,000-seater stadium was named after a young
Tipperary footballer, Michael Hogan, who was murdered
along with thirteen other people in 1920 by British soldiers
who drove onto the pitch during a match and opened fire. If
the Queen was to walk out from the Hogan Stand tunnel onto
that hallowed sward, so familiar to the Irish at home and
around the world, it would be a powerful symbol of British–
Irish reconciliation. Equally, the respect shown by her to the
GAA would be of massive significance, and not just in Ireland, for the GAA has a hinterland that embraces the Irish all
over the world. At that point no one had approached Croke
Park to test the feasibility of a visit from their point of view,
and I already knew from discussions around the visit that
there were some officials who thought the idea ludicrous. I
would need to know from the Queen if she was willing to visit
Croke Park before I broached the subject with the authorities.
I was at pains to say I could not guarantee a positive answer
from the GAA, but my instinct was that they would be
delighted.

The final thing I asked was that the Queen might consider
beginning her speech at the state dinner with some words in
the Irish language. Even one sentence could set to rest so
much historic angst and resentment around the dire treatment of the language by the British when they were in power
in Dublin Castle. I knew that the Irish and British diplomatic teams had already discussed this possibility, and that it
was seen as highly unlikely. To push it on our side would be
impolitic. However, I believed Her Majesty should at least be
aware that I was certain of the massive impact that five simple words could have. Edward remarked that the Queen

would be justifiably concerned about getting something wrong and giving inadvertent offence at the very start of the only speech she was going to make. It was high-risk. I said I completely understood that concern, and so was not pressing the point; but we were talking about five words, no more, and they could make history. I left the matter in Her Majesty's hands and entirely to her discretion, fully accepting that she would have her own good reasons for or against.

Edward listened carefully and said he would bring the suggestions directly to Her Majesty. Almost immediately on his return to London he was able to say that the Garden of Remembrance and Croke Park were both possible as far as the Queen was concerned, but the use of the Irish language raised fears in case it went wrong and caused umbrage. I was happy with two out of three, for the fears were understandable.

An immediate job now was to put Croke Park on the agenda at our end and to get the agreement of the GAA. I raised it through the normal channels and felt the sharp pushback immediately. The idea was not popular for a number of reasons. The first was the certainty within officialdom that the GAA would not agree and that in floating the idea there was the risk of a leak, which could provoke an unseemly public controversy. Also, officials felt there was not a snowball's chance in hell that the Queen's advisers would agree to her visiting such a neuralgic place. I was delighted to be able to dismiss the last argument. There was consternation that I had privately broached the matter through Edward Young. As I had done so, there was nothing for it but to diplomatically approach Croke Park.

At that point I should have insisted on letting Martin handle the approach, but instead I agreed that a retired senior diplomat would do so. His feedback, when it came, was resoundingly negative – so negative I became suspicious and wondered if he had actually talked to anyone in authority at Croke Park or had merely looked into his own heart. The identity of the diplomat was not known to me, so I asked for him to be named, and it turned out to be someone we knew of old to be hostile to the entire Building Bridges concept; a man so resolute in the infallibility of his own judgement that he was perfectly capable of taking a unilateral decision that the Queen was not going to Croke Park. I asked Martin to find out how the GAA had been approached. He phoned the Director General, Páraic Duffy, who told him that there had never been any approach about the matter. Martin checked with the other senior GAA figures and the story was the same. We were incensed at having been misled, but that was a matter for another day. For now, the possibility of a visit to Croke Park was back on the agenda, and it was up to us to make the case to the GAA authorities.

The Director General and President thought the idea had merit, but they had a worry that the association's Ulster Council might veto it, since Sinn Féin was not backing the visit, and there was a lot of support for Sinn Féin among GAA people in Ulster. If Ulster said no, that would spell the end of the idea. I did not share the concerns about Ulster. Aogán Ó Fearghaíl from Monaghan was the President of the Ulster Council, and as open and far-seeing a man as it was possible to encounter. But I knew the key opinion would come from the Ulster Council Secretary and Chief Executive, Danny Murphy, who was from Burren near Rostrevor.

A meeting was arranged at Croke Park between Martin, GAA President Christy Cooney, Páraic Duffy, Aogán Ó Fearghaíl, Danny Murphy, and David Cooney, Secretary General of the Department of Foreign Affairs. Martin was interrogated closely as to why the GAA should have the Queen at Croke Park. He explained simply that if she was coming on a state visit to Ireland, I wanted her to see the best we had; and the GAA and Croke Park were the best. Danny Murphy memorably summed it up: 'If this is what our President wants, then it is our duty to do it and to do it well.' Páraic Duffy said, 'Tell us what you want us to do and we will do it.' And they did.

David Cooney returned to the Department of Foreign Affairs to break the news that they had been misled by their original emissary. The Queen was going to Croke Park. She wanted to, the GAA wanted her to, the President wanted her to, and that was that. If flabbers were gasted, which they likely were in retired-mandarin circles, it was well away from my earshot. When, as happened occasionally thereafter, we met the now-deceased original emissary at functions (some of which were held at Croke Park) the subject was never raised.

As we had now nailed down the main history-making set pieces of the visit, I assumed the Queen's use of the Irish language was completely off the agenda. However, I had reckoned without Edward Young and Her Majesty's capacity to chew over and revisit things.

The following weeks went by in a frenzy of organisation and planning, and much public prognostication about the details of the Queen's itinerary, which were still under wraps. Out of the blue we had a visit from a close friend, who dropped by on his way home from Karachi, where he was British deputy high commissioner to Pakistan. Francis Campbell has a unique CV. A County Down Catholic, he had gone to school at St Colman's College with my youngest brother. He was a former private secretary to Tony Blair, and made history by becoming the first Catholic to be appointed

British ambassador to the Holy See. His family home was in the North, not far from our home in Rostrevor, and it was not unusual for him to drop by in between postings or on visits home to see his father and a mutual elderly priest friend who lived in Rostrevor. Nor was it unusual for members of my family to descend upon him in Rome.

On this occasion Francis was heading on to London from Islamabad by way of Dublin. Over lunch he nonchalantly asked how preparations were going for the Queen's visit. Without giving any details, I told him that I believed the visit would be better than anyone could anticipate. I need not have been so discreet, for as usual Francis knew just about everything that was knowable. 'I will be meeting a friend of yours tomorrow,' he announced. 'He tells me that you have five words in Irish that might be useful to Her Majesty.' I told him that that matter had been respectfully closed off on both sides. 'Even so,' he said, 'just for your friend's own record, can you write the five words out phonetically? He forgot to ask.'

Francis dragged a used envelope from his inside pocket, and a pen. I wrote the words out reluctantly, emphasising that on no account was anyone at the London end of the conversation to think I was revisiting a closed subject. 'Would Ulster Irish do?' said the mischievous man who went to the same Gaeltacht as me. 'Leave it!' was my terse reply, indicating as firmly as I could that the piece of paper was not for Her Majesty's eyes but for Edward Young's curiosity only. The language issue was closed at my end, and I was not prepared to risk looking like I was trying to embarrass our guest. Francis reassured me he understood the position. I mentioned the conversation to no one.

*

The desire for reconciliation was evident from the moment the Queen's plane touched down at Casement Aerodrome, the headquarters of the Irish Air Corps in Baldonnel. The aerodrome was named after Sir Roger Casement, a senior diplomat in the British Colonial Service who was knighted by the Crown in 1911 for his investigations into human rights abuses in Peru. Born in Dublin to an Anglican military family, he was raised in England until, at the age of thirteen, he was orphaned. He moved back to Ireland and was educated at Ballymena Academy in County Antrim, living during his six years there at Galgorm Castle with his cousins the Youngs, wealthy linen merchants. Casement and his contemporary Rose Young became great friends. They shared a developing interest in Irish nationalism and Gaelic culture that was at odds with the militant unionism and anti-Home Rule views of the rest of their Young relatives, who were intimately involved in gun-running for the Ulster Volunteer Force in 1914 and threatening the British government with civil war if Home Rule was granted to Ireland.

Casement's support for the 1916 Rising, including trying to get a supply of arms for the Irish Volunteers from Germany, resulted in his trial for high treason in London and his execution. The British establishment's attempt to ruin his good name, by publishing diaries detailing homosexual acts in Congo and Peru, has been a running sore in Irish nationalist and republican circles. It would probably be true to say that the touchdown of the Queen's flight at Casement Aerodrome likely meant very little to the British public, whose limited knowledge of Irish history has not always been helpful to reconciliation. But that the first state visit by a British monarch, a hundred years after Casement was first knighted, should commence in a national institution dedicated to his name was itself indicative of the quiet yet powerful symbolism that was implanted into so many aspects of the visit.

The Queen emerged from the aircraft wearing the first of several elegant outfits in various shades of green. The fabrics had been carefully sourced in Ireland by her dresser, Angela Kelly. The white dress designed for the state dinner at Dublin Castle had a bodice of finely wrought three-dimensional shamrocks. If we had been busy organising the visit at our end, it was clear with every appearance by the Queen that absolutely nothing had been left to chance at the Buckingham Palace end, and everything that could be done had been done to reassure the Irish public that this was a mission with a considered and considerate purpose, and not a simple social call.

The first public event of the visit was to the Garden of Remembrance. The journey was strange, for security dictated that the streets of central Dublin, which would otherwise be thronged, should be empty. The Queen and I travelled together, gratified to see that wherever there was a cramped viewing point behind the barricades there were groups of people smiling and waving. There was one small group of 'BRITS OUT' protesters close to the garden, but they were neither visible nor audible to us at the time. Only later, watching them on television, did I see that some were wearing English soccer club jerseys. Geniuses – or, as Father Ailbe used to say of Ardoyne's serial stone-throwers, 'If they had brains they would be dangerous!' Protesters made virtually no impact at all during the four days.

The brief ceremony at the Garden of Remembrance was solemn and formal. The Queen placed the wreath and took a pace back as per the protocol, and then did something as unexpected as it was powerful, and definitely not per the protocol. She bowed her head in respectful homage. It was an unadorned gesture and there was no mistaking its message. All over Ireland, people stirred. Could this really have happened?

On the second afternoon, a very different wreath-laying ceremony took place at the Irish War Memorial Garden at Islandbridge. The guest list had caused headaches for us. The British side and the Irish Department of Foreign Affairs were resolutely opposed to any invitations to loyalist former paramilitaries. We were equally resolute that after long years of working with them, building trust and treating them as welcome guests, we were not going to overlook them on this occasion, which meant so much to them.

Martin, Denis Moloney and Harvey Bicker organised several busloads of former loyalist paramilitaries, and not a few republicans who were now happy to acknowledge their ancestors who had fought in British uniform. Their presence created a situation that had to be managed carefully. The Queen's exit from the gardens would involve her walking along a path flanked by random guests, and the British side were very anxious that the royals would not be caught on camera shaking hands with, or even in the vicinity of, former paramilitaries. Neither Martin nor I had a problem shaking their hands, and in fact we wanted to make sure they felt welcome. So the choreography involved the two of us briefly meeting some members of the general public gathered on our side of the pathway, among whom were some loyalists. The Queen and the Duke of Edinburgh, flanked by security, passed by an the other side as they were guided to the waiting cars. Thus no one felt publicly snubbed and no one was compromised. The loyalists had already figured out that they were likely to be bypassed, and were pleasantly surprised to be made a fuss of, even if the handshake was from the President of the Republic and not their own beloved Queen. No matter. They understood, and it was enough to be part of the emotional solidarity at Islandbridge, which was felt by all there and many more watching on television. There were no speeches, just a set of images many of us thought we would never see in our lifetime. For Harvey Bicker, the day was a vindication of all the risks he had taken fourteen years earlier in pinning his colours to my mast. It is his beaming tear-stained face I remember when I think of that day.

On day three, Her Majesty arrived at Croke Park to be greeted by Christy Cooney and Páraic Duffy, the senior GAA officials who had embraced the idea of her visit so willingly. Croke Park was pulsating with its big-event energy, full of colour and music, children in jerseys from thirty-two counties, bands of footballing and hurling heroes and an almighty assembly of GAA greats. The mood was festive, confident and proud. It turned solemn when the Queen, Christy and I stepped out from the tunnel and she walked for the first time on that famous pitch, then turned and looked up at the Hogan Stand. Christy quietly told her that this was the stand named after Michael Hogan, who along with thirteen others had died there on Bloody Sunday 1920. She looked as if she might cry. Almost in a sigh she sadly and slowly said: 'I know, I know.'

We went back into the fray of handshakes, line-ups, introductions and chatter. There were so many people I wanted the royal visitors to meet, for a greater collection of my heroes would be hard to find in one place; but I especially wanted to introduce the Queen to Danny Murphy, since it was his call that had given us this phenomenal day. I also was intent on introducing her to a former GAA President, Paddy McFlynn of Derry, who had struggled out of bed at the age of ninety-four to be there and was almost levitating with joy at this remarkable turn of events. We watched bemused and pleased as the Duke of Edinburgh was handed a hurl with respectful humour. Mercifully he did not attempt to puck a sliothar in that crowded room.

There was not the faintest trace of unease or resentment, obsequiousness or false deference. Their Majesties were clearly enjoying themselves at Croke Park, and Croke Park was enjoying their company. On the way back to the Áras I thought of one of my unionist colleagues in Northern Ireland, who back in September 1991 had told me she was terrified by the outbreak of black and red flags in a nationalist area that she had to travel through to get home. She wondered what ominous thing it could portend. Could I explain it to her? I told her the only people the black and red flags were designed to put the fear of God into were the Meath supporters that County Down would meet that year in Croke Park in the All-Ireland football final, for it was the Down GAA flag. The very flag that effortlessly lifted my heart to altitudes where oxygen was required was unknown to her, as was the entire interlocking hinterland of sport, culture, community and identity it represented. I hoped that, for her and many like her, the Queen's visit had opened the mystery of the GAA to a benign curiosity.

Since that day in 1991, she and I and our respective families have become very close, our lives interwoven by shared holidays and events; but still I am conscious that there is a long road to travel before she might be inclined to stay up all night waiting in a state of euphoria for the Sam Maguire Cup to reach Rostrevor on an open-topped bus. She will never know what the name Liam Austin symbolises, or what it means to just say 'Pete' without need of the surname McGrath . . . Why should she? Her husband's twin was callously murdered by the IRA not far from where I grew up in Belfast, so just to have her (and her husband's) enduring friendship is enough. But I dare to hope that there will be a generation of children to come in Northern Ireland who might kick a Gaelic football or puck a sliothar without a care in the world about their religion or politics, as happens effortlessly south of the border. If it does happen, and already work is going on to bring it about, there is little doubt that on a certain day in May 2011, a Queen of England and a royal prince helped turn the tide of fear and unfamiliarity.

Treatises could be written about the at times unseemly bunfight for tickets to the state dinner at Dublin Castle that took place on the second night of the Queen's visit. That was someone else's nightmare, thankfully. I had long adopted a view that there were certain things that, once delegated, should stay delegated. Decisions about which politicians should attend the state dinner were well inside the delegated category. My response each time the door opened and a plea from another quarter was reported was to say, 'And good luck with that, then!'

On the day of the dinner, my special adviser briefed me after her long final run-through with the caterers, musicians, security, protocol and many many others. During the conversation she dropped an enigmatic reference to the Queen rehearsing Ulster Irish at the government guest house at Farmleigh – then immediately said that of course we all knew that was not going to happen. I thought it was a joke at my expense, but a doubt began to gather in my mind. Was it really possible the Queen was going to speak in Irish?

My contribution to the state dinner, apart from writing a speech and agreeing the menu, was to make sure that the first person the Queen saw and heard as she ascended the stairs to the Battle Axe Landing was Ireland's most distinguished piper, Liam O'Flynn, whose music had been like a soundtrack to my life since the early 1980s. There he was, playing the poignant piece he had composed fourteen years earlier at the outset of my presidency: 'An Droichead', 'The Bridge'. It was exactly right for the moment. I had the feeling that, miraculously, everything the Ulster poet Louis Mac-Neice had fretted over in *Autumn Journal* was beginning to straighten out:

> I note how a single purpose can be founded on
> A jumble of opposites:
> Dublin Castle, the vice-regal ball,
> The embassies of Europe,
> Hatred scribbled on a wall,
> Gaols and revolvers.
> And I remember when I was little, the fear
> Bandied among the servants
> That Casement would land at the pier
> With a sword and a horde of rebels.

That night in Dublin Castle, the Queen in her speech and I in mine were to commit to founding that single purpose from the jumble of opposites that characterised our interlaced and difficult histories. No routine recitation of worthy floridities would cut the mustard that evening, for in these set-piece speeches every word would count, would be counted, parsed and analysed for posterity. Especially the Queen's speech.

I welcomed Her Majesty, noting that hers was the first ever state visit to take place between our two countries.

> This visit is the culmination of the success of the peace process. It is an acknowledgment that while we cannot change the past, we have chosen to change the future . . . Inevitably where there are the colonisers and the colonised, the past is a repository of sources of bitter division. The harsh facts cannot be altered nor loss nor grief erased, but with time and generosity, interpretations and perspectives can soften and open up space for new accommodations.

I acknowledged the 'peacemakers, who, having experienced first-hand the appalling toxic harvest of failing to resolve old hatreds and political differences, rejected the perennial culture of conflict and compromised enough to let a new future in'.

> The journey to peace has been cruelly slow and arduous but it has taken us to a place where hope thrives and the past no longer threatens to overwhelm our present and our future. The legacy of the Good Friday Agreement is already profound and encouraging. We all of us have a duty to protect, nurture and develop it . . . Though the seas between us have often been stormy we have chosen to build a solid and enduring bridge of friendship between us and to cross it to a new, a happier future.

When the Queen stood up to make her speech, her first words were the five I had written phonetically on the back of that envelope, Ulster Irish, pronunciation perfect. I was stunned into muttering a lame 'Wow!', and looked across at Edward Young sitting at the next table. He gave me a long laughing wink. No better gift could I have been given, or the Irish people.

Earlier that day I had given the Queen a facsimile of a book of Irish phrases, a primer prepared for a meeting in 1593 between the Irish Pirate Queen, Grace O'Malley aka Granuaile, and Elizabeth I in London. When she sat down at the end of her speech, I complimented her on the speed with which she had become fluent in Gaelic. It had quite obviously been her personal decision to use Irish, to trust my instinct and to show her willingness to go as many miles as it took.

Her Majesty's speech, beginning with those five words in Irish, *'A Uachtaráin agus a chairde'* – 'President and friends' – brought the visit to an emotional level not usually associated with state visits. It was, according to the *Daily Telegraph*, 'one of the most important speeches of her reign'. It was no exercise in diplomatic-speak obfuscation or ceremonious banality. Her words affected people deeply, and not just those who were there:

> Madam President, speaking here in Dublin Castle it is impossible to ignore the weight of history, as it was yesterday when you and I laid wreaths at the Garden of Remembrance.
>
> Indeed, so much of this visit reminds us of the complexity of our history, its many layers and traditions, but also the importance of forbearance and conciliation. Of being able to bow to the past, but not be bound by it.
>
> Of course, the relationship has not always been straightforward; nor has the record over the centuries been entirely benign. It is a sad and regrettable reality that through history our islands have experienced more than their fair share of heartache, turbulence and loss.

These events have touched us all, many of us personally, and are a painful legacy. We can never forget those who have died or been injured and their families. To all those who have suffered as a consequence of our troubled past I extend my sincere thoughts and deep sympathy. With the benefit of historical hindsight we can all see things which we would wish had been done differently or not at all. But it is also true that no one who looked to the future over the past centuries could have imagined the strength of the bonds that are now in place between the governments and the people of our two nations, the spirit of partnership that we now enjoy and the lasting rapport between us . . .

So we celebrate together the widespread spirit of good-will and deep mutual understanding that has served to make the relationship more harmonious, close as good neighbours should always be.

The Queen's words were universally welcomed, even by Sinn Féin, which had opposed the visit. The slightly tense mood all over the island had shifted quickly to one of warmth, welcome and ease.

There was an intriguing sequel within Sinn Féin on the final day of her visit. The party had boycotted the entire affair, despite serious efforts on our part to get them to engage with it, going as far as talking directly to Martin McGuinness and meeting privately with Gerry Adams. We could not disclose any details of the visit, nor did McGuinness and Adams ask us to do so; but we asked both men to trust our judgement on its content, which we emphatically believed would augur well for the peace process. We argued that by excluding them-selves from the visit they were sending the wrong message to the very people we needed to reconcile with, our unionist neighbours to whom the Queen meant so much. Their absence, we argued, could be construed as a failure to fully honour parity of esteem. That would be a loss to Sinn Féin but possibly also to nationalism in general, something we were very anxious to avoid.

We gave them the opportunity we had afforded to others to let us know what they would like Her Majesty to say and do. They later offered some ideas in writing about what she might say, and these we relayed back to her team, for they too were hoping that the visit would embrace every possible constituency and leave none on the outside looking in. In the end, however, Sinn Féin could not and did not make the leap of faith. All their elected representatives and officials were instructed to stay away from the events associated with the visit. We held seats for them at the state dinner, with Martin continuing to try to persuade them right up until the last minute, but to no avail, even though after the Croke Park visit it was evident that they had missed an important and unrepeatable opportunity. The first sign of a realisation within Sinn Féin that it was missing out on a significant and hugely popular national reconciliation event occurred immediately after the Queen's speech, when Gerry Adams was complimentary about it and welcomed its content.

On the final day of her visit, the Queen visited St Patrick's Rock, a famous historic monument associated with the ancient kings of Munster in the town of Cashel, County Tipperary. The welcome on her arrival was to be offered by the Minister for Public Expenditure and Reform, Brendan Howlin. The local mayor, Michael Browne, was a member of Sinn Féin. Since his party had instructed him to stay away, he was not scheduled to attend at any stage of the event, although of course he had been invited. There was no mention of his name in the visit protocol, but much to the surprise and annoyance of Sinn Féin, he decided somewhat peremptorily that it was his civic duty to greet the Queen in the name of all the people of Cashel. With a handshake and the words 'Welcome to Cashel, Your Majesty, and I hope you enjoy your stay', Michael Browne single-handedly made a nonsense of the Sinn Féin position and managed to inveigle them in from their self-imposed exclusion. He died of cancer two months later. The terminal nature of his illness had rendered meaningless the threats from party headquarters, and therein at least in part lay his courage to defy the party diktat.

From Cashel the Queen travelled to Cork for her final engagements, which included a visit to the city's legendary English Market and an encounter with one of its equally legendary characters, fishmonger Pat O'Connell. In answer to a question from the Queen as to the name of a particularly ugly fish, he told her it was known as 'the mother-in-law'! Prince Philip pointed to a display of fishcakes and asked what was in them, only to be told, 'Yerra, fish.' These were easy-going encounters full of smiles and laughter. The nation breathed a collective sigh of relief. Outside on the street, for the first time in four days, security slackened off sufficiently to allow random members of the public to gather and shake Her Majesty's hand.

After a farewell from An Taoiseach Enda Kenny, the royal guests departed from Cork International Airport. Edward Young phoned from London as their plane touched down to say that it was by far the best state visit ever, and he had never seen Her Majesty so happy. There was a definite sense on both sides of the sea that the visit had brought all of us over a historic watershed to a new platform of mutual affirmation and friendship. It augured well for the future as much as it helped reconcile the past. We had pushed through walls of woundedness and emerged stronger for offering our hand and having it firmly gripped.

Both Her Majesty and I received a huge number of congratulatory letters in the wake of the visit, more than had been generated in either jurisdiction by any previous state visit anywhere. Many came from Irish men and women living in Britain for whom the visit marked a new era of self-confidence and pride. I got one memorable letter from an elderly Irish republican lady who wrote that she had been completely against the visit, having no time at all for monarchs and in particular for 'the monarch next door'. She thought I was wrong to invite the Queen. At first I thought the letter was going to be a torrent of abuse, but the tone changed in the second sentence as the writer described turning on the television to catch the first five minutes from Casement Aerodrome and then watching every televised moment from start to finish over four days. She described how she had cried throughout and how so much pent-up anger and resentment had just washed right out of her. As the Queen's flight took off from Cork airport, she prayed for her safe return home and concluded that the visit 'had been choreographed by the angels'. There were certainly a lot of prayers said!

For Martin and for me, the visit was a decisive realisation of the Building Bridges project. It capped fourteen years of sustained effort to help straighten out the skewed relationships between Northern Ireland's unionist community and their neighbours south of the border, as well as the historically fraught relationships between Ireland and Great Britain. The Queen was in the sixtieth year of her reign when she came to Dublin, a mere hour's flight away, for the first time in her life. She was eighty-two years old. The road taken to her visit was long, arduous and twisted. It would take time to absorb its legacy and to put it to good effect.

Almost immediately I was invited to make a return state visit to Britain before my term of office ended in November. I saw the invitation as a personal courtesy and appreciated it as such, but it was not the norm to make return state visits within such a short time frame, and I decided against it, believing that there was a lot more to be gained from letting the many benefits and memories of the Queen's visit linger in the public mind. I suggested the invitation be extended to my successor and that it should take place after a gap of about two years, when it would be another tremendous opportunity (as indeed it proved to be) to showcase how far relationships between Ireland and Great Britain had improved.

It was evident from Sinn Féin's boycott of the visit that there was still work to be done. The party had misread the public mood and underestimated the impact of the visit. The leadership had been afraid to go out in front ahead of their followers, believing they were not ready to embrace the new dispensation between Ireland and its unhappy imperial past. Yet opinion polls after the visit confirmed that it had been popular among a majority of Sinn Féin voters. Sooner or later the party leadership would have to follow where members like Michael Browne were leading.

It took a full year. On 27 June 2012, Martin McGuinness shook the Queen's hand for the first time, at a community event in Belfast's Lyric Theatre. In 2014, when President Michael D. Higgins made the return state visit to Great Britain, Martin McGuinness was a guest at the state dinner at Windsor Castle. His presence there was unforced and natural, almost unremarkable, for time had moved on and what had been a mountain too high to climb in Dublin Castle in 2011 was barely an incline in Windsor Castle in 2014. Martin and I were fortunate to be among the other diners that night, and watching people from every possible constituency gather around that table, I was more convinced than ever how right I had been to insist that the return state visit be deferred for a couple of years, to let the import of the Queen's visit do its work as a leaven and a loosening of old tight bindings, particularly among the most disaffected. The last of the bridges seemed to be firmly in place.

At both the start and end of my presidency I visited Irish troops on peacekeeping missions in Lebanon. They were the first and last foreign visits I made, and for good reason. No Irish President had visited the troops abroad before, and when I indicated in November of 1997 that I was intent upon going to Lebanon, the advice from Foreign Affairs was resoundingly negative. In the end it proved to be doable, and it was important that it was done to highlight the vital work that a small neutral country can do, to give recognition to the men and women who make that difficult and dangerous work their vocation, to honour those who had died or been injured on service abroad, and especially to draw attention to the long wasted years of human misery that unresolved conflicts over land, identity and religion inflict. For Lebanon the misery continues. For Northern Ireland the seeds of peace were planted by every vote cast in support of the Good Friday Agreement in 1998. Things are better, but still not good enough. That is why the bridges we have built to one another have to be strengthened and crossed again and again.

\*

When I left office on 10 November 2011, many of the trappings of office fell away automatically, and others I turned down. No more police protection, no official car, no diplomatic passport, no VIP lounge. I went back to regular life, just as it should be in a republic of equals, and to a plan for the next chapter.

The plan was probably forged in Ardoyne long ago, when I discovered from some of our Protestant neighbours that God wanted Northern Ireland to remain Protestant and British, and from Catholic clerics that the same God wanted a Catholic Ireland, an all-male priesthood and a male magisterium that demanded the obedience of all those baptised as Catholics, male and female. A strange set of contradictions in the name of Christ. Now I would have time to figure out how that divisive legacy could be interrupted and reset. Within a few weeks of leaving Áras an Uachtaráin, I was on my way to Rome and to the Pontifical Gregorian University. No more high heels or elegant suits; just a hoodie, jeans, a backpack and a student card.

## 14

One September morning at the start of the new academic year in Rome, at the entrance to the Gregorian University, I noticed a man dressed in a floor-length white cassock, a broad white *fascia*, or sash, and a white *pellegrina*, or shoulder cape – an ensemble for all the world like the everyday dress of the Pope. I began to wonder if there was an unannounced papal visit that day, for from the back it looked like the Holy Father. Worse still, if it *was* the Pope, then the Pope was smoking like a chimney under his matching white ecclesiastical straw-brimmed hat (the *saturno* or *capello romano*). Eventually I established that it was not the Pope and headed for breakfast, followed by the gaggle of new students to which the papal lookalike belonged.

I was with a group of fellow students whom I had known for several months, but the young man in white was now behind me in the queue with his friends, and one of them struck up a conversation with me, beginning predictably with: 'What order of sisters do you belong to?' When I answered that I was not a member of any, the next question was: 'Are you a consecrated virgin?' That was my opportunity to flash my wedding and engagement rings, and to mention my husband and children. The reaction was bemusement, followed by incredulity when I disclosed that I was a student in the Faculty of Canon Law. The idea that anyone in their right mind would voluntarily study canon law was widely dismissed among students at the Pontifical Gregorian University. It was a view I had already encountered at home

from my clerical friends. Not a single word was offered by
any of them that could have been even loosely described as
encouraging. Almost all launched into horror stories about
studying the subject in seminaries. One, a philosopher, told
me what he had been told: 'Study philosophy, lose your mind;
study theology, lose your faith; study canon law, waste your
time.'

It emerged that my new friend's extraordinary costume
was the habit of the Norbertine order. He was English, and
on that first day he realised who I was, and also that I did not
particularly want it to be generally known. One of my fellow
canon law students was Irish, and so my immediate classmates knew my identity; but most people in the Greg did not
know, and I wanted to keep it that way. My Norbertine friend
could not contain his bewilderment at the idea that a former
President of any country would in retirement come to Rome
to study canon law. I countered that I was likewise thrown
by the idea that any young person would come to Rome from
England to study theology, or indeeed to compromise their
lungs with the well-known consequences of cigarette smoking when they could have cappuccinos and gelati instead.
We called a kind of truce. He would not reveal my identity to
anyone else at the Greg, or mock canon law; and I would
continue to give out to him about smoking. It wasn't long,
however, before he let my identity slip to a student in his
class. She happened to be a student at the Passionist lay
centre, where I had stayed, and I knew her quite well. She
was sure he was making fun of her, and was very put out that
I had not filled her in. I had simply told her I was a retired
university teacher – which was true up to a point. I was
happy enough for people to find out about my presidential
past, just not from me on day one, for I wanted to meet

student to student, person to person, and to avoid any eruption of awkwardness.

I was interested to know why any young man would join the Norbertines these days, after the pasting the order had rightly taken thanks to the depredations of the Irish Norbertine sexual predator Father Brendan Smyth. Over a forty-year period he had sexually assaulted countless children in a number of places around Ireland, including the parlour of my old Belfast school, St Dominic's. When he was first arrested, in Northern Ireland, he fled to his order's Kilnacrott Abbey, south of the border in County Cavan, hoping to avoid trial. The botched handling of a request for his extradition resulted in the fall of the Irish government in 1994. Smyth was eventually extradited, and in 1997 he died in prison in Northern Ireland while serving a twelve-year prison sentence.

The Norbertines had knowledge of Smyth's abuse from the 1970s. The Church hierarchy was aware of it too. In 1975, two teenage boys who reported Smyth to Church authorities were interviewed by a team acting on the authority of the Bishop of Kilmore. The team included a canon lawyer, Father Sean Brady, later Cardinal and Archbishop of Armagh. The boys' allegations were not reported to the police. The Church did nothing, and the Norbertines simply moved Smyth from place to place – in Ireland and in various foreign countries – while he continued to abuse children. Smyth's career as a vile sexual predator ended only thanks to the courage of victims and the intervention of the secular media. Had the matter been handled differently by the Church authorities, it is likely many of his later victims might have been saved from his assaults.

My young Norbertine friend seemed well versed in the awful story. He was not, however, put off by it in the least, even though the order came out of it badly. I explained that the Smyth affair had played some small part in my decision to study canon law. Without the secular media and their forensic journalism, Smyth would have gone unpunished. Not one single case of clerical child sex or physical abuse subsequently came to public knowledge as a result of information volunteered by the Church itself. In fact, the Church authorities had done their utmost to prevent these matters becoming known to the public. Where, I had asked myself, was canon law in all this?

In 2009, the Report of the Dublin Archdiocese Commission of Investigation (known as the Murphy Report) recorded: 'The Commission heard evidence from canon law experts that the status of canon law as an instrument of Church governance declined hugely during Vatican II and in the decades immediately after it . . . Since the 1960s, canon law itself has been in a state of flux and considerable confusion, making it difficult even for experts to know what the law is or where it is to be found.' Worse still, the commission disclosed the shocking finding that, at the end of its forensic trawl through the archdiocesan records and stories of victims, it had not encountered a single case where canon law 'was invoked as a means of doing justice to victims'.

Before the Murphy Report was published, but while the commission was working, I noticed an advert in the *Tablet*, a tolerably reflective Catholic weekly magazine, for a week-long summer school in canon law at Dublin's Milltown Institute. The course director was to be Dr Elizabeth Cotter. I knew she was good, for she had been my daughters' school principal at Loreto on the Green in Dublin. Having sorted my daughters out, she gave up teaching and became a canon lawyer at the request of her religious order. A few people in

Ireland had similar qualifications, but none had done what Elizabeth was now doing – offering in our capital city, to anyone, lay or clerical, the chance to become literate in canon law, the institutional legal architecture of the Catholic Church.

I signed up to the summer school, little thinking that it would change the course of my life. My family, knowing nothing at all about canon law, were marginally more enthusiastic than my clerical friends. They thought it was a better bet than my previous summer-school studies of the bodhran and the tin whistle, the consequences of which, even in a house as big as Áras an Uachtaráin, could be fairly unpleasant for anyone with passable hearing. Martin was particularly thrilled that this was not yet another summer school of set-dancing in which he would be a reluctant conscript. There was a high level of demand for the services of men from the females of the set-dancing species, to the extent that some men, mentioning no one in particular, began to get notions about themselves and their film-star allure. A halt was put to that unhealthy gallop the year Daniel O'Donnell joined our class and thereby became the sole object of female attention. He was also one almighty good dancer, not to mention a very good sport.

It was our hero Daniel who retrieved the situation when the key to the summer school went missing – along with the school's director, last seen on the road to Killybegs – on a bitterly cold wet night with a hundred people queued up at the door to hear Donegal's best sean-nós singers, most of whom had travelled long distances to perform, including from the outer islands. The high, narrow slice of a window to the gents' toilet was found to be open. All that was needed was a volunteer who was willing to be hoisted inside, slim enough to get through the window and flexible enough to avoid drowning in the toilet bowl. Daniel stepped forward, followed by thirty women who were anxious to support various parts of his anatomy as he was propelled upwards with something less than speed, a lot of territorial claims, and raucous merriment. Only when he shouted that he was heading straight into the toilet bowl did his male comrades take control of the situation. He emerged a few minutes later, apparently unscathed, through the fire-escape door, the undisputed champion of the hour.

News of Daniel's presence at the summer school spread quickly, and the set-dancing class was packed to capacity the next day. Martin took one look and went to Portnoo to play golf. Rules were hastily but efficiently established for the equal distribution of Daniel as a dancing partner. I managed to get the fifth figure of the Ballyvourney Jig Set. Some years later, when he was sent home from *Strictly Come Dancing* for perceived flaws in his waltz technique, we were adamant that had the dancers been required to perform the Connemara Reel Set, he would have made smithereens of the rest.

At the first tea break of our dance-free canon law course, I sat beside Father Frank Morrissey, an eminent canon lawyer from New Brunswick in the Canadian Maritimes. I mentioned that I had a lot of relatives not far from him, in Nova Scotia, among them a couple of priests, one of whom, Father Albert Cosgrave, was about his age. Maybe they knew each other? Maybe we do, he said, laughing as he pulled from his pocket a letter from Albert, his former classmate and long-standing friend, received before he left for Ireland.

Frank and Elizabeth offered a compelling vision of the possibility of making canon law a force for change. After the summer school, I undertook a master's degree by research on the constitutional framework of the Church and the Second Vatican Council's concept of 'collegiality'. I had by that point come to know the writings of many canonists, some of it drab and much of it overly defensive. But one writer stood out with a special energy: the Jesuit canon lawyer and theologian Ladislas Orsy, whose work inspired me to believe that studying canon law might not be such a waste of time after all. I decided to turn my recreational interest in the subject into something more serious, a post-presidential project to qualify as a canon lawyer and then to make the rights and obligations of the Church's three hundred million child members the focus of doctoral research.

In some ways it was a return to the past, for when I had started out as an academic lawyer at Trinity College in 1975, my first area of research interest had been the rights of children in custody in Ireland and the United Kingdom. The official reports into Catholic institutional and clerical abuse of children, and the mismanagement of credible allegations of abuse by the Church hierarchy, seemed to me to be corruption in action. The Church's capacity to overlook the rights of children and to ignore the damage to victims struck me as so endemic and systemic that simplistic theories about the causes – priestly celibacy, or poor seminary formation on sexual matters, or protection of the institution of the Church – were unlikely to tell the whole story. I looked for the books and articles that would explain how children were treated by canon law. There were virtually none, and that told me where I ought to begin.

Canon law had developed rather haphazardly over many centuries, and was first officially codified in 1917. Its authoritative language is Latin, and there was never any official translation of the 1917 code into any other language. The

1917 code should be compulsory reading in every Catholic school, for it is a repository of embarrassing drivel, and stands as a useful reminder of just how prone to egregious errors the institutional Church has always been.

When Pope John XXIII announced in January 1959 that he was convening a Second Vatican Council for the spiritual renewal of the Church, he also announced the complete reform of the code of canon law. The drafting of the new code took almost twenty years, before it was finally promulgated by Pope John Paul II in 1983. It was an improvement on the 1917 code, but its fitness for purpose was tested and found wanting in the following decades amidst the avalanche of child-abuse scandals. There was an irony in this, for the Church saw itself as a champion of children, and early canon law had helped develop the idea of children as holders of rights on their own account.

It was a Catholic priest, Canon Joseph Moerman, who had pushed the idea of the United Nations International Year of the Child in 1979, and it was he who had helped bring about the 1989 United Nations Convention on the Rights of the Child, which the Holy See was among the very first state parties to ratify. Yet, inexplicably, there had been no attempt by the Church to review and update canon law in the light of the convention. I looked for scholarly writings by canon lawyers who had researched this area, and with the exception of some fine tangential work done by Frank Morrissey, there were none. If I was to make this my area of specialisation, then I had to start by qualifying as a canon lawyer.

In deciding to become a canon lawyer, a qualification available only through the pontifical universities, I faced the same problem that had faced Dr Elizabeth. There was nowhere to study for the licentiate (professional qualification) in canon law in English except in Washington or Ottawa – neither of which was a realistic prospect for me, given their distance from Ireland. A Jesuit friend, Father Gerry Whelan, persuaded me that Rome, a two-and-a-half-hour flight away, was a good option. Study would be in Italian, but Martin and I already loved the city and I hoped my passable proficiency in Spanish would help until I managed to get to grips with the language.

I applied to be admitted to the Pontifical Gregorian University's Faculty of Canon Law to study for the licentiate. Like all prospective students I had to get a reference from my bishop. In my case it was Dr Christopher Jones, Bishop of Elphin and a Roscommon man and long-time close friend. His late brother Bunny was married to Pauline Delaney of Castlerea, sister of Father Ailbe, who had married us. Christy wrote a hearty recommendation, my higher diploma and master's degree in canon law gave me some welcome exemptions, and I was accepted to commence studies on leaving office at the end of 2011.

All foreign students at the Greg have to offer proof, through a national exam, that they have acquired the necessary level of Italian for matriculation, so in the summers of 2010 and 2011 Martin and I headed off to a language academy in the Umbrian town of Assisi. It was run by a prominent linguistics scholar, Professor Angelo Chiuchiù, and his equally talented son Lorenzo and daughter Gaia. Our familiarity with Assisi up until then had consisted of several one-day trips to the famous thirteenth-century Basilica of St Francis, with its stunning frescoes by Giotto and Cimabue. We had previously trundled up and down the hills and through the squares of that exquisite little town perched high and dizzily on the edge of Monte Subasio without paying them very much attention. We had also observed on those past trips that the stories of St Francis and St Clare had more or less completely obliterated the story of St Gabriel of Our Lady of Sorrows, the Passionist clerical student who had also been born in Assisi and who had died at twenty-four before he could be ordained. His name adorned Ardoyne's second-level parish boys' school. It was Gabriel who had been the role model for Ardoyne's Catholic teenagers, especially the young men of my day, some of whom ended up in paramilitary organisations and many more of whom did not. I was to encounter Gabriel again, somewhat unexpectedly, in Rome.

Unwittingly, Martin and I were about to become deeply immersed in the invisible side of Assisi, the daily non-touristy life of the small number of residents who continued to live in the town after the earthquakes of 1997. Apart from the damage and loss of life, another consequence of those terrible days had been a huge and permanent exodus of many townspeople. The older men who stayed on liked to meet up each day in the Piazza del Comune, moving around the square's benches during the day, following the shade. We rented a small apartment off the Piazza, walked through it four times a day on the way to and from the academy for morning and afternoon classes, and within a week were on first-name terms with the men, whose curiosity had been aroused by the police cars that seemed to appear when we were around. At first they thought we were Mafia under observation, or protected witnesses. Having discovered the less dramatic truth and the link with Ireland, the casual salutes gave way to longer conversations as they cross-examined us daily about politics, the economy and the Church. It was a great way to practise our faltering Italian.

Not much happened on the Via San Gregorio, where we

had our apartment, and the police activity was a great novelty to our neighbour Vilelma, a widow who ran a bed and breakfast next door. She waylaid us most days on the way home, invited us in for an aperitif and cakes the size of car tyres, and between the sign language of gesticulation and pidgin Italian we covered a lot of subjects. She was a tonic on any subject, full of curiosity, wit, wisdom and that natural graciousness so characteristic of rural Italians.

When we eventually extricated ourselves each day from Vilelma's terrace and succeeded in reaching our building next door, there waiting for us were Giuseppe and Marian Pace, Maltese linguists who taught Italian at the academy during the summer holidays. They rented the apartment next to ours, and we shared a small rooftop balcony. In the evenings we met there, tried to get to the end of the never-ending cake, drank a glass or two of Coke or Prosecco, practised our Italian and looked at the starry night sky. On most evenings there were concerts in the Piazza, so we would ramble up to a café on the square and generally join with groups of fellow academy students, most of them seminarians preparing, like me, for studies at one of the pontifical universities in Rome.

With the help of our friends and teachers we rapidly acquired basic Italian, which is to say I could fling together Italo-Spanish attempts at conversation with no regard for tenses or pronouns or prepositions, while Martin, who eats grammar books and dictionaries for breakfast, refused to speak a single word unless it had been processed through the grammar mill and came out perfect in every respect. When a walk in a local forest resulted in me being bitten by a snake that I neither saw nor felt but the consequences of which I later definitely saw and felt, we became acquainted with the doctor, pharmacist, local cottage hospital and big hospital in

Perugia. The doctor arrived, took a look at my scarlet elephantine leg and began to recite what sounded like a litany to
the Blessed Virgin: 'Madre de Dio, O Madre de Dio!' I sur-
mised my leg was the cause of his consternation. ''Ospital,'
he announced, using up his entire English vocabulary. He
indicated that he and Martin would carry me downstairs.
Martin enquired if we should send for an ambulance. The
doctor pointed at his watch to indicate that time was of
the essence, and so I was bundled into his little car and off to
the cottage hospital, to be put on an antibiotic drip.

The hospital was fastidiously clean and I appeared to be its
only patient. A very pleasant young female doctor sprang into
action. She had good English. I was able to tell her that this
had occurred before as a result of an insect bite, and had
developed into septicaemia. Within seconds an ambulance
was at the door and I was on the way to Perugia, attached to
the drip. It was another fastidiously clean hospital, and in the
early hours of the morning a team of experts was on the case.
When the infection began to respond to the treatment a few
days later, and they discovered that Martin, being a dentist,
could give injections, I was allowed back to Assisi and into
the care of the doctor and pharmacist and Martin.

The doctor lived round the corner, but mostly those days
he lived with us, for he never seemed to leave. If he wasn't
there, the pharmacist was. We discovered he stuck up a back-
in-ten-minutes sign on his shop, also around the corner,
while he delivered the white powder, needles and accoutre-
ments with which Martin took delight in delivering my
injections. He was never back in ten minutes, so impatient
customers took to coming to our apartment to look for him.
Anyone visiting the flat and seeing four adults gathered
around a kitchen table on which were syringes and white

powder would have been forgiven for not thinking immediately of cellulitis and antibiotics. A lot of people did visit, the distraction of which greatly helped my recovery, and soon I was fit to be wheeled up to the square for the night-time café life.

I arrived in Rome in the first weeks of 2012 to begin my post-presidency life as a full-time student. I had packed my ten-kilogram Ryanair-sized carry-on suitcase with a few light clothes, having sent ahead by courier a lot of heavy canon law tomes. I was prepared for an idyllic Roman spring and for the years of intensive study ahead as a student of the Greg, situated one minute from the Trevi Fountain. My first Roman home was to be at the Lay Centre on the Caelian Hill right behind the Colosseum. It occupied part of two floors of the Passionist fathers' massive headquarters. Martin was due over a couple of weeks later, bringing with him with some more of my summery clothes.

It started snowing heavily the day after I arrived, and the snow continued for days after. The little electric bus taking me home from the Greg on my second day slipped and slithered down the appropriately named Via dei Serpenti, provoking groans from the passengers and finally a shrug from the driver, who stopped it dead as it spun wildly to the left, opened the door and told us he and it were going no further. I managed to get so disoriented in the driving snow that I walked back the way the bus had come and turned a ten-minute ride home into an epic freezing hike in ballet shoes to where I had started. Making the best of a bad lot, I thought to take in a visit to what I assumed would be a deserted Trevi Fountain to capture photos of it covered in snow. I assumed wrong. Multiple representatives of every nation in the world, all except me appropriately dressed for the weather, were queued eight deep around the fountain, camera or phone in hand. I gave up and set off again in what I hoped was the right direction.

Temperatures plummeted to depths unseen in Rome for almost three decades. Traffic stopped. People bum-boarded down the slope at the Colosseum. Groups of tourists had snowball fights at the Trajan Forum. For a full week, as if in complete denial that Rome was snowbound, I plodded the thirty-minute walk to class through the foot-deep snow and slush in sneakers, a light rain jacket and multiple layers of everything I had packed. My room had no heating. The building had no heating. The monks wore long woollen soutanes and thick woollen capes. Borrowing them or even requisitioning them was not an option, no matter how desperate the frozen laity were. When Martin arrived at the weekend and saw the refrigerated state of his wife, he frogmarched me into a shop on the Corso and I emerged with one of the millions of black Michelin Man coats that are the go-to wardrobe item for every woman in Italy from October to April, even on warm days. It doubled as a duvet.

I was not the only one ill-prepared for the weather. A couple of days after my arrival, a young American girl appeared at the Lay Centre wearing a T-shirt and high-heeled sandals, and dragging two monumental suitcases full of more T-shirts and high-heeled sandals. Her taxi had left her at the bottom of the virtually impassable road about three hundred yards short of the entrance to the Lay Centre. Unable to find the doorway, which was hidden in a giant wall, she had teetered up and down the road until hypothermia set in, at which point a man in a car stopped and offered her a lift – this on a road no car had risked for a couple of days. The elderly male driver, also unable to locate the doorway, took her home to his wife. Meanwhile all hell had broken loose in the Lay Centre when the young woman did not turn up as expected and no word had been heard. Finally, hours later, the doorbell rang. We gathered at the door and watched in disbelief as our new housemate and her elephantine cases were safely disgorged from a car the size of a tumble dryer. She wobbled in, her vertiginous sandals looking somewhat the worse for wear. Donna, the Lay Centre director, nerves shredded with worry, just said: 'Sandals – you wore high-heeled sandals?' Back came the response: 'What can I say. I'm a girl!'

We were definitely a mixed bunch. There was also an aviary full of chirruping birds and a marauding band of Roman cats, among them the handsome black-and-white Moses, who insinuated himself from being an outdoor to an indoor cat during the great freeze. The cats' favourite pastime was frightening the living melt out of us by bolting from the bushes in the dark or, in the case of Moses, by jumping from his indoor perch on the ground-floor bathroom window just a split second before the automatic light came on. I suggested we needed a defibrillator installed there – either that or Moses had to go – but he had the Lay Centre director completely under his little paw and there was no shifting him.

The next person to show up in sandals, a few days later, was my dear friend Sister Bernadette from the Poor Clare Convent in Ennis. She was a contemplative sister, but held an office in the order that obliged her to attend a meeting in Assisi, with a stopover in Rome. It was a great chance to meet up. Martin and I went to meet her at her order's Rome convent, and there she was in the only footwear she had: her old faithful brown (very flat) open-toed sandals. 'She is actually worse than you,' said Martin as he picked her up and carried her through the twelve inches of snow to the taxi that had been due to take us to lunch.

We diverted to a shoe shop on the Corso, which was mercifully open on a Sunday and completely empty, as was the Corso itself. Two bored teenage girls in miniskirts stood behind the counter. I wondered what they would make of Sister Bernadette in her pre-Vatican II habit and unseasonal sandals. Martin, his Italian a bit rusty, just pointed to her frozen toes. The girls sprang into action, fussing over her like clucking hens and with genuine concern insisting on fur-lined bootees, arguing among themselves as to what would best suit her. When they heard she was going to Assisi, where the weather was worse and the convent had no heating, the four boxes of boots that had been brought from the bowels of the store were summarily cast aside and another lot appeared that would have prevented frostbite at the summit of Mount McKinley. Bernadette protested the whole while that she would never get the wear out of them, as once home she would be back into the regulation sandals. No matter. The sandals were wrapped, the boots were acquired and she fairly danced up the Corso in total comfort and delight. Martin was particularly pleased, for no matter how noble one-way nun-carrying was, it had not done wonders for his back.

Outside temperature notwithstanding, I had arrived at the Lay Centre to a warm welcome from my old American friend Donna Orsuto, Professor of Spirituality at the Greg. She was the director of the Lay Centre, which she had co-founded years before to carry on the work of hospitality and ecumenical dialogue conducted by an order of Dutch nuns called the Ladies of Bethany. At their Rome house on the Piazza Navona, they had hosted many of the ecumenical observers during the Second Vatican Council. When their mission ceased in the mid 1980s, Donna and the Dutch icon artist Riekie van Velzen founded the Lay Centre as a place of ecumenical and inter-faith hospitality and formation for lay students of the pontifical universities, athenaea and institutes in Rome.

Originally the Lay Centre had been situated on the Piazza Navona, but I first got to know about it when it later operated out of a small convent building in the grounds of the Pontifical Irish College, a seminary near the Lateran Basilica. I had often visited the Irish College over the years, for a number of our close friends had studied or worked there. In 1990, the aforementioned Sean Brady, then the rector of the college, had provoked much muttering when he invited me to lunch in the communal dining room in breach of its then strict no-women rule. In those days the convent next door was occupied by a group of highly educated Irish nuns who had all held very senior positions in Ireland but whose job in Rome was to attend to the feeding, washing and ironing of the seminarians in the college. We took them out to dinner, and if ever there was a mutinous crew, they were it. Times were changing, but not for women in the Church, and shortly afterwards we heard they had decamped back home and suggested 'the lads' learn those thankless domestic skills as an investment in their future as pastors rather than princes.

The empty convent soon became the home of the Lay Centre, but even that building became too small, and in 2009 there followed a move to the Passionist Generalate, about ten minutes' walk away. Afterwards the Irish College's old convent was completely refurbished and is now the Villa Irlanda, a bed and breakfast establishment owned by the Irish College and very popular with Irish wedding parties.

Next door to it is the little St Joseph's cottage, which I was later fortunate enough to live in for two years.

The Lay Centre now occupied an unused part of the Passionist fathers' enormous headquarters and retreat house, set in acres of elegant gardens overlooking the Colosseum. It had once been the site of a temple dedicated to the Emperor Claudius, built by his wife Agrippina, mother of Nero. I had occasionally visited the beautiful ancient church attached to it, known as the Basilica dei Santi Giovanni e Paolo, or in Ardoyne as 'John's and Paul's'.

I had visited the Passionist campus once before, in June 2007, when I was in Rome to attend the canonisation of St Charles of Mount Argus CP. Charles Houben (1821–93) was a Dutch Passionist priest who gained fame as a healer in Dublin. Some class of a clerical genius then sent him to Holy Cross, Ardoyne, for a rest. Even in 1885, there was not much chance of getting a rest in Ardoyne. The short time he spent there, however, secured for him the local status of folk saint, and during my childhood many people still prayed to him.

The Vatican Mass in 2007 at which he and three others were canonised by Pope Benedict was possibly the wettest canonisation in the history of canonisations. It was a truly miserable endurance test, a very, very long outdoor ceremony in relentless torrential rain. While the Pope and cardinals remained dry under a canopy, thirty thousand others were assaulted by the monsoon. We guests in the VIP section for the diplomatic corps – who had been told the event was to be indoors, and were therefore dressed accordingly – sat wrapped in large black bin bags. Our plastic seats were of the variety that dipped into a depression in the middle. When we stood up for the opening procession, the seats filled up with three inches of water; and when we sat down as per the instructions on our commemorative leaflets, water squelched in all directions. I took particular note of the British ambassador, whose quaint plumed helmet was now a sorry sight, and with the feathers plastered to his face he looked the perfect picture of misery. I decided that I was not going to risk standing up again, and so sat throughout the entire ceremony, glowered at by Cardinal Bertone, Sodano's successor as Cardinal Secretary of State, from the comfort of his dry zone.

I did not realise that the entire diplomatic delegation took their cue from the lead VIP, who happened on that particular day to be the President of Ireland, though no one had informed me of that. If I sat, they sat, and so we all sat even when the instructions clearly said 'Stand'. It possibly did look to Bertone as though there was a slight protest going on in the diplomatic ranks. Bad as our situation was, it was considerably worse for the thousands of standing pilgrims, many elderly, frail and disabled. It was pitiful to see a number of them picking their way to avoid falls amid the deluge as they carried to the altar the gifts in the offertory procession. The apparent lack of care for those who had made long journeys was difficult to comprehend. Many people just drifted away, defeated by the weather.

When the Mass ended, we were invited to meet the Pope inside the basilica. I was the first to be greeted by him. He was flanked by Cardinal Sodano and Archbishop (now Cardinal) Harvey. I had not anticipated representing my country looking as if I had just done the annual Tiber swim. Trying to make light of the sodden state of those queueing to greet him, I offered Pope Benedict my hand and said, 'Congratulations, Holy Father. Today you created four new saints and thirty thousand martyrs, among whom I count myself!' Benedict and Harvey laughed. Sodano, never my favourite prince of the Church, looked as if he might disgorge his innards on the spot. Still, the only audience for the remark was we five. Who would ever hear of it? Ah, Roma . . .

By the time I arrived later that day to the Villa Spada, then the home of Ireland's ambassador to the Holy See, Archbishop Diarmuid Martin (whose waterlogged mitre had to be binned) had already heard the story, and so had the entire saturated ambassadorial corps. It is fair to say there was a more than decent level of support for the remark. Next morning early, as Martin and I wandered near the Pantheon in brilliant sunshine eating a litre of gelato, we ran into Archbishop Martin exiting from an ecclesiastical outfitters and carrying a bag with his new mitre.

On that day of the unforgettable inundation, I got my first glimpse of life behind the mammoth walls of the Passionist Generalate, which runs up from the back of the Colosseum along one entire side of the Via Claudia. Once through the extremely discreet entrance and up the narrow lane, we were greeted with a vista of endless fine buildings, acres of pristine clipped lawns, shrubs and trees, orange and lemon groves and families of ducks waddling about as if they were in the countryside. Above all there was a compelling sense of peace to be found in this place just a few yards from the bustle of the Colosseum, the Metro, the forums, the hawkers and sellers, the tourists and ordinary life of Rome. We had a fine lunch there with the Passionists in their refectory, saw their trove of St Charles memorabilia, and reminisced about Belfast's Ardoyne and Dublin's Mount Argus, two Passionist parishes in which I had lived. When I mentioned that I had visited their basilica a few times before, I was asked if I had ever seen it dressed up for a wedding, as it was that day. I had not, but I did know of its reputation as a favourite place for Roman weddings. We entered it from the sacristy, and to say it was breathtaking would be to do it little justice. I could not believe my good fortune when, five years later, I discovered this magnificent place with its stunningly beautiful chapel and grounds was to be my first home in Rome.

There were twenty or so of us staying at the Lay Centre while studying in Rome, and for the first time I encountered Catholics who belonged to one or other of the twenty-three eastern Catholic churches, which are headed by the Pope but allow married priests and have their own separate code of canon law. There were also Jews, Muslims, Orthodox Christians and a Sufi dervish. We lived together in community, sharing dinner, washing-up and weekend cooking. We chatted over hasty breakfasts, walked or bussed together to class, explored Rome together, explained ourselves and our cultures to each other, grew in friendship and in exasperation at the official bureaucracy that we newcomers had to navigate, especially those from outside the European Union. The old hands obligingly helped the new. I was older than all of the others by a mile, but they were a tolerant lot.

Our dinners began with a blessing prayer and ended with a short hymn: '*Magnificat, magnificat, magnificat anima mea dominum, magnificat, magnificat, magnificat anima mea*' – 'My soul doth magnify the Lord'. The Magnificat is one of the oldest Catholic Marian hymns, attributed to Mary the mother of Jesus and believed to have been said by her when she visited her cousin Elizabeth to announce her pregnancy. One of the Lay Centre's young imams, who sang it with gusto each evening, told me of his interest in and devotion to Mary, who plays an important role in Islamic spirituality. It was news to me, and part of the rich process of mutual discovery that the Lay

Centre offered. Respect for and interest in each other's beliefs and culture was embedded in the place.

There was evening Mass on a Wednesday for anyone interested, even just as a spectator. Since we had no resident priest, a different guest celebrant would join us each week for dinner and a discussion, sometimes with other invited guests who brought interesting scholarly perspectives on aspects of Church life or ecumenism or inter-faith matters. Some of the residents were devout or pious, but none were sanctimonious. None of them were wealthy, and they were often making great personal sacrifices to study in Rome. Our Passionist landlords were not unduly friendly, and sometimes an outbreak of laughter on the main student corridor or late-night phone calls heard through an open window became a subject of complaint, which Donna, the consummate diplomat, always managed to mollify.

My study/bedroom was in an attic above the main student corridor. It had a high ceiling, a drab tiled floor, a window that overlooked nothing in particular, a bathroom with noisy plumbing, a single bed, a desk and a bockety office chair that tended every so often to lurch suddenly to the left and throw me onto the floor. There was a small wardrobe, an armchair that I never used, and an IKEA throw, bought in bulk during the big freeze, in which I wrapped myself as I studied Italian, Latin and canon law.

A couple of yards from my bedroom door was a glass wall, the demarcation line between the Lay Centre and the monastery, through which I saw the occasional Passionist heading to or from his room. The great bonus of my room and that window was that I was wakened every morning by the chanting of the Passionists at early-morning Mass. Their private chapel was off-limits to inhabitants of the Lay Centre, but I loved last thing at night to listen to their stout rendition of my favourite hymn, the Lourdes Salve Regina. Less welcome was the noise from the thudding bass of rock concerts at the Colosseum or the Circus Maximus.

My room was a long way up, and on that first day, as I dragged my case up the stairs, passing the Passionist glass barriers on each floor, I stopped to catch my breath before trying for the summit. There, through the glass, I could see a very familiar portrait: St Gabriel of Our Lady of Sorrows. Suddenly I was back in Ardoyne, for the weekly novena in his name, and the memory sprang from somewhere of Father Justin telling us the story of Gabriel. He was just the sherpa I needed to get me to the top, though any satisfaction in arriving there was rendered null and void when I discovered that in order to eat I would have to go back down those blessed stairs to the ground floor. St Gabriel and I were going to have many conversations.

On the same level as the Lay Centre's chapel was an obscure door that opened onto a balcony, where we could hang our washing, sunbathe, eat lunch or just marvel at the magnificent vista over ancient Rome and the stunning pinky-orange sunsets. I discovered the balcony a month after I arrived, when the snow had finally disappeared. Here was a place to watch the night sky and the moon over the Colosseum.

The front door of the Lay Centre opened onto a part of the monastery gardens we were permitted to use for walks, occasional garden parties, football matches or just sitting in the shade. It had tall trees, shrubs, lawn and a pebbled perimeter walk. The first time I took that walk was some weeks after my arrival. The snow had just gone and the evenings were lengthening, so I set out to explore my surroundings. I arrived two minutes later at the far perimeter and gasped out loud, for there right under my nose in all their unrivalled glory were the Colosseum and the Arch of Constantine, and it seemed I had them completely to myself. Every visitor I brought to the same spot had the same stupefied reaction. No one lived nearer the Colosseum than we did, and no one had such a breathtaking hidden vantage point from which to see it. Walking to and from college each day past the Colosseum, up the Via dei Fori Imperiali, past the Trajan Forum into the Piazza Venezia, the Corso and the Piazza della Pilotta, I never lost the effervescing sense of awe, happiness and joy at this new life chapter. That in itself was a miracle, for I was studying canon law, and if any subject is designed to drain the joy out of life, then canon law has to be it.

For the previous fourteen years I had been watched over more or less constantly by police protection officers. This might have lulled me into a false sense of immunity to danger, at least at first. I had no car in Rome and no desire to use anything but public transport and Shanks's pony. The area immediately bordering the monastery could be a bit spooky at night. I entered and exited the monastery grounds on foot, often on my own in the dark. Two large graffitied metal gates creaked fully open as if to admit a car, and then took forever to close. We were instructed that we were to hang around until the gates clanged shut behind us, in case an unauthorised person tried to enter. Apparently we were expected to challenge any intruder as if the Angel Gabriel himself was guarding us. In reality, as soon as the aperture was wide enough to squeeze through, we sprinted up the long unlit path to the Lay Centre door about two hundred yards away.

What did not help was to discover, through a casual conversation with a Passionist friend I happened to bump into, that our monastery was sometimes used to temporarily house priests with a history of abuse. They could have been among the men we sometimes encountered when we were going in and out or simply enjoying the gardens. We had not been told. Nor had the Lay Centre personnel. Donna was apoplectic, particularly since there were regular Lay Centre family events involving children. She does not do apoplectic as a rule, for you would be hard put to find a more serene, tolerant, happy and trusting human being. She had spent almost thirty years ploughing a lonely furrow as one of the few females working in the Gregorian University and was not given to confrontation. She made an exception in this case and the matter was resolved quickly and satisfactorily so that the centre's famous lawn parties, with Riekie's grand-children running about, continued happily.

The beautiful gardens had orchards of lemon and orange trees, the fruits of which were clearly removed for use in the monastery, but I was interested in the elder trees near the gate. No one seemed to remove their blooms or berries. One of my favourite summer rituals back in Ireland was making elderflower cordial. I got permission from the Passionists to harvest their elderflowers, but the trees were so high and the blossoms so hard to reach that I had to engage the help of a visiting Jesuit priest who was conveniently very, very tall. The superior general of the Passionists, who also happily supplied the lemons needed for the recipe, got a bottle of my cordial, as did the secretary to the canon law faculty, Dr Mirjam Kovac, who lit up with delight, for it reminded her of summers at home in her native Slovenia. Without her endless help and enthusiasm, many a time I would have given up, headed to Ciampino airport and home. She had a doctorate in canon law, worked incredibly hard as the faculty secretary and also taught methodology, a subject as fundamental and necessary as the ability to use a computer. She was far and away the best teacher I encountered at the Greg, with a real gift for communicating a complex enough subject and for making sure that every student was making progress. If I managed to settle into the Greg's flummoxing clerical culture, it was thanks to Mirjam, the library staff, and the team in the Greg bar, who made my new student workplace on the Piazza della Pilotta a place of welcome.

It soon became evident that, probably alone of the institutions that surrounded me, the Lay Centre was dynamic, vibrant and genuinely hospitable. Donna and Riekie seemed to be creating an altogether warmer, more inclusive, less judgemental experience of the Church. It was a view that was to become more and more convincing with each passing day, and each experience of what proved almost invariably to be the disappointingly jaded ecclesiastical side of Rome.

In my first encounter with the canon law faculty, I explained that I would be entirely on my own, there were no security implications for the Gregorian, and I would be plodding in and out on foot, carrying my books and lunch in a backpack. I would appreciate it if no one was told my background. Father Michael Hilbert SJ, the previous dean, had reason to know I was no dilettante, for he had been the examiner of my master's thesis on Church governance at the Milltown Institute. Still, I felt like an exhibition piece just unboxed and being evaluated.

Also present at that meeting was Father Keith Pecklers SJ, a liturgical scholar at the Greg and an ecumenical expert whom I had met briefly at an Irish event in New York some months earlier. Although not a canon lawyer, he volunteered to help me navigate the notoriously bureaucratic admission system. Things had been very casual in the months before I came to Rome, but now they insisted on having even my A-level certificates from over forty years ago. With my sheaf of documents checked and double-checked, I joined the long queue of new students waiting to register in the secretariat. It was like an old-fashioned post office, with two seated clerks. I was fortunate to get the more pleasant of the two. The young priest from the Congo whom I had chatted to for the hour that we were stuck in the queue was not so fortunate. He was brusquely told his documents were not in order and summarily sent back to the end of the queue. It turned out his documents were fine.

Some days later, I had to present a certificate that showed I had attended a course in the Italian language and passed the requisite exam. This time I met the awkward clerk, who waved my certificate away on the grounds that it was not from the Gregorian's Italian course. I pointed out that it was from the Pontifical Lateran University's intensive autumn course up the road, and was at a higher level than that demanded by the Gregorian. I had read nothing that said students had to learn their Italian at the Gregorian. He was having none of it, and out came the brusque dismissal, at which point I asked to speak to his superior. An elegant older man appeared and engaged in a heated conversation with my adversary, not a syllable of which I understood. Suddenly my level B2 Italian did not seem all that impressive or even useful. To my surprise, the older man turned to me and in excellent English announced that I was absolutely correct, my certificate was perfectly acceptable and he hoped I would accept his apology. Almost every day thereafter I ran into the officious clerk in the Greg bar, where he studiously blanked me until my persistently cheery '*buongiorno*' eventually produced a glimmer of a smile.

*

Not far from the Gregorian University is the Jesuit Oratory of Francis Xavier, home of the Caravita Catholic community, which has a particular focus on ecumenism, inter-religious dialogue and peacemaking. Just about every kind of Christian and many other faiths turned up to the services at Caravita. The relaxed atmosphere and genuine liturgical sharing gave an insight into what successful, active ecumenism could produce. The Archbishop of Canterbury's representative to the Holy See was formally installed there as part of a dynamic relationship with the nearby Anglican Centre, and almost immediately I made friends with the then representative, the Australian archbishop David Richardson, and his wife Margy.

Caravita had fine music and a beautiful location in central Rome. It wasn't a parish, more of a loose gathering. I wandered over after class on my first Ash Wednesday in the city, forswearing the Greg's chapel, which I never warmed to. In front of the simple altar, ashes were being distributed by a number of people. I joined a queue randomly and received my ashes from the head of Rome's Methodist Church. By the time I got back to my seat I was overcome with trembling and tears of joy. This was exactly how it should be. It was exhilarating, and I could not help thinking how very different life would have been if this had been the norm in Northern Ireland.

When I returned to Caravita in September 2019, I found the community reeling from the news that Father Keith Pecklers, one of its founders, had shortly before been listed among priest abusers by the diocese of New Jersey and had left the team of pastors. Shocking as that news was, I remain very grateful to Caravita for its lived ecumenism. I relished those Sundays when I walked from the Colosseum to Caravita and always stayed too long chatting after Mass, so that I had to grab a bus back to do my stint in the Lay Centre kitchen, setting tables, making lunch and doing dishes.

Long before I reached the end of the doctoral road, I had to spend an entire year studying medieval Latin (via Italian) at the Gregorian. I still have no idea how I managed to get through the year or the exam. My best pals in the class – a pair of young Jesuit priests, Mike from Canada and Brian from the United States – also passed, and to say the three of us had exhibited no great facility for the subject at the outset of the year would be an understatement. Yet we all eventually aced it, thanks probably to two things.

The first was that early on in the year we realised the chances of us individually getting through the weekly workload of Latin translations were zero. The Italian and Spanish speakers in the class whizzed through them, but we were completely tongue-tied in class, even after sixteen-hour days battling with the subject. After several humiliating classes I suggested we divide the work in three and share our translations with one another the night before class. That worked to the extent that at least it looked as though we had done all the prescribed work, no matter how poorly. The second reason for our unexpected success had to do with the answer to a question I asked the teacher/examiner the week before the dreaded exam. We had already been told emphatically never to ask questions in class, so when I stuck up my hand the professor vented on that rule for a minute; but I insisted that the question was legitimate and we were entitled to an answer. He relented, and I asked if he would require a polished or a literal translation of the exam text. With what can only be described as scorn, he emphasised that we were not to even attempt a polished translation. What was required was a literal one.

We three glowed with delight, for a polished translation lay far beyond our capabilities. I arrived at the exam with my three dictionaries – medieval Latin into modern Latin, Latin into English, and English into Italian. I had twelve coloured felt-tip pens with which to identify verbs, tenses, nouns, adjectives, adverbs, nominative, accusative, dative and genitive cases, and unknowns. The examiner was nonplussed at the sight of them, for it must have looked as if I was about to colour in the exam paper rather than do a translation. God knows I was tempted.

The text to be translated had not photocopied well, so the exam paper was a bit of a mess, but we said nothing when the examiner interrupted us to correct his own errors. Until the tenth time. I had lost my concentration, one student had walked out and the tension in the room was close to exploding. My fluency in the language of complaint surprised even me, and before I knew it I was threatening to go to the dean, expressing outrage at the amount of time the examiner had wasted and saying that if this had happened in Ireland he would be answerable to Joe Duffy. I imagine the reference to Joe Duffy, which was lost on all concerned, was not what persuaded him. But suddenly he became humbly apologetic and helpful, offering us as much extra time as we needed. My classmates gave me the thumbs-up. My two Jesuit friends, knowing me a bit better than the rest, drew their fingers across their throats to indicate *Quit while you're ahead – now!* I spent the evening explaining the national pastoral and judicial role of the Joe Duffy radio show, on which all Irish problems are aired and solved, more or less.

The day of the exam results dawned, and I sat nervously in

the Greg bar contemplating the horrible possibility of a resit while the rest of the class headed off to check the results list. My two mates returned dancing on air. To the evident horror of the rest of the class, we lesser Latin scholars had taken the top three places, with me at the very top. We gulped down glasses of Prosecco offered by the bar manager Fabio, our number-one fan and friend, and then got out of there fast before the Premier League scholars turned their wrath on us unlikely winners from the Fourth Division. The three of us headed for a ten-euro eat-and-drink-all-you-can Japanese restaurant, where we spent the rest of the day in a delirium.

Our joy was short-lived, for during that bizarre year of medieval Latin we had also been working on finalising and submitting for approval the plans for our doctoral theses. Mine was given immediate approval, but my two Jesuit friends kept hitting irritating minor hitches so that the summer they had planned at home in the US and Canada now looked as if it would have to be spent in Rome rejigging their projects with no guarantee of success and no conviction that the effort would be worth it. They were both seriously considering just giving up when the possibility of changing university came up in conversation, and I mentioned that I knew Frank Morrissey, by then professor emeritus at St Paul's, Ottawa. Both had been considering a transfer to Ottawa without knowing if it was even possible. I phoned Frank. He talked to the canon law dean. She talked to my friends. They sent her their thesis projects and in no time they were gone.

Their departure was a big loss to me, left behind in Rome without their camaraderie and craic, but for them it was the beginning of really happy and fulfilling years when they stormed successfully through their doctoral research in the richly student-affirming environment of St Paul's. They were and remain without doubt the two most sincere and impressive young priests I have ever met. One ended up working on an American Indian reservation where a senior lay colleague was a classmate of mine from schooldays at St Dominic's. He felt the Lord had already prepared him well for this apprenticeship to yet another feisty Belfast woman.

Growing up in Ardoyne next door to a Passionist monastery had already introduced me to the saints commemorated in the Basilica of Giovanni e Paolo, where St Gabriel and St Gemma had their own dedicated side chapels. Each also had a school in Ardoyne named after them. In the excavations beneath the basilica is one of the best preserved ancient Roman houses, said to incorporate a tunnel to the Colosseum and a holding place for the wild animals who 'entertained' audiences there. Its frescoes are a wonder, but it is the more modern additions to the basilica that seem to attract Romans to queue up to book their nuptials there despite an unprepossessing exterior.

In the 1940s, Cardinal Spellman of New York, the then titular bishop of the Basilica of Giovanni e Paolo, raised funds with the help of Joe Kennedy, JFK's father, for the refurbishment of the basilica. Among other changes, they recycled thirty-three very grand chandeliers from the first Waldorf Astoria Hotel in New York. Romans call it the Chandelier Chapel, and when the chandeliers are lit and the aisle is resplendent with rows of large urns bursting with fresh white flowers, it really is an idyllic picture-perfect wedding backdrop. I got into the habit of dropping in there shortly before it closed each evening at six, when there was no one there but me and the elderly amiable caretaker who did not seem to mind me lighting candles at the last minute.

I had the chapel of St Paul of the Cross to myself, and it was there that I thought of Ardoyne, the Troubles, the dead, the wounded in body and mind, and the past we could not allow to be repeated.

One evening as I left, I encountered the former Bishop of Down and Connor, Dr Paddy Walsh, who was visiting the Irish College for a few days' holiday. He had been the chaplain to the hospital beside my Dominican school back in Belfast of the 1960s. When I was seventeen, he gave us a talk on Pope Paul VI's encyclical *Humanae Vitae*, which provoked a very lively and, for the time, frank debate. In my first year as a student at Queen's University, he was one of our Catholic chaplains. I often met him at Mass or events in the chaplaincy before he moved on to become head of St Malachy's College, a second-level diocesan grammar school for boys. The years of his tenure as Bishop of Down and Connor were a nightmare of violent deaths and daily ugly dramas. It visibly wore him down, and he was never comfortable in front of a microphone or camera. He was more likely to turn up in a house of the bereaved than on television.

In 1995, while I was pro vice chancellor of Queen's, I hosted the first ever dinner in the university for chaplains past and present. They were a group of about twenty, of mixed Christian denominations. The most senior among them was Bishop Paddy Walsh. What intrigued me and not a few others that night was just how overtly frosty he was with me, his host. I put it down, rightly or wrongly, to clerical hostility towards articulate women who did not always toe the Church line, a hostility I occasionally encountered, though Walsh's predecessor, Cardinal Cahal Daly, did not suffer from that particular attitude.

If Walsh was shocked to find me leaving the church he

was about to enter, I was even more surprised to find him visiting the Passionists' heartland, for when he was Bishop of Down and Connor there were times when it seemed there was no love lost between him and the Ardoyne Passionists. During the loyalist siege of the Holy Cross girls' primary school in 2001–2, the Passionist rector of Ardoyne, Father Aidan Troy CP, and his confrère Father Gary Donegan CP had become well known through television and radio coverage of the shocking affair. They handled an explosive situation with courage, dignity, charity, calm and forgiveness, but there were local mutterings about a perceived absence of overt support from Bishop Walsh. I was in regular touch with the priests and other people in Ardoyne during those days and was taken aback to learn that the view had formed, rightly or wrongly, that the bishop's main concern seemed to be that the priests were getting too much publicity.

Events came to a head when Father Troy was summoned to the bishop's house to explain why he had left the diocese over the weekend without notifying his ordinary – that is to say, the bishop. Father Troy was burying his father that weekend in Bray, County Wicklow, and had left a message on the bishop's phone to that effect. The encounter with his ordinary added greatly to the strain he was already under. He came to discuss the situation with me, in visible anguish. He was seriously considering leaving Ardoyne in order to mollify the bishop, a course of action that would have been nothing short of disastrous, given his pivotal role in keeping an alarming mess from turning into something even worse. I persuaded him that it was essential he remain, and he was reassured when I told him I would find a way of dealing with the bishop. I had no idea how I was going to do that without running the risk of making matters between them worse.

By pure luck, the day after my meeting with Father Aidan I attended a lunch in Dublin to mark the anniversary of a ground-breaking television documentary series made by the all-priest Radharc team. I sat beside Father Martin Clarke, spokesperson for the Episcopal Conference, which was meeting that same afternoon. I told him the story and asked what could be done. He listened and said to leave it with him. Before the day was out, both Bishop Walsh and his auxiliary Bishop Donal McKeown had been in touch by phone with the Passionists to offer support, and Bishop Walsh turned up to say Mass in Ardoyne a few days later. He spoke in private with Aidan, with generosity and graciousness, which was just as well, for outside the door there was a tense gathering of fellow priests, all of whom supported Aidan and were spoiling for a showdown. One word the wrong way from the bishop and there could have been quite a scene. Father Aidan was delighted with the turnaround and rang me to ask: 'What on earth did you say to him?' I replied truthfully: 'Nothing.' I never did find out what the late Father Martin said, but it certainly worked.

Now, in the portico of the Basilica of Giovanni e Paolo in Rome, not another sinner about, Bishop Walsh and I exchanged no more than brief small talk, itself remarkable given what we had both lived through back home. There would be no chewing of the cud over coffee, as usually happened with the Irish visitors I often ran into in Rome. He was uncomfortable, monosyllabic and anxious not to dally. Tellingly, though, he spontaneously revealed that he found solace in Rome and the memories of his student days. The confident young priest of my school and student days was now bent, care-worn and bordering on wretched. At one level he had had a stellar career as principal of a leading

Catholic boys' school and as bishop of his home diocese, but in reality the relentlessness of the Troubles had drained him, as it had so many. Now this man who had insisted on deference and strict obedience to the letter of canon law was thoroughly demoralised, even lost, in the cold climate generated by widespread episcopal betrayal of abused children.

## 15

Across the street from the Lay Centre is the church of Santo Stefano Rotondo, where Donnchad mac Briain – King of Cashel and Thomond, and son of Brian Boru, High King of Ireland – lies buried since around 1064. The road from the church leads up past the Pontifical Irish College, where I sometimes attended Sunday Mass.

The Irish College is a handsome building. Its small chapel has been transformed into one of the most beautiful in Rome by the gloriously distinctive work of Slovenian artist Father Marko Rupnik SJ. A fine wraparound cortile is home to a monument to Daniel O'Connell, who, horrified by the Famine and weakened by a spell in prison for political activism, set out on a pilgrimage to Rome but died en route at Genoa in 1847. He left 'my body to Ireland, my heart to Rome, my soul to heaven'. As a result, his heart was placed in a casket in the Irish College, which was then at San Agata de Goti, not far from the Lateran Basilica and the Basilica of Santa Maria Maggiore. Sadly, when the college moved to its new premises there was no sign of the casket, and its whereabouts is an unsolved mystery. However, in the cortile there is a monument to O'Connell by Benzoni, which ensures that all pilgrims remember him still. It was a privilege to have the chance to live there for two years towards the latter part of my tenure in Rome, for the two-bedroomed cottage in the college garden allowed me to make a home in Rome for Martin and our visiting family and friends.

Beginning in childhood, Daniel O'Connell has been an inspirational figure to both Martin and me. We sometimes visited the imposing but gloomy Theatine Basilica of San Andrea della Valle, where part of O'Connell's many funeral obsequies took place over two days on 28 and 30 June 1847. I often dropped in as I passed it on Wednesday afternoons on the way to a café in the quiet nearby Piazza Farnese, just off the Campo de' Fiori, to meet my friend Barbara Donovan, the Irish administrator of the Venerable English College. Just as her sister Eleanor had been a great friend during my days working for RTÉ, Barbara became the best of company in Rome.

Sitting in San Andrea's sober interior, I sometimes recalled March 1976 and our honeymoon pilgrimage to O'Connell's home at Derrynane House in County Kerry. Being reminded there of O'Connell's life and his commitment to non-violence had helped calm the unshakeable sadness that clouded those early days of marriage. The sectarian murders on the morning of our wedding of my neighbours, friends and surrogate big brothers Tony and Myles O'Reilly had shrouded our honeymoon in a grief that was capable of overwhelming me even forty years later in a church in Rome.

My attitude to that small part of old Rome was not helped by an invitation to lunch with the Legionaries of Christ, who have a house close by. I had little time for the cult-like Legionaries, founded, as I have mentioned, by the arch-criminal, thoroughly corrupt but hugely influential Father Marcial Maciel. The vast sums of money he gathered, allegedly from wealthy Catholic Mexicans, allied to his strong public defence of the magisterium, provided him with a protective veil behind which his repugnant crimes continued through the papacies of John XXIII, Paul VI, John Paul I and John Paul II. When continuing to overlook Maciel's crimes became impossible, Pope Benedict, who had known of his double life for years, gently consigned him to a monastery. He authorised an investigation into the Legionaries, the results of which have never seen the light of day, and while many believe the order should have been wound up, it continues today. For such a relatively small order, it still wields considerable influence, in particular through the number of members of the curia who are associated with it. This phenomenon, it was explained to me, arises because the order's generous donations cover their salaries and the Holy See is happy to be absolved of that burden.

By the time I met members of the order in Rome, Maciel was dead and the truth about his appalling catalogue of crimes – from rape to child abuse to bigamy to money-laundering for drug cartels – was well known and irrefutable. The men I met were not unimpressive, and the impact of Maciel's crimes hung over them visibly. Among them was a former law student of mine from Trinity days, Eamonn O'Higgins, now teaching philosophy at the Legionaries' own university in Rome. Also there was a Father Edward McNamara, more worldly than Eamonn but willing to look the Maciel demons in the eye and comment in a non-defensive way. The most interesting person at the lunch, however, was a young zealot with staring eyes. The group showed no signs of being scandalised when I told them how ashamed I was of my church's attitudes to gay people, women, collegiality and human reproduction. They were courteous and willing to engage, though their beliefs were rigidly orthodox. They asked if I would meet one of their members, Father Michael Mullan, who was based in Dublin and whom they thought I might be able to advise, as he was experiencing some problems. I agreed to meet him in the Greg bar.

Father Michael turned up with his brother Peter, a seminarian and fellow Legionary. Both had the conventional central-casting good looks of Maciel's typical recruits: the perfect grooming, the amazingly white teeth, the expensive tailored black suits, but also the glazed-over intensity and impenetrable logic that made a meeting of minds unlikely. Born in America of an Irish father from Omagh, they were nephews of a well-known Irish priest for whose ecumenical work I had great respect, Father Kevin Mullan. Father Michael, for his part, had been director of the Legionaries' Faith and Family Centre in Blackrock, south Dublin, since 2007, and things were not going well. He had come to Ireland, he told me, because the Irish had brought the faith to America, and now that it was falling apart in Ireland, America was returning the compliment. Oh dear Lord! The Blackrock centre offered courses in marriage preparation, marriage renewal and spiritual direction, retreats and family-oriented activities, among other things. He complained that it was not attracting enough Irish families. Could I help him understand why it was not flourishing as he hoped it would?

I suggested that perhaps the explanation was relatively simple: that the association with the name of the Legionaries of Christ was seen as problematic, given its founder's reputation as a criminal, not to mention the Legionaries' reputation for protecting him and for being – there was no nice way of saying it – a cult. With great forbearance he explained to me that Maciel was not a criminal. He was simply a Mexican, and he had behaved as Mexicans behave. I pointed out that it was pretty clear that most Mexicans are not criminal priests who rape their own children and seminarians, launder money and use it corruptly to buy influence and protection.

When it became obvious I was making no headway, I asked Father Michael what services he offered at the centre. This he talked about enthusiastically. He held classes for children as young as three, and, among other things, he was proud to say that at that age they could recognise chasubles. I was not sure I had heard correctly, and asked him to repeat it. Yes, sure enough, it was indeed 'chasubles'. Chasubles are the ornate outer liturgical vestments worn by priests when saying Mass. Why, I asked, would three-year-olds need to recognise chasubles? He patiently explained it was 'because you cannot start their priestly formation soon enough'. A full hundredweight of loose pennies dropped. Half afraid of what I was about to hear, I asked if he was referring only to male three-year-olds. Of course he was. Sure what else?

When I asked how the centre dealt with gay teenagers, Michael and his brother grinned broadly, as if I had just offered them a strawberry gelato. Michael said, 'Oh, that is no problem. We can turn them easily. The Legionaries do it all the time.' Homosexuality, he told me, was a disorder that was curable and that arose from poor parent–child bonding. I asked if he knew what was the biggest killer of males aged 15–25. He thought it was AIDS. I told him it was suicide, and the biggest at-risk group within that age cohort was gay males. He thought that was because homosexuality and mental illness often went hand in hand. I asked if he thought a culture of heterocentricity, of treating homosexuality as being intrinsically disordered and evil, of criminalising, of bullying, of making people fearful and excluded even in their own homes, schools, and faith communities might just possibly lead to mental health problems? No, he didn't.

I asked what his qualifications were to undertake such 'cures' and was told of his degrees in philosophy and theology. My gasket was pretty close to blown by that point, and I reckoned it was time to disabuse him of any weird notion he might be entertaining that I thought his centre was worth having, never mind helping. I admitted that I was very concerned about the nature of the centre's work with minors and that I would be making my view known immediately to the archdiocese. The brothers were still smiling happily as we parted, as if we had just shared a pizza and a laugh, and Michael sent me a kind email of thanks for taking the time to meet and engage with him. I sent a full record of the conversation to Dr Elizabeth Cotter, the Vicar for Religious in the Dublin archdiocese, and left it at that. It came as no surprise subsequently to learn that Father Mullan had left Ireland, moving first to England and then back to his native United States.

A community of Jesuit scholars lives on an upper floor at the Gregorian University. I got to know the head of that community, Father Mark Rotsaert, a pleasant, calm Belgian, through Caravita. Father Mark was organising a series of seminars at the Greg on reconciliation, and asked if I would do one on the peace process in Northern Ireland. I agreed to do it by way of an interview with a mediator and an audience question-and-answer session. A few days later he told me the interviewer was to be my old friend the Irish Jesuit Father Gerry Whelan, who had suggested I could study canon law in Rome.

Gerry and I met in the Greg bar to map out the questions. He had been away from Ireland for a very long time and was not up to date on the politics of peacemaking. We passed a very pleasant hour and I got up to leave. As I did so, he said there was just one more thing he needed to say. I was under no circumstances to mention LGBTI rights. We had just spoken for an entire hour, covering everything to be raised in our forthcoming public discussion, and the subject had not been mentioned by either of us. I was perplexed and not a little annoyed. I explained there would be a live audience and if a question on the subject came up, then I would most assuredly answer it. I left him in no doubt that his attempt at censorship was unwelcome and in my view very telling of the repressive and unhealthy culture of the institute in which I was studying. I told him I was rather tired of encounters with fake-hetero homophobes, of whom there seemed to be rather a lot in Rome, and in particular among its student seminarians. Then I told him a story.

In 1984, I was asked by Cardinal Ó Fiaich and Archbishop Ryan to be a member of the Catholic Church's delegation to the New Ireland Forum in Dublin Castle. I was at that time a founder member of the Campaign for Homosexual Law Reform, and I raised with Archbishop Ryan the problem that if I was asked about Church teaching on LGBTI issues in a public forum, I would not be able to defend it. He simply said, 'Did I ask you to?' The answer was 'no', and so I went to the forum. But as I remarked to Gerry, times have since changed, particularly in clerical Rome.

I realised that Gerry's warning was likely related to an event that had happened a few weeks earlier. A very fine young Irish priest had invited me to meet up with some of his colleagues for a pizza. Most were American priests in their late twenties and early thirties. They turned out to be a rough, loud bunch on the whole, much given to making homophobic and sexist jokes, no doubt deliberately amplified for my benefit. My Irish friend was mortified, as were a couple of other non-Americans in the group. I told them how disappointing it was to find young pastors who were so insensitive and uncaring, pointing out that within their own group there were likely young gay men who were inwardly hurting at the toxic attitudes of their peers, not to mention the well-known phenomenon of 'methinks he doth protest too much'.

I raised the matter a few days later with one of their superiors. His answer was to openly acknowledge that many were viciously homophobic and deeply sexually conflicted, but I was not to worry because most did not last more than five years in the priesthood. I asked if he agreed that people could do a lot of damage in five years, to others and to themselves. He did not appear to be too bothered. I asked how much it cost to educate one of these young men both before and after ordination, for the group in question had all spent two years studying theology, three years studying philosophy, plus three years of postgraduate study, all in full-time residence in Rome with full board in fine accommodation, flights home paid for, and all at the expense of the laity. He shrugged that question away too.

Disillusionment about priestly training was not hard to come by at the Gregorian. Some of the young priests and seminarians studying there found the cynicism and silence as oppressive as the gossip and sexually loaded backbiting. One encounter just plain depressed me. It was with a recently ordained priest, now doing postgraduate studies but returning to his diocese in England during the holidays to help out. He had a cheery, good-humoured personality and I could see why he would relish parish work and why people might find him a breath of fresh air. I asked what he was most looking forward to on returning to a parish. He didn't miss a beat. 'The money!' he said. 'We have a lot of funerals of elderly

Irish people and I get loads of Mass cards to sign and every one of them comes with money. The Irish in Britain are great for that. I'm saving up for a car.' I asked if it was not the case that most of that money had to be given to the parish priest. 'Yeah. The trick is to always give a little. It keeps you right . . .' Later that summer, he sent me a picture of himself standing proudly by his new second-hand car, keys in hand. I suppose a lot of old Irish people must have died that summer.

Upon his election in 2013, Pope Francis inherited a church in the Western world where vocations to the priesthood and religious life had collapsed and large numbers of Catholics were exercising their human right to simply walk away. The story was very different in Africa and Asia, where the Church was growing, but the decline in the West, the cradle of Christendom, was steep and rapid. On Francis were pinned the unlikeliest of hopes and expectations that he would turn the tide. He was barely in office when the hagiographers were detailing his saintly qualities, his credentials as a reformer, his grand plan for renewal. Francis was imbued with an earthy, winning personality, and a spontaneous kindliness when talking to journalists on planes. His language has hinted at possible change. But despite having supreme authority over the universal Church, he has been hesitant to use that power to make even minor doctrinal amendments.

With regard to the position of women in the Church, it became evident that he was all talk and little action, just like his predecessors. A product of the usual clerical formation, which patronises and idealises women with a sentimental slush that is dishonest and anti-egalitarian, he seems to have thought that a token appointment here and there would keep the female wolves from the door. Meanwhile, victims of abuse were stunned to discover that despite his new Commission for the Protection of Minors, he like so many of his colleagues had a default position of believing the best of alleged abusers and the worst of alleged victims. The contradictions in his views were highlighted during his disastrous visit to Chile in 2018, and again during an underwhelming visit to Ireland later that same year. It was clear in both countries that the laity's estimation of him was more nuanced than that of the tribe of hagiographers and supporters who portrayed Francis as a radical reformer.

Martin and I were in St Peter's Square the night Francis was elected in March 2013, and we were among those enthusiasts who prayed for a pope who would bring hope and real change. I wrote to him that night wishing him well in his mission. Next morning we woke to discover that the hagiographers were already busy spinning the new Pope's simplicity, his insistence on returning to pay his hotel bill, his decision not to occupy the papal apartments but to live in the Vatican City state hotel, known as Casa Santa Marta. The contrasts with the ermine-clad, Prada-shoed Benedict were churned out thick and fast, but already the worrying signs of a different Francis (later highlighted in Paul Vallely's excellent biography) were there to be seen.

The morning after his election, Pope Francis paid a visit to the Basilica of Santa Maria Maggiore. We were told it was because of his devotion to Our Blessed Lady. But it seemed an odd choice, since as pope he was the titular bishop of Rome and his proper basilica was in fact the Lateran, up the street from Maria Maggiore. What made it odder was the fact that he was greeted there by Cardinal Bernard Law, who had been controversially appointed Archpriest of the Basilica of Maria Maggiore after being run out of the Boston archdiocese when the appalling extent of his cover-up of priestly abuse was revealed by the secular press. The curial brotherhood, headed by Pope John Paul II, had given a metaphorical two fingers to the Catholics of Boston, and to the hundreds of victims of clerical sex abuse there, by rewarding Law with one of the most prized sinecures in Rome. By the time of Pope Francis's elevation, Law had retired, but was still Archpriest Emeritus.

One of Law's talents was fund-raising, and he was known for distributing large sums of money to worthy causes, including causes in Argentina. Since his fellow cardinals indulged his sense that he had been hard done by and was something of a martyr to aggressive secularism, it was mooted in some local quarters that Francis too felt sorry for his old colleague, from whom he may have received funding to help with his work on behalf of the poor, and wanted to send an early and clear message to those pursuing the clerical scandals agenda. It was a very telling visit, but it scarcely got a mention in the press, which had collectively decided that Francis was the Messiah the Church had been waiting on.

I spent almost three years full-time in Rome, but at the end of my first doctoral year I began to divide my time between Rome, home, and teaching semesters at Boston College, the University of Notre Dame in Indiana, and St Mary's University in Twickenham.

At the Jesuit-run Boston College I was reunited with the rector of the Irish College, Monsignor Liam Bergin, who is now a very highly regarded tenured professor there and a lot happier than when in Rome. He was great company, and the months there whizzed by, with weekends spent with him and other friends at football and basketball matches. Notre

Dame, which is run by priests of the Congregation of Holy Cross, is also a top-class academic institution, with a more spiritually conservative atmosphere. It was from a radio studio in Notre Dame that I first told the Irish broadcaster George Hook of my support for changing the constitution to allow same-sex marriage, in the referendum that would be held shortly after Martin and I came home from the United States. We both became caught up in the campaign at home, believing fervently in marriage equality as a human rights issue and increasingly unhappy with the ways in which our church makes LGBTI Catholics feel excluded and unloved. We were thrilled when the referendum passed so comprehensively. I experienced it as a day when grace flooded the land, a holy day, a day of wholeness.

The Church's response was to announce that the World Meeting of Families would be held in Dublin in 2018. The idea had originated with Archbishop Paglia, head of the Holy See's Pontifical Academy for Life. It was expected that Pope Francis would attend the event, and Paglia himself told me in 2017 that he hoped a visit from the Pope would head off the then mooted referendum to liberalise Irish abortion laws. I thought the Pope would be much better advised to come on an open pastoral visit, as John Paul II had done in 1979, and to complete that unfinished papal pilgrimage by going to Northern Ireland, where peace now prevailed. The World Meeting of Families had been created in 1994 notionally by John Paul II but in reality as the brainchild of Cardinal Alfonso Trujillo, who was its director. It became a platform for Trujillo's ultra-orthodox and often venomously expressed hostility to homosexuals, divorce, reproductive rights and more. It was a perfect veil for the reality that he was in fact a violent sexual predator.

Since the die was cast and the World Meeting was to be held in Dublin, I wrote to the Archbishop of Dublin expressing the hope that it would be welcoming and inclusive for all families, such as those with gay members, single parents and divorced and remarried partners. I hoped that if the Pope came to Ireland he might help heal the divisions among Catholics that had been highlighted by the clerical abuse scandals, the marriage referendum and the debate on the forthcoming abortion referendum. I was asked to help with the input into the preparatory catechesis, and spent a day with the main catechist, Martin Kennedy, whose vision seemed to be similar to mine. When the catechesis was published and went out to the parishes there was real delight. It used the language of Pope Francis to show that the World Meeting was going to be inclusive of single-parent families, gay families, the divorced and remarried, and others who felt excluded because their situation was irregular according to Church doctrine. Unfortunately, that catechesis was summarily withdrawn and the inclusive language edited out of the replacement version. It is not clear who was responsible for that, but Cardinal Kevin Farrell was in charge of the World Meeting as head of the Dicastery for the Family, the Laity and Life, and there is no doubt that he was lobbied intensively by those who wanted the event to be what it had always been: a rally for the orthodox. It was now certain that families like mine, with our gay son and his husband, were not going to be welcome.

In March of that year, I had been invited to speak at a conference on the role of women in the Church. The conference was to be held in Vatican City, as it had been for the four previous years without any difficulty. Cardinal Farrell was the Vatican figure recently made responsible for liaising with the organisers, Voices of Faith. When they sent Farrell the list of speakers, he vetoed three of them. I was one of the three, and each of us had campaigned for gay rights. The cardinal gave no explanation, so I can only surmise that was the reason.

I realised immediately that this was not an ideal prelude to the papal visit five months later, and efforts were made, including by the Archbishop of Dublin, to get the cardinal to change his mind. In the end, the conference organisers decided not to agree to Farrell's conditions. The Jesuit curia offered their very suitable premises, located just outside the Vatican wall. It was a place I knew well, for it was where my thesis supervisor and I had met regularly over the previous three years.

Cardinal Farrell's intervention ensured that a routinely overlooked conference became the subject of huge international press interest. I described the Church as an 'empire of misogyny' and the exclusion of women from the priesthood as 'codology dressed up as theology'. I had used precisely those words at a conference on women in the Church at Milltown Institute in Dublin thirty years earlier. They had even appeared in a Catholic publication of the conference proceedings, but no one seemed to notice. Now, thanks to Cardinal Farrell, they were trending on Twitter (or so I was told), and the next day the word 'codology' was heavily googled!

With attendance at the World Meeting of Families now problematic for many families, I suggested to a group of disappointed Catholic supporters of gay rights that one way of showcasing Ireland's egalitarian and inclusive attitude to families in advance of the papal visit would be to make the annual Pride event into a big family celebration. Pride was due to be held at the end of June 2018, two months before the papal visit. My son Justin and the journalist Ursula Halligan were deputed to persuade the organisers to embrace the theme 'We Are Family', which I believed would attract a huge attendance and tell its own story. The organisers took up the idea with enthusiasm, and the festival was an outstanding success, with twice the anticipated number attending – mothers, fathers, grannies, grandads, babies in buggies toting their rainbow flags. The chief of staff of the armed forces was there in uniform. A uniformed army band sporting rainbow wings played to a rapturous crowd.

At the invitation of Roger Childs, RTÉ's head of religious affairs, I made a TV documentary on Irish families, for transmission in advance of the papal visit. It was designed to show families' strength in adversity and diversity, their mixed views on churches and faith, their deep moral sensibilities and their views on the forthcoming visit.

The visit itself was a bit of a damp squib. It rained virtually non-stop throughout, and attendances at the big open-air Mass in the Phoenix Park were modest, with little more than one tenth of the numbers who had turned up there for Pope John Paul in 1979. I attended the only state-run event in honour of the Pope, hosted by the Irish government in Dublin Castle. Leo Varadkar, our young gay taoiseach, born of an Indian Hindu father and an Irish mother, shone through the entire affair with the well-chosen words he spoke on welcoming Pope Francis to Dublin. He graciously acknowledged Francis's leadership on care for the earth, for migrants and for the poor. He expressed gratitude for all that the Catholic Church, through its people, priests and religious, had contributed over centuries to Irish Christian values, to education and healthcare. He spoke of our pride in the work of Irish missionaries. But he also spoke bluntly of the dark side of the

Catholic Church in Ireland, openly acknowledging the state's and society's complicity in much of it:

> It is a history of sorrow and shame ... The Ireland of the twenty-first century is a very different place today than it was in the past. Ireland is increasingly diverse ... I believe that the time has now come for us to build a new relationship between church and state in Ireland – a new covenant for the twenty-first century ... one in which religion is no longer at the centre of our society, but in which it still has an important place.

There was a palpable sense of tectonic plates shifting.

I left Ireland for Rome the weekend after the Pope's visit. There was the small matter of the defence of my doctoral thesis to be attended to. It was scheduled for the end of September, and although the thesis was written in English, the rule in the Faculty of Canon Law is that the defence must be in either Italian or Latin. The latter not being a serious option, Italian it would have to be.

I went back to my old room in the Lay Centre, now renovated and sporting a leather lounger bequeathed by the departing Canadian ambassador. I never used it. Instead I was glued to the desk, sitting on my old bockety swivel chair with its capacity for keeling over, practising my verbs and pronouns, identifying likely areas of questioning, and emerging only to attend Italian classes in the Gregorian, to run through answers with a friend to see how my Italian sounded, to go to the chapel to ask for God's intercession on defence day, and to eat communal meals with the Lay Centre inhabitants. As it had the previous September, the centre was hosting a group of Hebrew University students from Jerusalem, a lively mix of young Muslims and Jews. All they wanted to talk about was the Northern Ireland peace process. How did we get there? How long did it take? I tried to encourage them. Do what you are doing here. Build bridges to one another. There is no other way.

The defence went well, or as well as could be expected when discussing canon law in the simplest Italian present tense. It was public, and packed with family, friends, fellow students and colleagues as well as serial defence-attenders. Archbishop Diarmuid Martin made the trip specially. So did my two-year-old grandson Mossie, who was taken for an ice cream for the defence's two-hour duration. We had a monumental party back at the Lay Centre, where the cook had created a dazzling display of Irish-themed food. I was presented with the garment that marked my award of a doctorate from the Pontifical Gregorian University. Trimmed with emerald green, the colour of canon law, it is a black biretta of the type designed for and usually worn only by male clerics.

There has been a church at Ardcarne, in north Roscommon, since 500 AD. The current church of St Beo-Aedh is Protestant (Church of Ireland) and was built in the eighteenth century. It hosts the twentieth-century addition of Evie Hone's first stained-glass window, depicting the Lamb of God. The Famine monument in the grounds hints at the misery that particularly afflicted that area, with stories of bodies lying nine deep in the ditch all the way back up the hill for miles past the site that became my grandparents' home.

I now live on the banks of the River Shannon within sight of St Beo-Aedh's, as well as the old monastic site at Tumna and my father's family home at Carraward. St Michael's

Church in our local village, Cootehall, is where my father was baptised. Ardcarne is our past and our present hinterland, with Ardoyne and a few other places in between. I am thus the first of our long-dispersed clan to return permanently to Roscommon, and to Ardcarne, though thankfully not yet as a corpse.

Plantation, penal laws, famine, partition, poverty and emigration crippled that world of ancient settlements, strong clans and centres of scholarship. It ripped apart communities of friends and families, and their grief at what was lost to them always seemed to haunt the place. It was generally agreed by all our relatives and friends, including my father, that Martin and I were entirely absurd in choosing to live in a very mucky field on the side of a very windy hill in Roscommon. However, when the house was built my father found every opportunity to visit and to just sit looking across the Shannon at his own old childhood home, reminiscing about the families who had once lived where we now lived, and the hard lives they had endured in those times when emigration seemed the only option and when childhood ended at fourteen with a train or boat ticket to an independent working life far from home.

One sunny day, as my father sat outside chatting with my cousin Eugene McGreevy and looking across the fields of yellow-green meadow to the lake shore, the quiet afternoon was pierced by what was to me an unfamiliar sound: the less than melodious *krek krek* of the corncrake. When my father was young, the sound was often heard in the countryside, though the bird itself, being notoriously secretive, was rarely seen. Farm mechanisation had meanwhile brought about the corncrake's virtual disappearance hereabouts. My father and Eugene were enthralled to hear it for the first time in many years. A slew of childhood memories were evoked, and we gathered to hear them and to listen out for our musically challenged visitor. I had no idea what a corncrake looked like, and my father was just starting a description when, as if on cue, it rose up out of the grass and swooped away, heading north as he once had.

# Acknowledgements

Special thanks are due to my husband Martin, and to Brendan Barrington of Penguin Random House Ireland, who encouraged me to begin and helped me all the way through to completion of this memoir.

# Index

MM indicates Mary McAleese